ACTS OF CONSPICUOUS COMPASSION

Acts of Conspicuous Compassion

Performance Culture and American Charity Practices

SHEILA C. MOESCHEN

The University of Michigan Press

Ann Arbor

First paperback edition 2016

Copyright © 2013 by Sheila C. Moeschen

Published in the United States of America by
The University of Michigan Press
Printed and bound by CPI Group (UK) Ltd, Croydon, CR0 4YY

2019   2018   2017   2016   5   4   3   2

A CIP catalog record for this book is available from the British Library.

Library of Congress Cataloging-in-Publication Data

Moeschen, Sheila C.
Acts of conspicuous compassion : performance culture and American charity practices / Sheila C. Moeschen.
    pages   cm
Includes bibliographical references and index.
ISBN 978-0-472-11886-1 (cloth : acid-free paper) — ISBN 978-0-472-02927-3 (e-book)
    1. Theater and society—United States--History. 2. Charity in literature. 3. People with disabilities in literature. I. Title.
PN2226.M56 2013
792.0973—dc23   2013000019

ISBN 978-0-472-03655-4 (paper : acid-free paper)

To Mom & Pat (I win!)

Mike, for your love, support, and patience

Tracy, Gay, and Maryrita, my mentor dream team;
I owe you all more than I can say

Portions of Chapter 2 appeared in much-altered form in "Debutantes, Disease, and Democracy: Discourses of Gender and Nationhood in the 1930s Polio Pageants," *Women's Studies: An Inter-disciplinary Journal* 41, no. 3 (2012): 303–23.

CONTENTS

CONTENTS

Introduction

Introduction

"How fabulous is that?" purrs Ina Garten, referring to the steaming contents of the casserole dish held captive between her oven mitt–clad hands. Known more widely under the moniker the Barefoot Contessa, Garten is one of a stable of Food Network culinary superstars. Like her contemporaries Paula Deen, Emeril Lagasse, and Giada De Laurentiis, Garten has successfully stayed atop the entertainment cooking industry wave that propels and transforms seemingly obscure chefs and amateur foodies into highly lucrative commodities. Think Julia Child under the tutelage of *Entourage*'s Ari Gold.

Garten built her empire out of her highly successful gourmet food store, the Barefoot Contessa, in New York's renowned vacation enclave the Hamptons. Her Food Network show, *The Barefoot Contessa*, features Garten presenting sophisticated and elegant dishes made simple and inviting, culled from ingredient lists that read like superlatives in a high school yearbook: the best, the freshest, the ripest, the most perfect, and so on. Garten portrays an image of homespun chic; she comes across to viewers as cheerful, neighborly, and unfailingly positive. She is part Martha Stewart, part Snow White. Periodically she breaks from her preparations to admire her (and presumably the viewer's) skill, cooing one of her signature phrases such as "How fabulous is that?"[1]

In March 2011, however, life became much less fabulous and rather difficult for the cooking show star. A report surfaced on *TMZ*, the celebrity news and culture web site, alleging that Garten had refused to grant a six-year-old terminally ill boy his Make-A-Wish request to cook with the famed chef. Enzo Pereda, a young boy with acute lymphoblastic leukemia, and his family had approached the Make-A-Wish Foundation, an organization that helps make unique experiences a reality for terminally ill individuals, in

2010 with the request for Pereda to meet and cook with Garten. According to reports, Pereda was one of Garten's biggest fans; he watched her show faithfully from his bed every day, including times when he was hospitalized for treatments. Journalist Sheila Marikar writes for *ABC News* that at the time "Ina gave a 'soft no' supposedly because she had a 10-month book tour." Make-A-Wish asked Pereda how he wanted to proceed based on that information. "He said 'I will wait,'" stated Pereda's mother. "And he did."[2]

A year later Pereda's second request was denied, prompting his mother to write on her blog:

> I told him [Enzo] the unfortunate news, [and] his reply was simply "Why doesn't she want to meet me?" (As he is looking up at me with those big, beautiful brown eyes!) I would be lying if I said that I don't find this to be shocking. To know that out of EVERYTHING (material Enzo could choose to have) or ANY PLACE (in the world Enzo could travel to) and out of EVERY PERSON on this earth he chose Ina and she cannot see what an honor that is.[3]

The online response to Pereda's implied heartbreak was immediate, swift, and overwhelmingly critical of Garten. Major news aggregates such as *ABC News*, *Huffington Post*, the *Los Angeles Times*, and *Business Insider*, as well as numerous blogs, picked up the story. On social media sites such as Facebook and on forums such as Café Mom and The Stir, people voiced their outrage with Garten, excoriating her for her insensitivity and elitism. "I'd never thought I'd see someone turn down a dying child," posted one woman. Another wrote, "Sorry, but I won't be going back to admire her now that the Empress has no clothes and apparently no soul." Fueling the online ire was an item in the story about Pereda posted on *Business Insider* that mentioned Garten had recently thrown a $100,000-a-plate charity luncheon for six women to benefit the Hamptons' Historical Society.[4] Many people called for boycotts of her show and products. Others were quick to point out that she had an obligation as a celebrity and public figure (as well as a fellow human) to wholeheartedly participate in this act of conspicuous compassion.[5]

At first Garten's representatives remained silent, but within days of the snub felt around the world they released a statement claiming that Garten had only recently been informed of Pereda's request:

Ina receives approximately 100 requests a month to support charitable causes that deeply affect peoples' lives. She contributes both personally and financially on a regular basis to numerous causes, including Make-A-Wish. Sadly, it is, of course, not possible to do them all. Throughout her life, Ina has contributed generously to all kinds of important efforts and she will continue to do so.[6]

Another press release came shortly thereafter, announcing that Garten had contacted the boy personally to invite him on the set. His parents gave word that they had declined Garten's invitation. Citing no ill will toward the celebrity cook, the Peredas explained that Enzo had chosen to pursue his second wish, to swim with dolphins. The entire family wanted to move on and put the uncomfortable episode behind them. Presumably, Garten felt the same.

Though relatively short-lived, the Barefoot Contessa's public relations nightmare raises provocative questions about the cultivation of charitable sentiment, how need is expressed and decoded. It also highlights the social relationships formulated through charity and, most notably, what transpires when one or more of the individuals involved become resistant or reluctant social actors. Assuming that Garten was aware of at least one if not both of Pereda's requests, why did she refuse? Was she insufficiently moved by his plea, which might suggest an issue of pathology on her part, or was his request presented to her in a way that was insufficiently moving, which might suggest a breakdown of the narrative and affective devices used to effectively convey Pereda's wish? What is at stake, and for whom, in the cultural ritual of charity? How does explicating the mechanisms behind the creation of charitable sentiment shape political, ideological, and social understanding of one particular community most deeply implicated in the American charity industry: the physically disabled?

In *Acts of Conspicuous Compassion*, I take up these questions by examining the process and effects of creating charitable sentiment in American society. Benevolence is a fundamental moral and civic ideal that shapes ideas about individual character; reveals information about a nation's collective identity; and contributes to beliefs about and representational perspectives on social, physical, class, and racial difference. The designation between benevolent patron and needy Other must be made distinctive, which is to say "have-nots" are either marked as such or self-identified through materials and rhetoric designed to signify lacking or duress. The politics and impacts of making need intelligible in this manner earn a considerable amount of analytical focus in the proceeding chapters of this book.

Benevolence and *charity*, it is important to distinguish, are used interchangeably in this book due to their generative associations with "fellow-feelings," the innate emotional mechanisms related to matters of the heart and spirit. Concepts such as volunteerism and philanthropy, while sharing many of the same core values as charity (i.e., a preoccupation with assisting underserved populations or supporting social causes), connote a different set of practices and philosophies. Volunteerism becomes a component of charitable works. It persists as a highly subjective act that does not necessarily require intimate knowledge of a problem or cause or give an indication of how benevolence figures into the person's motives for volunteering. Many volunteer because they enjoy performing a skill; the emotional and spiritual facets of their activities may not figure into their involvement at all.

Likewise, philanthropy is often viewed as a private act that is largely financial. Moreover, philanthropy typically constitutes a voluntary gesture, "in the sense of it being intended and uncoerced." Historian Mike Martin defines philanthropy specifically in terms of its anonymity: "[Philanthropy involves] acts of voluntary private giving for public purposes. These acts, however, are rarely eccentric gestures."[7] In order to more fully explore the wide-ranging effects of benevolence, it is vital to understand its power to engage, excite, and captivate the masses, which often does depend on eccentric gestures. This is a crucial factor that sets philanthropy and charity apart.

Charity also encompasses a significant and necessary economic component of civic culture. A report posted on the site Charity Navigator states that in 2010 charitable giving topped out at $290.89 billion, spread across organizations in medicine, education, the arts, and organized religion.[8] With such a large sphere of influence, charity warrants both critical attention and reappraisal. Historically, charity has evolved from a spiritually based obligation to provide for those less fortunate to a social practice seamlessly incorporated into the fabric of our daily routines. Cause-related marketing (CRM) from the business and consumer culture sector has increased exponentially in the last decade on pace with the rise of integrative technologies and social networking.[9] People may participate in charity by purchasing a favorite pair of shoes; texting on their smart phone; or partnering with a social networking site such as Facebook, Crowdrise, or Care2Com. The integration of benevolence with our quotidian experiences makes it no less meaningful for participants or recipients. In fact, the ubiquitous nature of this cultural practice at this time in our country's history raises new questions about how organizations and movements compete for our benevolent attentions; why certain mechanisms used to communicate the charitable plea have been sustained in light of the changing avenues to engage in charity; and what this current moment reveals about cultural constructions of class, race, and embodied difference.

To track charity's lineage in the United States is to simultaneously elucidate the fraught legacy of physical disability as both a concept and a social position. For over a century, disabled people have defined and redefined their collective identity in relation to and against a wide range of assistive networks. From nineteenth-century workhouses designed to contain and rehabilitate physically and mentally disabled individuals to contemporary charity organizations established to service the needs of specific types of disabilities and disabling diseases, organized benevolence has served as a complicated and rich "disability locale."

According to disability studies scholars Sharon Mitchell and David Snyder, disability locales define "cultural spaces that have been set out exclusively on behalf of disabled citizens." "Locales," write Mitchell and Snyder, "represent a saturation point of content about disability that has been produced by those who share certain beliefs about disability."[10] While it may be tempting to identify any number of charity organizations as the logical repositories for these locales, this does not sufficiently account for the *ways* in which the disabled community becomes consolidated around the respective health or bodily issues that these entities address. Nor does it help dislodge the common perception that charity polarizes disabled and able-bodied people, positioning the former as lacking agency and autonomy.

For this reason, I move charity out of its exclusive association with the domains of organizations, conglomerations, and relief programs to restore it to its earliest incarnation as a moral sentiment, or what seventeenth-century Enlightenment philosophers referred to as a "fellow-feeling." Popular writings by philosophers such as Adam Smith and David Hume espoused the notion that moral sentiments guided behaviors and informed social interactions in civil society. The impetus for "fellow-feelings" came from an interaction between emotions and cognition. In the case of charity this meant bearing witness to the suffering of another, emotionally and cognitively processing the situation, and then taking action to alleviate distress.

This recapitulation of charity shares a relationship with the operations of compassion. Lauren Berlant's foundational work on compassion as a social relation between individuals is important to understanding how charity functions as a dynamic of civil society. Berlant performs a similar analysis of this fellow-feeling to take issue with the accepted belief that compassion exists as "an organic emotion" and to argue, instead, that compassion denotes "a social and aesthetic technology of belonging."[11] This helpful distinction refocuses the lens on this moral sentiment to take into account *how* compassion is manifest and what this exemplification means politically as well as socially, ethically, and on a humanistic level. The principles of compassion, Berlant states, "derive from social training, emerge at historical moments, are shaped by aesthetic conventions, and take place in scenes that are anxious, volatile, surprising, and contradictory." The same can be said about charity. Charity is neither innate nor granted through divine right, but rather constitutes a cultural practice instigated by and made intelligible through the production of different affective, rhetorical, and visual signs.

Berlant engages with this theoretical perspective in an effort to disclose what the production of compassion means for members of the American welfare state, broadly conceived as all populations characterized by lack of resources, means, or materials that citizens *should* care about under the most general terms of the social contract. In contrast, my examination of charitable sentiment proceeds with the notion that, in addition to consisting of a set of cultural operations, charity is a political apparatus deployed to bring a sophisticated level of attention to highly distinctive communities, individuals coded as "worthy" of charity for supposedly extraordinary reasons that surpass those of the basic social contract. That is to say, the creation of charitable sentiment is a directive that *compels* citizens to act on their benevolence in a way that compassion does not. Relief is only one of many complicated outcomes of this process. Another is the forging of subjectivities that often collapse the cause with the individual. Where this is most pronounced is in the case of the disabled community, where charity is a metonym for socially constructed ideas about the loss of citizenship and erosion of personhood.

In the last decade, those working in the field of disability studies have effectively pushed against the theoretical frameworks that form the basis for our understanding of disability and the social forces that shape this concept. For some, this has involved concerted efforts to reintegrate the lived realities and corporeal experiences of people with physical diversity. Michael Davidson discusses this approach in his book, *Concerto for the Left Hand*. Incorporating the material perspective of the disabled body into research "brings this body to the fore, reminding us of the contingent, interdependent nature of bodies and their situated relationship to physical ideals."[12] This concern is echoed in Rosemarie Garland-Thomson's seminal work on staring. In her analysis, the act of staring takes on physical properties as an "interrogative gesture" that forges social relationships and produces knowledge about self and Other, especially in respect to physicality.[13] A focus on the phenomenology of disability unveils new ways to more adequately account for the lives of those with disabilities; it also exposes the limitations and problems of accepted policies and belief systems.

Other researchers have made the case that disability deserves new consideration as an identity formation, and it is within this body of work that I situate *Acts of Conspicuous Compassion*. For instance, Lennard J. Davis renews the need to take critical advantage of what he situates as the "dismodern era," the contemporary period marked by disability's productive instability. In Davis's formulation difference becomes a unifying aspect that gives identity politics flexibility. Moving away from exclusivity-based identity politics, Davis argues that "disability studies can provide a critique of and a politics to discuss how all groups, based on physical traits or markings, are selected for disablement by a larger system of regulation."[14] This outlook also figures into the ways in which disability contests individual and collective formulations of subjectivity.

Building on this view in his book *Disability Theory*, Tobin Siebers persuasively argues for the recognition of disability as a "minority identity."[15] Identity is not fixed or immutable for Siebers, nor can it be consolidated to exclusively biological or social factors. Instead, identity connotes a means of associating with a group or society on symbolic and material terms. Minority identities in particular, Siebers contends, bear the additional task of "representing the experiences of oppression and struggle lived by minority peoples separately but also precisely as minorities, for attention to the similarities between different minority identities exposes their relation to oppression as well as increases the chance of political solidarity."[16] It is from this vantage point as a minority identity that people with disabilities possess the capacity to unsettle and promote change to the networks that comprise the cultural status quo, that is, those that uphold standards of normalcy.

The creation of charitable sentiment is one such system that reflects accepted conditions of mainstream society. The appearance of disability disrupts these conditions, which becomes part of the impetus for benevolent intervention: to ameliorate the specter of physical deviance that makes individuals uncomfortable, confused, or scared. As a result, I reconsider the conventionally held perception that people with disabilities belong to a two-dimensional cohort of "poster children," objectified and helpless in their inclusion in the charity industry. This notion not only reinforces a pejorative and misleading representation of people with disabilities, but it also diminishes the political and social agency of both able-bodied patrons and disabled benefactors of charity.

To be clear, I am not suggesting that those individuals taken advantage of, exploited, or denigrated by the charity industry are responsible for their abuses. Rather, I make the case that the inherently manufactured quality of charitable sentiment makes the tension between ideology and identity, between representation and social reality, palpable. Within this friction questions emerge about the stability of disabled and nondisabled subject positions, as well as the reliability of the political, ideological, and economic structures that underpin organized benevolence.

A useful model for conceptualizing the way physical disability interacts with benevolent networks can be found in the idea put forth by Siebers understanding disability as a "complex embodiment." Siebers borrows from feminist theories that espouse the notion that all knowledge exists on a phenomenological level to make the case that disabled subjects, by virtue of their physical diversities, offer renewed perspectives of these epistemes. "The disposition of the body determines perspectives," writes Siebers. "But it also spices these perspectives with phenomenological knowledge—lifeworld experience—that affects the interpretation of perspective."[17] The charity industry responds to the physicality of the disabled individual by attempting to speak for those perspectives, to authorize an envisioned "lifeworld experience" that bears a narrow scope of meanings. This is evident in the aesthetic choices made when a wheelchair user appears in a public services announcement (PSA), in the rhetorical choices present in the copy of a charity drive announcement, and in the visual choices that accompany participants in parades or other public events.

However, not only does complex embodiment attempt to more fully incorporate the phenomenological perspectives of people with disabilities; it also seeks to broaden the way disability is conceived as an amalgam of social and environmental restriction *and* physical variability that exists within all beings. Siebers writes: "The theory of complex embodiment views the economy between social representations and the body . . . as reciprocal. Complex embodiment theorizes the body and its representations as mutually transformative. . . . The body possesses the ability to determine its social representation as well."[18] This relationship becomes salient when the mechanisms behind the cultivation of charitable sentiment are divulged. It is the recognition that a certain degree of contrivance accompanies the shot of the wheelchair user in her PSA that simultaneously engenders new methods of reading and relating to the disabled body. Suddenly the "lifeworld experience" offered in the film becomes suspect, open to interpretation as well as cognitive and affective renegotiation. When contextualized within the American charity movement, complex embodiment fosters awareness of how people with physical disabilities respond to the representational systems in play, thereby also troubling attitudes and beliefs that contribute to upholding dominant discourses of ableism.

Charity depends upon an array of representational devices to make need apparent, legible, and ideally emotionally provocative. In the unfolding drama of the Barefoot Contessa's humanitarian gaffe, Pereda was exemplified as angelic and soulful, imploring his mother "with his big, beautiful brown eyes" as to why Garten refused to meet him. This description, combined with information about Pereda's life-threatening illness, coalesced to create an image of the young Pereda that likely resonated in the cultural conscious as synonymous with qualities such as innocence, weakness, and purity. Despite its accuracy or inaccuracy, this portrayal no doubt exacerbated Garten's public image problems, setting her up as the "heartless" woman who denied the request of a "dying" child, while permitting people to readily demonstrate an uncomplicated moral stance on the incident. For people with physical disabilities, these visual, rhetorical, and affective conventions guide public perception and offer moral instruction on how to engage with corporeal difference. They are the tools that facilitate the social and economic ritual distinguished as charity, which makes them ultimately unstable, susceptible to countless modification and reconfiguration.

The devices under consideration here—borrowed from stage work, film, advertising and print media, television, and public spectacle—owe their ontology to performance culture. Unfortunately, charity and pretense have shared a lengthy, historical entanglement. The mid-nineteenth century gave rise to evolving anxiety over populations marked in the public sphere as threatening, a list that included immigrants, criminals, and mendicants among others. Beggars posed a serious affront to the American work ethic, appearing to flaunt the conventions of honest labor to instead rely on the public's assistance either in the form of individual handouts or through the assistance of the institution. Most significantly, the figure of the mendicant became synonymous with deception. "Supposedly, the beggar only pretended to seek work," writes social historian Amy Stanley, "coining his unblushing falsehoods as fast as he can talk."[19]

As the nineteenth century fell away, ushering in a new era dominated by industrial advances and swift urban expansion, the mendicant "problem" became increasingly prevalent. The lengths to which beggars would go in order to procure aid from the public appeared increasingly sophisticated, prompting newspapers to publish prescriptive articles such as the one that ran in a December issue of *New York Times* in 1904 titled, "New York's Holiday Beggar and his 'Graft.'" In it, the author discloses a system devised by the Mendicancy Department of the Organized Charity of New York to divide beggars, much like the police categorize criminals, into distinct classes, identified by their chosen method of deception. "The Flopper," for example, "is a fake cripple [who] sits down or flops on the sidewalk, usually at the entrance of an elevated railway station." A class of beggar described as the "Throw Out" "pretends that he is paralyzed and is able to throw his wrists or ankles out of joint." The article goes on to state that of the 2,000 beggars infiltrating New York streets, "nearly all are fakirs," adding, "the profession of the beggar is now as well established as the profession of the thief."[20] Physical disability encompasses an essential component of the beggar's performative body work, placing it and those who live authentically with a disability in a fraught position. In one respect, this exposé stresses the nature of contrivance as a provocative way to engender sympathy for and, presumably, benevolence toward the needy Other. However, yoking disability to deceptive practices diminishes the realities of people with disabilities, while also enforcing a distinctive, negative visual, affective, and representational framework within which to read the disability experience.

As the case of the nineteenth- and twentieth-century mendicant makes unambiguous, performance conventions play a critical role in communicating need, in making distress comprehensible, and in enabling subjects to become affectively engaged in the presentation of want. This is not to sug-

gest that all those seeking assistance are maliciously dishonest or that charity organizations act unethically in their attempts to garner public support.
The fact remains, as I evidence throughout the chapters in this book, that
artful contrivances are both accepted and compulsory components of the
charity plea and vary in their transparency and effect. Performance culture
is a critical repository for these mechanisms that individuals and organizations become progressively reliant upon as the competition for people's
attention and financial resources widens.

Performance culture can be characterized as the organizing systems of
devices, properties, instruments, and conventions that support the creation
and dissemination of theatrical events including but not limited to stage
performances, filmed works, television shows, public performances, spectacles, rituals, and ceremonies. Due to its diffuse locations and multiple facets,
performance necessarily involves merging human, nonhuman, material, and
immaterial properties together. These constituents make up the expansive
network of performance culture. Scripts, acting styles, film technologies,
costumes, genres, star icons, fan culture, dramatic criticism, and the properties of ritual may all fall under the rubric of performance culture. At the
same time, it is important to point out that each of these items contains its
own theoretical and artistic logic; political structures; and aesthetic, cultural,
and historical particularities.

Performance culture is not a discipline, nor is it a methodology. Rather,
it is a designation that accounts for the different processes, approaches,
theories, artistic and professional roles, forms, and applied techniques germane to performance. This designation delineates between the influence of
performance-based methodologies and an assertion that charity is a performance.

It is worth briefly discussing how the field of performance studies has
expanded the parameters around what constitutes performance and its relational concept performativity. Theorist Richard Schechner's foundational
notion that performance relies on "restored behavior" helped to bridge the
gap between social and theatrical practices. Similarly, anthropologists and
sociologists seized on the idea of using the principles of performance (i.e.,
proscribed, rehearsed, restored behaviors) to understand cultural phenomena such as historical events, communal actions, and significant occasions.[21]
To this body of work, feminist, queer, literary, and performance scholars
among others contributed to a growing interest in the notion of "performa-

tivity." Like performance, performativity has accrued critical attention for developing new insight into areas as varied as speech acts, cultural trauma, and political scenes.[22] In their introduction to the *Sage Handbook of Performance Studies*, performance scholars D. Soyini Madison and Judith Hamera remark on this pervasiveness: "For many of us performance has evolved into ways of comprehending how human beings fundamentally make culture, affect power, and reinvent their ways of being in the world."[23] There are few areas of inquiry that remain untouched by performance studies' analytical and theoretical feelers.

However, as many scholars also contend, such an inclusive and encompassing view of performance threatens to neutralize its political impact and artistic efficacy. By ostensibly relegating all interactions and occurrences within the purview of performance and performativity, critics risk misconstruing important cultural, historical, and material distinctions that complicate how we understand performance as a unique expressive mode and a notable social enterprise. Theater historian Tracy C. Davis concludes:

> No doubt it is pleasing to subsume the various scholarly disciplines in the arts, humanities, social sciences, and sciences under the rubric of performance, but perhaps with a sense of humility, rather than hubris, we probably should recognize that all human thought and behavior cannot be usefully explained by the single idea of performativity.[24]

Researchers must resist the propensity to tidy up the whole of experiences, events, and behaviors for study as products of performativity or performance without at least acknowledging the analytical limits of this approach.

Yet it is tempting to make the case for examining charity as a performance. I could argue that charity is a civic custom that involves participants adhering to a collective social script, reducing the concept to little more than a collection of learned and reiterated behaviors. However, this line of inquiry misrepresents the *process* of creating charitable sentiment, which takes into account the agency of both the benevolent patron and the recipients of aid. It also fails to illuminate the various social and historical forces impinging upon charity that contribute to its adaptability and malleability. Additionally, to argue for a performance of charity places the focus on benevolent actions, which is to say gestures, postures, or behaviors that reflect one's spiritual, moral, or civic design. This emphasis reveals little of how charity impacts cultural norms, influences political ideology, or affects marginalized identities such as disabled or impoverished people.

Consequently, this book illuminates a correlation between performance culture and charity in an effort to keep the materials and politics of performance distinct from the concept of benevolence. My research evidences the developing sophistication of devices, technologies, and conventions made available through performance culture to engender charitable sentiment throughout the nineteenth, twentieth, and twenty-first centuries. The relationship between performance culture and charity exists in tandem along a historical spectrum that speaks to a generative cultural consciousness about how to adequately combine, manipulate, deploy, and comprehend these elements. Performance culture serves as a means to explicate the social and political impacts of charity and, most important, is responsible for exacerbating our current climate of benevolence, marked by a social penchant for conspicuous compassion.

Chapter 1 presents an examination of America's first experience with organized benevolence in the nineteenth-century crusade to educate and reform blind and hearing-impaired individuals. Sentimentalism and sentimental culture played pivotal roles in the earliest attempts to mobilize the public around this worthy cause. I discuss the contributions of Common Sense philosophers in developing theories about sentimentalism as a mode of expression and communication, drawing a correlation between sentimental culture and the ability to experience charitable "fellow-feeling."

Sentimentalism also informed popular representations and perception of disabled individuals. Nineteenth-century theater, namely melodrama, offered provocative portrayals of "deaf/dumb and blind" communities. I recuperate an array of widely performed affliction melodramas, plays featuring impaired characters, to show how these dramas not only produced sentimentalized images of disabled people but offered a way for spectators to understand and replicate the ideal charitable dynamic. Reformers directly utilized these theatrical practices and their dramatic models in their own public, educational performances showcasing the rehabilitation of their "woefully afflicted" pupils.

The legacy of staging distress using public performance and spectacle takes on new complexities and sophistication in the highly political, theatricalized efforts of the twentieth-century National Foundation for Infantile Paralysis (NFIP), an organization that takes primary focus in chapter 2.

The war on polio (infantile paralysis) galvanized Americans around what scientists and health officials characterized as a mysterious, lethal enemy that posed a threat regardless of age, race, class, or gender. This chapter highlights the NFIP's efforts in its formative years. The foundation emerged as a revolutionary entity that explicitly exploited the social, educational, and entertainment aspects of performance culture in its attempt to raise funds and resources in the fight against polio. The NFIP fundamentally changed the way people thought about and responded to disease, while also instigating a novel approach to brokering charitable sentiment.

I consider the NFIP's aggressive implementation of live and mediated performance in its annual fundraising campaigns to explore how this approach broadened the charity's appeal to resonate politically and socially. For example, I illuminate the seemingly contradictory practice of staging elaborate pageant performances within lavish annual charity balls. These pageants, created and executed by upper-class white women, excised disability and illness from the national mythology in order to reify American ideals and reiterate a republican narrative of progress, innovation, and prosperity.

This type of aggrandized spectacle became a hallmark of NFIP practices, inarguably altering how citizens understood charitable sentiment. Depressing, maudlin, melodramatic representations of those impacted by polio were carefully reengineered to engender the right combination of sentiment and civic pride. Capitalizing on the visibility of America's most famous polio survivor and founder of the NFIP, President Franklin D. Roosevelt, the foundation's campaigns revolved around interactive events and public performance to reconfigure the polio crusade into a cultural drama that cast children as casualties, citizens as heroes, and polio as the unknown foreign enemy threatening the future of the country. Additionally, the foundation's novel use of emerging media such as film, radio, and later television helped to further the organization's ideological imperatives and corroborated its performance-based methodologies. Public service announcements, radio broadcasts, and the inclusion of celebrity icons driving these endeavors solidified public support for the NFIP and set the stage for a new era of spectacular benevolence.

Chapter 3 traces the technological and cinematic influences of the NFIP in the charity telethon phenomenon. Television, as the NFIP effectively demonstrated, offered up an apparatus to educate as well as entertain. Looking for ways to continue to demonstrate television's positive effects as an entity capable of facilitating social good, programmers welcomed the charity telethon event: a self-contained novelty program designed to raise a large amount of funds in a constrained amount of time. The telethon acquired popularity amid other quirky cultural "stunts" such as dance-a-thons. Telethons appealed to charity organizations for their ability to capture a massive demographic and bring immense exposure to an association's cause.

The Muscular Dystrophy Association's (MDA) annual telethon materialized as one of the most lucrative, popular, and highly contested charity fundraising events in American history. As many scholars have adequately demonstrated, the telethon produced representations of those living with neuromuscular disease that echoed the same sentimental portrayals put forth in nineteenth-century melodramas: the disabled individual was conceived as hopeless and pitiful. However, I offer a different way to understand these depictions as part of the telethon's performance gestalt, which depends upon distinct visual and rhetorical strategies for its cultural and economic effects.

Television created an opportunity to poignantly "speak for" the disabled experience by circulating narratives about the lives of those with neuromuscular disease. Telethon producers seized on this to incorporate filmed vignettes of disabled individuals interspersed among the telethon's entertainment diet of jugglers, singers, and dog acts. These filmed vignettes, what I term *telemonials*, are essential parts of the telethon, designed to promote comprehension of the muscular dystrophy narrative and invite emotional investment in the impaired individual. However, due to their contrived nature, telemonials also produce a distancing effect that reinforces difference. This separation is further exacerbated by the unique, intensely physically comic performance style of host Jerry Lewis. I reexamine Lewis's comic machinations to make the case that his performance work allows for critical breaches in the sentimentalized and often oppressive flow of images during the telethon that permit the spectator to make the transition from experiencing charitable sentiment to performing charitable action.

Performance culture and benevolence intertwine in the contemporary moment in the cultural preoccupation with excessive voyeurism, unencumbered consumption, media saturation, and conspicuous compassion. The ABC show *Extreme Makeover: Home Edition* was the first reality television show to earn critical and popular success by exploiting the cultural fascination with bearing witness to radical transformation. In chapter 4, I focus on the contributions made by reality television to this current period in America's charity history. Reality television, fully embraced as a viable, commercial enterprise by television networks in the early 2000s, provides a logical forum for the generation of charitable sentiment. Its aesthetic properties, borrowed from documentary cinema, endow reality TV with an inflated sense of liveness, immediacy, and inclusion. Furthermore, much of its content, which centers on placing ordinary people in extraordinary, life-changing circumstances, compliments the seminal notion that charitable sentiment engenders life-altering intervention. In this case, the results are broadcast in spectacular terms for millions of viewers across the world.

Extreme Makeover: Home Edition gestures back to the sentimentalized tenets instituted in nineteenth-century America in its conceptual framework that highlights deserving families facing perilous circumstances and enormous personal challenges. In the course of the televised hour, the lives of the family are forever altered vis-à-vis the reconstruction of their dilapidated and, in some cases, dangerous homes into technological, ecological, and domestic dreamscapes. This reality show, indebted to performance culture with its highly mediated, cinematically controlled dramatic rendering of the American "rags-to-riches" mythos, offers a new way for the public to experience and consume benevolence. Furthermore, its cast of anonymous volunteers, stable of celebrity guest stars, and, most important, host of corporate donors and sponsors exhibiting their benevolence on national television raise ethical questions about the appeal of this type of conspicuous compassion in the wake of a perilously diminished public welfare state.

The contemporary social environment dominated by self-conscious exhibition and celebrity culture figures into the issues raised in the book's conclusion. While charity still remains the domain of institutional entities such as religious, environmental, and health organizations, its prevalence as part of our entertainment and leisure spheres signals a shift in the way citizens comprehend and respond to the call for benevolent action. The increased desire to demonstrate charitable acts through buying and using products such as rubber wrist bracelets or by sharing one's efforts on Facebook or YouTube suggests that we have moved beyond cause-related marketing's "give to get" model to one where display and affirmation become virtues prized over moral or civic obligation. In the wake of this moment, the role of performance culture in the production of charitable sentiment seems particularly vital. Furthermore, the inclusion of the disabled community in this exchange, influenced by a society obsessed with hyperidealized bodies, preoccupied with prolonged life spans, and concerned with the politics of visibility, raises fresh apprehensions about the way disability is represented, understood, and experienced by mainstream culture.

At its core, *Acts of Conspicuous Compassion* offers a way to recognize and deeply consider the various rhetorical and representational systems that enable individuals to identify and act on the request for charity. In the process, the discourse about why people invest in benevolence changes, no longer exclusively tethered to issues of ethics, spirituality, or civic obligation that can be highly individualistic, idiosyncratic, and even oppressive. Instead, a portrait of American charity practices emerges where contrivance is necessary and permissible and where a sense of productive artifice that helps neutralize uncomfortable class, racial, and embodied realities is, for better or worse, the preferred critical mode.

1 *Dramatizing Distress*

Sentimental Culture, Melodrama, and Nineteenth-Century Reform for the Deaf/Dumb and Blind

The Connecticut Asylum for the Education of the Deaf and Dumb opened its doors to the public in April of 1817. The first of its kind in America, the crusade to instruct deaf/dumb individuals how to read and write flourished in the early decades of the nineteenth century under the efforts of the Reverend Thomas H. Gallaudet.[1] Up until Gallaudet's intervention, people characterized as deaf/dumb dwelled in isolation, living either as wards of the state in workhouses and orphanages or as familial specters sequestered from the public in private homes. Without the ability to communicate and, more important, understand the word of God, deaf/dumb individuals were characterized as hopeless, pitiful souls destined for a life of sorrow. In his inauguration speech, Gallaudet performed a type of ventriloquy for his students, personifying their tortured plight:

> What mysterious darkness must sadden their souls! Must not each one of them, in the language of thought, sometimes say, "What is it that makes me differ from my fellow-men? What is that strange mode of communicating, by which they understand each other? Why do I not posses it, or why can it not be communicated to me? What are those mysterious volumes over which they pore with such delight, and which seem to gladden the hours that pass me by so sad and hopeless!"[2]

The rhapsodic nature of his speech amplifies the type of emotional discourse necessary for entreating the public to join in supporting his benevolent efforts. It also contains traces of the popular oratorical presentation style prevalent in early nineteenth-century American pulpits and theaters. Gallaudet's rhetorical choices and the representational framework they create not only served as his most effective and controversial tool in generating support for his educational asylum they also produced a model of how to understand and respond to people with this particular kind of physical disability.

Gallaudet's foray into organized benevolence, the first consolidated and mobilized endeavor of its kind, was a natural outgrowth from his interest in serving in the ministry. Religious doctrine clearly outlined the importance of tithing and assisting the impoverished and needy as part of God's divine work. However, these fundamental ideas took on new significance in the wake of the Second Great Awakening: a period of religious revivalism that spread throughout America. It is within this cultural climate that, ironically, the concept of charity shifted from an exclusively spiritual practice to a tenet that informed both religion and civil society.

According to historian Kathleen D. McCarthy, the "rush of religious enthusiasm" typified by the Second Great Awakening spanned from the 1790s to the 1830s and indelibly changed America's spiritual and cultural environment.[3] Advocates of this spiritual movement preached a doctrine of salvation through benevolent acts, which ultimately contributed to the proliferation of relief societies that developed activities such as distributing Bible tracts; teaching literacy; and providing widows, orphans, and the poor with basic materials such as food and clothing.[4] This era of spiritual fervor resulted in what McCarthy characterizes as "religious disestablishment": the restructuring of religious doctrine that emphasized the individual's role in shaping one's own spiritual destiny. McCarthy writes:

> Disestablishment cleared the way for more vigorous proselytizing by evangelical sects: Baptists, Methodists, Presbyterians, and non-Calvinistic Congregationalists. Unlike many of their predecessors, these sects emphasized the power of individual conversion, grace, and human perfectibility.[5]

For the individual benefactor, this meant negotiating new codes of behavior enacted to demonstrate a commensurate relationship between the exterior and interior, the spiritual soul and the social self. McCarthy goes on to note that religious disestablishment granted the person control over his spiritual destiny; for average citizens, achieving spiritual elevation or salvation was no longer a matter of predetermination.

With its emphasis on the autonomy of the individual, this new ideological climate significantly altered the way people perceived their needy cohort. Specifically, the spread of evangelical Protestantism exacerbated attitudes that an issue such as poverty, one of the leading impetuses behind charity, was a result of personal failings or laziness.[6] People in need were subject to social scrutiny; their material lack signified a lapse in both character and ethical integrity. Work, personal rehabilitation, and moral uplift became antidotes to unmitigated giving, and people such as Gallaudet reflected these ideas in the institutional structures of their assistive organizations. Benevolent fellow-feeling served as the conduit to realize this model.

Humanitarians Cotton Mather and Benjamin Franklin joined with other critics in advancing the merits of charity for the health of the nation. Mather's widely circulated essay entitled "Bonifacious: An Essay upon Doing Good" advanced voluntarism as a form of civic duty. People should commit their lives, Mather exhorted, to the "perpetual endeavor to do good in the world."[7] Building on these views, Benjamin Franklin espoused a conception of charity that also took into account the tenets of Republicanism, which stressed "simplicity, patriotism, integrity, valor, and a love of justice and liberty." This further accorded with Republicanism's gendered principles, which McCarthy points out contributed to redefining manhood in terms of how men participated in civic duty.[8] The politics of the public sphere belonged to men, responsible for building the infrastructure, such as institutions, asylums, and schools, that would support the affective, sentimental, and spiritual work of benevolence, driven primarily by women.[9]

Under the rubric of Republicanism, charity involved an equal amount of compassion and practicality. For these reasons, Franklin, as well as others, advocated dispersing material or economic relief coupled with correctional measures designed to reintegrate the disadvantaged into society. "'The best way of doing good to the poor,' Franklin stated, 'is [by] . . . driving them *out* of it.'"[10] His philosophy gained momentum by midcentury as educators and reformers made this notion the foundation of their benevolent efforts. Relief organizations created in the late eighteenth and early nineteenth centuries to help populations determined worthy of assistance exhibited this combined ethos of Republicanism and spiritual enfranchisement: people required an amalgam of moral guidance and practical instruction.

A burgeoning cultural preoccupation with teaching self-control and discipline over physical appetites and ethical challenges also factored into the expansion of groups dedicated to advocating for self- and societal preservation. For instance, the Quakers sought to expand their efforts beyond the distribution of religious tracts that warned against the dangers of sloth, intemperance, and poverty to persuade individuals to reform by committing themselves to the Quaker community. Similarly, Philadelphia's first white, women's charity, Parrish's Female Society, aided African American and white women. Participants worked collaboratively to run a house where needy mothers received child-care help, acquired household provisions, and earned wages for spinning textiles such as cotton and flax.[11] By reinforcing the virtues of labor while concurrently offering moral direction meted out by religious texts, reformers outfitted the needy with renewed understanding of how to contribute as responsible citizens.

These earliest efforts instituted new material measures to address what many critics saw as alarming problems plaguing America in antebellum society. In doing so, they instigated an unforeseen backlash against the people receiving assistance. Laziness, destitution, and intemperance became the discerning traits of "dangerous classes," which middle-class Americans strove to define themselves against. Social historian David Wagner argues that by drawing parameters around their own perceptions of acceptable behaviors, reformers manufactured distinctive categories within which to cast the Other. "Proper-thinking respectable citizens," writes Wagner, "developed a view of correct behavior which placed the poor, particularly, immigrants and people of color, women without husbands, and men without visible means, into the categories of deviant, dangerous, or immoral."[12] People with disabilities occupied a more complicated designation in the early decades of the nineteenth century. These individuals encapsulated an array of cultural meanings that ranged from pitiful "creatures" to living abominations of God's will. Within this environment that bred social unease over the presence of diverse communities, reformers took on the at times daunting task of inviting citizens to sympathize with and emotionally as well as materially invest in those threatening and, in the case of the deaf/dumb, mystifying populations.

Religious establishments were no longer the singular entities entreating individuals to assist the ill, disabled, destitute, or depraved. Women and men without formal spiritual training, but with passionate beliefs about shaping America's civil discourse, took the lead in driving benevolent aims. The rise of groups interested in servicing different communities with their own unique sets of needs produced two discernible outcomes: reformers began to drive representations of their targeted populations, as evidenced by Gallaudet's language in his inauguration speech, and they had to contend with competition from other entities equally invested in garnering the public's attention and resources. For localized relief societies in small or rural centers dependent upon individual acts of benevolence in the form of handing out tracts, sewing clothes, or conducting Bible classes, this latter aspect produced less of a strain on their resources. However, for people like Gallaudet, who envisioned comprehensive facilities for his students that spanned multiple cities and states, obtaining public and even legislative support was imperative. In an effort to bolster their causes and aggressively gain public sympathy, reformers employed strategies lifted from the pages of popular sentimental fiction and the stages of America's theaters.

THE RISE OF NINETEENTH-CENTURY SENTIMENTAL CULTURE

"If I meet a cripple moving with pain through the streets my pity is excited," writes an anonymous individual in a short item that appeared in 1792 in the periodical *Weekly Museum*. "At the same time," the person continues, "a sensation of pleasing gratitude arises, on the reflection, that such is not my case; and so likewise with every malady, and evil that I see."[13] The writer's confession to excitable pity testifies to an evolving social transition in the way people thought about and responded to emotions and their stimuli. Enlightenment philosophers, also called Common Sense philosophers, such as Thomas Reid, David Hume, Adam Smith, Francis Hutcheson, and the Earl of Shaftesbury, generated theories on the nature of social and personal relationships, taking particular interest in the mechanics of affect. By disclosing the workings of the interior as they related to actions that impacted the public sphere, people would be able to produce a more successful, prosperous, and morally sound community.

Sentimentalism as a concept and an emotional property become a pervasive element in the cultivation of charity in antebellum culture. This distinctive fellow-feeling formed the affective crux of the charitable plea, most notably when it involved bearing witness to another in pain or distress. As the writer for the piece in the *Weekly Museum* illustrates, an emotional reaction to someone in need determines the intellectual and moral responses of the spectator. The writings of Common Sense philosophers contributed to the growing awareness of the way emotion functioned to instigate a series of reactions comprised of complex cognitive and sensory facets. The role of reformers became focused on finding ways to manage and, at times, exploit this understanding for their own benevolent aims.

Intellectual forbears such as Descartes and Locke elevated the processes of the mind over the heart. In contrast, Enlightenment philosophers focused on sentient properties to contend that "the capacity to respond to the signs of others' woes" separated the human from animal.[14] The degree to which people responded to emotional stimuli such as suffering, grief, or love correlated to their moral aptitude. As cultural historian Janet Todd explains in her examination of nineteenth-century sentimental culture, physical and emotional manifestations of the interior were "justified by the belief that a heightened sense of one's virtue through pity for another" was ethically advantageous.[15] Subsequently, fellow-feelings served as organic ways to implement ethical checks and balances that ensured civic and individual propriety.

Sensibility fostered a different type of self-awareness in people. It produced a way for citizens to comprehend and control their behaviors as well as generated a method to decode or read others' actions. Shaftesbury attributed this conduct to each person's "inward eye" that discerns scenes, events, or moments and assigns them with affective value and meaning.[16] Viewed by many as a system of principles that offered crucial personal and moral instruction, sentimentalism gained momentum through its incorporation into nineteenth-century novels and short stories. Literary works became seminal texts that helped to circulate and instill sentimental creeds in the cultural imagination, providing ways to guide behavior and identify emotional signs.

Sentimental literature turned on heightened displays of affect, specifically showcasing the expansive heart and goodwill of its characters. Early sentimental novels such as Samuel Richardson's *Clarissa; or, The History of a Young Lady* (1748), Laurence Stern's *A Sentimental Journey* (1768), and Susanna Rowson's *Charlotte Temple* (1791) produced the seminal typology of the sentimental figure: an individual, often innocent, naive, and female, attuned to nature, inciting the passions of others through her transparent emotional makeup. The sentimental plot followed a simplistic formula that turned on the investment in the characters' spontaneous goodness where a higher moral purpose prevailed. The typical sentimental novel's resolution meted out punishments commensurate with the crime and proffered rewards that reinforced the highest ethical virtues.[17]

This type of writing presented more than engrossing characters or dramatic plots; it was engineered to *move* the reader. The reader or spectator, affected by the overwrought spectacle as a "true feeler," was "expected to match pang for pang, and sigh for sigh with the persecuted victim."[18] Women, viewed as the more delicate sex, were thought to be particularly susceptible to sentimental influence. Nineteenth-century beliefs about women cast them as "creatures of the heart" who possessed superior virtues. Primarily motivated by emotion, women were taken as possessing more innately authentic characters than their male counterpoints. Cultural historian Karen Halttunen points out:

> The woman of sensibility involuntarily expressed her feelings in swoons, illness, trances, ecstasies, and most important, tears, the "infallible signs of grace in the religion of the heart." Sentimentalists thus insisted that true women were constitutionally transparent, incapable of disguising their feelings.[19]

For this reason, sentimentalism became synonymous with women's culture. It grafted feminizing discourses of compassion, care, love, and vulnerability onto women's domains such as the home and church. Furthermore, sentimentalism positioned women, specifically white, middle-class women, as the ideal purveyors of benevolent initiatives, making them the vehicles for the creation and proliferation of highly organized public charity organizations and relief societies.

In *Women in Antebellum Reform*, feminist historian Lori D. Ginzberg examines the political, social, and economic implications of women engaged in benevolent activities during the first half of the nineteenth century. She states that society relied on women to set an example of moral and humanitarian ideals, not only due to their innate integrity but because women were excluded "from the greed and self-interest that characterized men, and [were] more likely to sympathize with the needy and the weak."[20] As a result, society sanctioned women's involvement in most humanitarian efforts. In turn, their activities as formidable organizers provided them with moral and social credibility as contributors to the public sphere.[21]

Removed from its sole confinement to literary or, later, theatrical realms, sentimentalism evolved into what literary theorist Shirley Samuels describes as a "set of operations" that transcended these discursive materials to "effect connections across gender, race, and class boundaries."[22] As both an ideology and a method of communication, sentimentalism was an imperative practice amid urban centers impacted by an emerging culture of hypocrisy. Cities offered anonymity for their residents, precluding customary and reliable ways of exchanging social information such as class and status. Outward appearance could no longer accurately convey a person's ethical makeup or moral intentions. Consequently, people attempted to discern these immaterial aspects by using a "sentimental typology." "A man's inner character," writes Halttunen, "was believed to be imprinted upon his face and thus visible to anyone who understood the moral language of physiognomy."[23] This belief governed the ways in which citizens read one another in the social sphere, and it also affected, in part, how people recognized and demonstrated the integrity of their benevolence.

Emotionalism supposedly leveled the playing field of antebellum identity politics, facilitated by a range of elements employed to produce a high degree of affective impact. Spectacle, demonstration, and display were primary vehicles in sentimental practices. It was just as vital to use whatever methods necessary to incite an emotional response as it was for the spectator to exhibit his or her reactions. The more poignant the presentation of calamity, the more readily and demonstratively spectators pronounced their affect.

In the case of sadness, anger, grief, or joy the commensurate behaviors (e.g., crying, wailing, laughing, acting violently, etc.) present themselves in straightforward, easily discernible ways. However, other sentimentalized emotions such as sympathy (a hallmark element of charity) and empathy produce more nuanced results. Philosopher Adam Smith devotes a lengthy section to the notion of sympathy in his work *The Theory of Moral Sentiments* (1759). For Smith, sympathy is an effect produced by the spectator's capacity to imaginatively transfer places with a suffering individual. "As we have no immediate experience of what other men feel," Smith writes, "we can form no idea of the manner in which they are affected, but by conceiving what we ourselves should feel in the like situation. . . . It is by the imagination only that we can form any conception of what are his sensations."[24] The person bearing witness to the spectacle of calamity, unable to literally experience the "torments and agonies" on display, may only approximate distress.

Smith exemplifies this when he states: "Though our brother is upon the wrack, as long as we ourselves are at our ease, our senses will never inform us of what he suffers."[25] The onlooker is simultaneously absorbed and detached from the scene and as a result is able to exercise cognitive and emotional self-awareness.

Theories of sentiment also hinged on the notion that these feelings were innately generated by various events, encounters, depictions, or exhibitions. Smith troubles this notion when he writes, "Sympathy does not arise so much from the view of the passion, as from the situation which excites it."[26] Emotion does not spring from the sight of tears alone, but rather from the *context* of the source of grief. Smith's distinction is an important one when it comes to the production of benevolence. The narrative framework for the emotion's source must be legible; it is this intelligence that enables the potential benefactor to, as Smith earlier notes, "imaginatively identify" with the person in need. It is also this contextualizing that permits the kind of emotional dissociation needed to not just emotionally invest in the Other but to critically act on their behalf.

Smith's treatise also raises questions of authenticity and contrivance in his insistence that affect may be attributed to external rather than internal or innate mechanisms. If a person produces emotion comparable to the type and degree of distress he witnesses, it follows that this spectacle may be inflated, exaggerated, or completely false in order to capitalize on an individual's sympathies. Concordantly, it is also possible for the benevolent patron to simply read and understand the signs of need and to produce an expected response. Smith's observations on sympathy introduce the idea that sincerity is a malleable concept and, more important, that both the spectator and the person soliciting charity are aware of the potential for mutual insincerity to exist between them.

The work of Scottish Enlightenment philosopher Thomas Reid bears relevance on this issue. In *Active Powers of the Human Mind* (1788) Reid contends that the ability to respond to another's trouble involves recognizing the "signs of distress." All individuals, he argues, possess an innate capacity to communicate emotional and psychological needs through a "natural language" conveyed through the body. "Looks, gestures, and speeches," Reid writes, "are the natural signs" one uses to express hurt, sorrow, joy, or need.[27] This language results from a system of physical signs that correlate to universally identifiable meanings that remain essentially stable. Focusing on an external manifestation of internal phenomena, Reid bases his claims on the belief that this language is inherent, organic, and therefore reliable.

Reid goes on to clarify that "we may sympathize with a perfect stranger, or even with an enemy whom we see in distress; but this is the effect of pity; and if we did not pity him, we should not sympathize with him."[28] Reid takes for granted that pity's arousal evolves from internalized comprehension of another person's pain or weakness. However, by locating the impetus to feel pity within a lexicon of visual and verbal signs, Reid inadvertently concedes that this emotion and its consequent relationship is predicated on fabrication; it is based on performing an act, gesture, or other kind of material signifier that communicates a desire for benevolent intervention. As charity evolved into a public practice with personal as well as social implications, these signs were subject to revision: the organizers of charitable endeavors learned how to deploy aesthetic and rhetorical devices that ensured a benevolent response. They mined many of these mechanisms from nineteenth-century theater, specifically those plays that bathed spectators in high emotion and spectacular tribulation: melodrama.

STAGING SUFFERING IN MELODRAMAS OF AFFLICTION

Nowhere was the palpable sight of sentimentalism in all its hand-wringing and tearful anguish more readily available or rendered more exquisitely pathetic than in popular melodramas performed on the stages of American playhouses. In this sense, drama outpaced sentimental literature for emotional release; its distinctive liveness engaged the workings of the spectator's imaginative faculties in a different way than could novels, poetry, essays, or paintings. Nineteenth-century writers on theater consistently invoked the dictum that the stage should "hold a mirror up to nature." The stage, many believed, reflected society's cultural and, more important, moral composition. Consequently, theater was held in tension by two schools of thought: for some, the drama existed as an economic enterprise that provided entertainment and possibly ethical instruction. In an article published in 1829 titled "The Modern Drama," the writer praises the theater for enforcing transparent ideas about good and evil: the dramatic exhibition of "the guilty as suffering the just punishment of their offenses, and the innocent and virtuous as receiving their merited recompense," notes the writer, ultimately affords the spectator with moral, social, and emotional instruction.[29] Other critics did not share this view, especially those individuals affiliated with Protestant religious sects. They believed that theater was a dangerous pastime that bred "vice and dissolution."[30] As such, theater managers and actors bore a considerable responsibility to the public, generating representations that possessed the capacity to either produce pleasure and moral guidance or else corrupt the public's sensibilities.

Theater enabled spectators to essentially "try on" emotional stances and moral decisions, whether contradictory or complementary, without lasting repercussions.[31] The dramatic contract brought Smith's theory about engagement and estrangement from an experience to life. A piece published in the *American Quarterly Review* about the drama's effects reinforces this notion:

> In witnessing them [dramatic exhibitions], we are excited by the passions of others instead of our own, as is the case in the real transactions of life; and that stimulus, which may be pronounced to be one of the actual wants of our nature, is thus afforded to us, without any of the evil consequences resulting from an indulgence of the passions in our own proper persons.[32]

In principle, theater *moved* spectators. Its art permitted an emotional investment in the narrative unfolding on stage, as well as insulation, in many cases, from the anxious presence of difference.

Melodrama, a nascent genre in the first decades of the nineteenth century, presented particularly compelling sentimental representations. Melodrama also created unambiguous paradigms of moral and ethical decorum, aligning itself with theater's capacity to instruct and elevate. In addition to its evil villains, brave heroes, beautiful heroines, and kind uncles, melodrama featured characters with noticeable disparities. Figures with disabilities, specifically those characterized as deaf/dumb and blind, populated a variety of plays.

These plays, distinguished here as affliction melodramas, staged the tragic plight and eventual retribution of the pathetic, physically disabled individual. Adapted from French and British sources and performed throughout the first decades of the nineteenth century, affliction melodramas capitalized on the public's growing interest in and concern with the situation of hearing-impaired and blind people. The inclusion of these melodramas in American theaters coincided with the charity work of Gallaudet and his predecessor Samuel Gridley Howe, a like-minded reformer interested in rehabilitating members of the blind community. Moreover, their formulaic nature and easily comprehensible ethical messages that touted benevolence as the highest form of intervention for these "trapped" characters offered the ideal aesthetic framework for making sense of Gallaudet's and Howe's mission.

Affliction melodramas also gave spectators new representations of the physically disabled that contradicted contemporary perceptions of disabled people as somehow nonhuman. Religious tenets that equated physical difference with monstrosity informed the earliest conceptions of physical disability; corporeal difference was thought to be the physical manifestation of evil and a punishment from God.[33] The proliferation of the nineteenth-century sideshow, cheap entertainment that featured the exhibition of congenitally disabled individuals (e.g., the "Armless and Legless Wonder" or conjoined Siamese twins), helped to advance and contain this distinction.[34] With the display of physical disability and other types of medical anomalies featuring prominently in the public sphere, meanings ascribed to corporeal difference changed, facilitated partly by the context for exhibiting disability and partly by the new range of meanings ascribed to disabled bodies.

A distinction between sideshow performers labeled "freakish" and those people possessing other forms of physical and cognitive disabilities arose by midcentury. "The difference between being a freak and being disabled," states historian Mary Klages, "lay almost entirely in the meanings assigned to the person rather than in any physical or mental quality per sey."[35] Blind, deaf/dumb, and in some cases cognitively disabled individuals signified in terms of affliction rather than freakishness. In regard to hearing and visually impaired people, eighteenth- and nineteenth-century theories on sense perception and mental acuity contributed to a reimagining of these disabilities in scientific terms.

John Locke, Voltaire, and Dennis Diderot circulated hypotheses about the mechanisms of the mind and senses that posited these disabilities as physical problems, not spiritual or supernatural omens. For example, studies of blind individuals conducted in the early 1800s focused on the results of experimental surgeries and treatments. Absent from these reports was consideration of the blind person's humanity or other aspects of their subjectivity. Reduced solely to medical terms, the blind person becomes little more than a vehicle for data collection, a kind of living "laboratory . . . where

empirical investigations and experimentation could provide useful knowledge about the condition of the nondisabled."[36]

What the scientific community elided in terms of the cultural significance generated by afflictions, the social realm supplied by way of literary
and artistic renderings of blindness and deafness. Nearly always framed by
tragic circumstances, blind and deaf characters inhabited lonely, sorrowful,
isolated worlds and exuded correlative emotional qualities such as despair,
melancholy, or hopelessness. Accounts of the deaf/dumb and blind appearing in mass periodicals reflected and strengthened these representations. In
an article published in the *American Monthly Magazine* in 1830, the writer
waxes poetic on the devastating situation of blind individuals:

> The blind are the most unfortunate. They are condemned to a prison of clay,
> dark, and helpless, and desolate, in the midst of a world, which is full of light
> and glory, and beauty; of which they continually hear, and after some concep-
> tions of which their souls must pant in vain, with all the sickening agony of
> unquenchable desire.[37]

Fiction and nonfiction critics (i.e., educators, religious leaders, physicians, social reformers, etc.) writing about disabled people during this time
helped to humanize afflicted individuals in their rhetoric, which presented
them as capable of feeling and emitting emotions. Unfortunately, these char-
acterizations tended to diverge into two categories, as disability and literary
scholar Martha Stoddard Holmes illuminates in her study of disability in
Victorian literature. She states, "Either they [the disabled] were innocent
sufferers—afflicted children grateful for charitable assistance—or they were
embittered, suspicious, and emotionally and morally degraded, begging
imposters willing to counterfeit suffering in . . . order to gather alms."[38] These
literary representations arguably oversimplified the disability experience in
the early nineteenth century. The reality—of disabled individuals who conformed to neither of these stereotypes but who lived fulfilling and even joy-
ful lives—remained largely undocumented. By the mid- to late 1800s writers
such as Herman Melville and Elizabeth Stuart Phelps would put pressure
on the contours of these seemingly one-dimensional renderings of physical
difference to offer more complicated and nuanced depictions of disability.
However, the views that Holmes outlines nevertheless appealed to reformers precisely for their rudimentary typology. Affliction melodramas further

supported these views of the disabled: deaf/dumb and blind individuals existed as unfortunate, pure souls, suffering a cruel fate, reliant upon the benevolence of able-bodied protectors.

More than literary representations, dramatic depictions engendered a dynamic of immediacy that factored into sentimental principles about instigating emotion. Theorist Michael Bell describes this phenomenon as one where the "immediacy of presence and the factual reality of distress" account for the spectator's emotional reactions.[39] Theater, with its claim to re-presenting action, events, behaviors, and characters in a way that attempted approximate simulations of similar errata in the public sphere, brought the spectacle of affliction into proximity with the average patron. Furthermore, it achieved this within a forum explicitly engineered to invite the audience members' emotional investment in the dramatized narrative. Affliction melodramas produced the unintended consequence of outfitting reformers interested in providing charity and education for the deaf/dumb and blind with a means to engage the public's collective sympathies in their cause, bring visibility to those considered by sentimental standards as "woefully afflicted," and ultimately invite benevolent intervention.

Philadelphia dominated the theatrical market in the first decades of antebellum America, with New York rising in popularity as a center of cultural and artistic activity. By midcentury over two dozen theaters existed in New York City alone.[40] As the number of playhouses, acting troupes, and managers increased, dramatic content became stratified, with everything from equestrian performance to the works of Shakespeare taking place on American stages. Though America lacked the same kind of patent laws operating in England, which differentiated legitimate from illegitimate drama, critics gave voice to an implicit delineation between "serious" drama and popular theatrical amusements. In 1823, a critic for the *New York Mirror* surmised:

> The Circus, in Broadway, has also a dramatic corps attached to it, for the performance of Melodramas, Pantomimes, Ballets etc. But as neither of these kinds of entertainment belong to the legitimate drama, they cannot properly be noticed in this department. The same remark will apply to the Amphitheatre and Circus in Richmond-Hill Garden.[41]

Melodrama, as noted, was often critically dismissed, and writers used the popular penchant for these plays to comment on class differences as well as artistic merit.

Another writer for the *New York Mirror* published a piece in which he derided spectators for embracing elements of melodrama such as "*real* horses, *real* dogs, *real* fire, *real* water, or *real* ice burgs." "The minor theatres," the author intones, "are ever ready to serve up those *monstrosities* which disgrace the drama."[42] Despite the attempts of these and other critics to exclude melodrama from the press and curtail the public's acceptance of this genre, it remained a popular fixture in many of the respectable theaters in markets such as New York, Philadelphia, and Boston throughout the nineteenth century.

If theater constituted a unique medium that strove to mirror nature, critics understood melodrama as the reflection of an idealized universe. Melodrama appeared at the turn of the century as a Parisian genre in venues restricted from carrying the "legitimate" (i.e., spoken) drama. It combined pantomime with music to form a drama of expression and movement appealing to the popular masses, many possessing little or no literary skills. The growing numbers of theater patrons who responded positively to the melodrama's exploitation of pathos and sentiment contributed to its propagation in both France and England. In the United States, early theatrical companies imported melodrama as a way to supplement native drama with well-known European fare. William Dunlap, an established playwright and theater historian, produced the "weepy comedies" of German playwright August von Kotzebue in the early 1800s. In the process, he opened up a new forum where American spectators could shed their "plentiful tears" and demonstrate "the purity and potential greatness of their own sympathetic hearts."[43]

Dunlap went on to translate French playwrights considered tawdrier than Kotzebue and other European translations. These plays added excitement, thrills, and "emotion-rousing" action to sentimental speeches, essentially offering a work designed solely to convey ethical platitudes. Their prescriptive composition enabled playwrights to easily adapt these plays to the American stage. Tropes such as mistaken identity, the return of a character to claim his birthright, the presence of supernatural intervention, and the dramatic rescue or resolution played out against a backdrop of elaborate scenery and gripping action, all of which accounted for portions of the melodrama's mass appeal. The sights, sounds, and emotions of such captivating stage action transcended class sensibilities, alluring to immigrants and the working class. What followed in the wake of these initial French and German translations was a steady output of melodramas from a variety of sources that presented themes, ideas, and characters indicative of a political, social, and economic climate in transition.[44]

Melodrama was especially adept at dramatizing the oversimplification of ethical choices and morally transparent characters. Literary theorist Peter Brooks presents a succinct characterization of this aspect of the genre:

> Melodrama starts from and expresses the anxiety brought by a frightening new world in which the traditional patterns of moral order no longer provide the necessary social glue. It plays out the force of that anxiety with the apparent triumph of villainy, and it dissipates it with the eventual victory of virtue. It demonstrates over and over that the signs of ethical forces can be discovered and can be made legible.[45]

As Brooks and other theater historians illustrate, melodrama held social significance for the way it enabled audiences to experience and make sense of the phenomena unfolding outside the playhouse.[46] The melodrama's distinctive portrayals of concepts such as paternalism and virtue were particularly resonant for citizens dwelling in a world of strangers. Melodrama bestowed on patrons a map and a compass, charting out a welcome terrain built upon nostalgic values such as truth, justice, purity, and benevolence. In this sense, citizens could authorize their own morality tales that adhered to traditional values in the midst of a social climate where those beliefs were becoming unstable. Spectators coalesced around melodrama to validate ideals and to participate in upholding what theater historian Jeffrey Mason identifies as a "sentimental vision of humanity" that resembled the primary tenets of sentimental culture, where affective exchanges governed interpersonal relationships and fostered social bonds.[47] Unruly or threatening entities were ultimately contained, and the right course of action triumphed as the only course of action.

A primary way for audiences to identify with the ideas presented in melodrama was through its stock characters. Figures such as the sweet, innocent heroine, the evil villain, or the familial patriarch embodied and communicated the melodrama's easily identifiable principles. Heroines were primarily portrayed as vulnerable, weak, and passive, making them the purveyors of salvation. In the melodrama, women required protection from the immoral forces of a world gripped in vice while they simultaneously personified the qualities of redemption and purity. Villains, in contrast, comprised the antithetical foil to the innocence and innate goodness of heroines as well as heroes. Whether framed in comic or dramatic sensibilities, the villain "directed his malevolence toward the citadel of virtue": the heroine.[48]

The spectacular clash between the persecuted innocents and the villain formed the dramatic crux of every melodrama, performed, in most cases, for maximum emotional and visual effect. Furthermore, the cultural implications of these characters correlated with their status within the play. Villains depicted the worst traits of humankind (e.g., greed, vice, depravity, etc.), while concurrently signifying the chaotic and morally corrosive forces supposedly threatening the American social sphere. Benevolent patriarchs, wise uncles, and virtuous judges worked against these forces. They stood for the qualities of stability, guidance, and control under attack by industrializing and urbanizing elements in the world outside of the playhouse.

Secondary characters, though just as culturally significant as primary ones, served unique functions in the melodrama. Roles for the ethnically or physically diverse or of a varied class status existed, in many instances, to challenge or satirize the moral truths advanced by central characters. They also played into stereotypes about class, religion, or ethnicity and were performed for comical effect. For instance, one character that became popular in the latter half of the century was the Yankee, a figure that was performed as either a fool, naive about local customs and behaviors, or a confidence man. Another type was the "low-comedy" character, often portrayed as racialized and ignorant and employed to humorously comment on the elite class of individuals performing and watching the melodrama.[49] Disabled characters, specifically deaf/dumb and blind youths or adolescents, offered another perspective on the ethics advanced in the melodrama. Performed by adult actresses cross-dressed as males, not only did these figures represent the epitome of sentimental discourses, but they also provided another source of excitement and intrigue within the melodrama's mise-en-scène.[50]

Within melodramatic plot conventions, disabled characters confronted murderers and thieves; eluded kidnappers; and even found themselves facing danger atop treacherous cliffs, on decrepit bridges, or in the midst of storms and fires. The plot of J. Farrell's *The Dumb Girl of Genoa; or, The*

Bandit Merchant (1823) involves Julietta, the "dumb girl," defending herself with a gun and dagger in order to foil a treacherous plot against her life. Likewise, in H. M. Milner's melodrama *Maseniello; or, The Dumb Girl of Portici* (1823), the deaf/dumb character Fenella meets an astonishing end when, despairing over the betrayal by her lover, Alfonso, and the death of her brother, Masaniello, she commits suicide by throwing herself off a balcony and into the sea. The play depicts the pathetic Fenella as a perpetual supplicant, subjected to the will of both Nature and the other characters. Her supreme sacrifices throughout the play, culminating in her catastrophic demise, reiterate a sense that the logical outcomes of marriage and motherhood associated with the able-bodied are not possible for those with afflictions. A reviewer in the *New York Mirror* summarizes *Masaniello* as involving "a most improbable love affair between the Spanish ruler of Naples and Masaniello's dumb sister."[51] Moreover, Fenella's spectacular demise excuses spectators from considering the social and moral implications of allowing this "improbable love affair" to meet its logical conclusion.

Playwrights exploited the envisioned tragedy of these subjects, confined by the limitation of their bodies and dependent upon the able-bodied for all of their needs. Affliction melodramas reinforced the conventional conceptions of physically disabled people while also generating a prototype for experiencing and enacting benevolence. The theatrical devices employed by several popular affliction melodramas helped to produce the "signs of distress" outlined in Reid's essay. In the course of the melodrama, these conventions primed spectators, both emotionally and cognitively, to cultivate benevolence as the appropriate response to what was understood as the pressing problem presented by deaf/dumb and blind communities in the public sphere.

A significant example of the way theater made this dynamic explicit and palatable is found in Thomas Holcroft's melodrama *Deaf and Dumb; or, The Orphan Protected* (1825). One of the more frequently performed and long-running melodramas, *Deaf and Dumb* places the charitable dynamic at the center of the plot. Set in France, the narrative turns on the events surrounding the mysterious "death" and triumphant return of the young Count Julio (also known as Theodore in the play), the deaf/dumb heir to the noble Harancour estate. The audience learns that eight years prior to the opening of the play, Julio's uncle Darlemont took him to Paris in a supposed effort to seek a cure for Julio's affliction. Once in Paris, Darlemont dressed Julio in rags and abandoned him on the streets to die as a beggar; following the apparent "success" of his scheme, Darlemont journeyed home to Harancour; broke the news of Julio's "death," which he attributed to the administration of bad medicine; and assumed his role as executor of the estate and Julio's fortune. The Parisian police discovered the abandoned Julio and, learning of his condition, delivered him to Monsieur De l'Epée, the renowned French instructor of the deaf and dumb.

Adopting Julio and renaming him Theodore, De l'Epée deduces that the boy comes from a wealthy or noble lineage. In an effort to locate Julio's family, he and the boy travel through France before finally arriving at Harancour. When the two arrive at Harancour, Julio dramatically reveals his familiarity with the estate. The stage directions state: "[Julio] sees the palace of Harancour; he starts, rivets his eyes to it, advances a step or two, points to the statues, utters a shriek, and drops breathless into the arms of De l'Epée."[52] St. Alme, Darlemont's virtuous and benevolent son, eventually recognizes Julio and confronts his father with the living proof of his misdeeds. Darlemont is denounced as the villain and exits the play "in the greatest agony," while De l'Epée and the other servants lovingly celebrate Julio's return to his rightful place at Harancour.[53]

The play codes Julio as the indebted recipient of De l'Epée's benevolence in sentimental conventions communicated through his body and gestures. As Julio recognizes that De l'Epée has brought him to Harancour, he "makes signs of gratitude to De l'Epée, and fervently kisses his hands."[54] Similarly, De l'Epée describes finding Julio in the streets of Paris: "I soon remarked ... a strange and sorrowful surprise in his looks, whenever he examined the coarseness of his clothing."[55] These affective expressions, generated through the disabled body, become their own signifying system of "sentimental semiotics," provoking responses predicated upon the affective meanings manufactured by these physical markers.[56] For a moment, audience members are captured in what Holmes recognizes as "currents of feeling" that briefly connect "people who are not disabled and people who are."[57] This identification is briefly realized once the artifice of theater makes itself known. Though patrons are able to weep along with Julio and, in doing so, display their own sentimental integrity, they are strategically denied empathy. In this sense, affliction melodramas produced a superficial comprehension of physical disability sustained on the ability to read and respond to material signifiers exclusively.

What these melodramas lacked in cultural sensibility toward difference they made up for in instructional potency. Ultimately, a powerful representational and literal dynamic was established on stage that positioned the benevolent patron and the disabled person in distinctive roles. *Deaf and Dumb* flattened out these respective figures so that they become entrenched in seemingly static positions, forming a dichotomy meant to facilitate benevolence as the only appropriate action. The emotional exchange fostered in theater inevitably occurs between the spectator and a representative of the able-bodied purveyor of charity. Holcroft's incorporation of Monsieur De l'Epée is evidence of how the play underscores the qualities of and the need for a charitable intermediary in both the world of the play and the world outside the playhouse.

Historians of Deaf culture credit the Abbe De l'Epée with inventing and implementing the teaching of sign language in France. His method, pioneered in the late 1700s, formed the basis for instructors such as the Abbe Sicard, Laurent Clerc, and later Gallaudet.[58] The character of De l'Epée operates as an ideal model of charitable sentiment; he is both a spiritual leader and an educator, making him a powerful amalgamation of qualities highly prized in the reform movement going on in the public sphere. Other characters in the play reinforce De l'Epée's characterization as a selfless charitable savior. For example, the servant Franval remarks to the other characters in the scene, "you see before you one who is an honour to human nature."[59] Julio expresses a similar sentiment. Using a writing tablet, he states, "Genius and Humanity cry out for De l'Epée; and him I call the best and greatest of human creatures."[60]

In the end, the depiction of charitable sentiment and its effects operates in this melodrama to serve the emotional and philosophical needs of the able-bodied community. In a lengthy monologue, De l'Epée describes the merits of his duty:

> If the labourious husbandman, when he views a rich harvest waving over the lands he has fertilized, experiences pleasure proportioned to his toils; judge what are my sensations, when, surrounded by my pupils, I watch them gradually emerging from the night that overshadows them, and see them dazzled at the widening dawn of opening Deity, till the full blaze of perfect intellect informs their souls to hope and adoration. This is to new-create our brethren. What transport to bring man acquainted with himself! Enjoyments, I own, there may

be, more splendid, more alluring; but I am sure, that, in the wide round of our capacities, none will be found more true.[61]

Like his predecessor Gallaudet, De l'Epée performs the function of surrogate deity in his ability to shepherd his pupils out of their perpetual darkness and into the "dazzling" dawn indicative of the hearing community. This is additionally reflected in the way he describes teaching the deaf/dumb to speak: "to new-create our brethren." De l'Epée's claim to essentially rebirth his pupils inscribes him within a discourse that connotes capabilities that are both Godlike and feminized. As such, the role of benefactor takes on new significance in this melodrama; the benefactor becomes a kind of supernatural persona, a privileged individual tasked with bringing to bear his superior morality and spirituality to effect social uplift. In short, De l'Epée's portrayal in *Deaf and Dumb* raised the bar for the average spectator, who, watching the play, presumably felt his heart surge with sentimental attachment to De l'Epée's endeavors. At the same time, De l'Epée occupies an alluring idealized icon for the serious reformer such as Gallaudet and Howe.

For those unable to identify with the impressive De l'Epée, other affliction melodramas offered more accessible benevolent characters. William Diamond's *The Broken Sword* (1817) dramatizes the story of Myrtillo, a displaced orphan who lost the power to speak after witnessing the murder of his father and subsequently enters the care of Captain Zavior and his family. The narrative culminates with a confrontation between Myrtillo and the villain who killed his father, the treacherous Colonel Rigolio. The pair struggle on a hazardous bridge suspended precariously over a raging current. In the fray, Rigolio breaks the tip of his sword on Myrtillo's torch, heaves Myrtillo into the current, and flees for his life. Estevan, a faithful servant, rescues Myrtillo and brings him to safety. Confident that Myrtillo has perished, Rigolio attempts to cover his treachery but is ultimately betrayed by the recovery of his broken sword, along with Myrtillo's confession. The play closes with a scene of moral and physical retribution: the restoration of Myrtillo's speech occurs as Rigolio is brought to justice.

Throughout the play, Myrtillo repeatedly demonstrates his gratitude and humility toward his family of "(S)Zaviors," making the deferential dynamic between the needy and the charitable unmistakable. As Captain Zavior recounts discovering Myrtillo in the woods, he notes the way Myrtillo "slipped" from a chestnut tree and "cast himself on his knees in the path before me."[62] In another scene, Myrtillo revisits these gestures of subservience and appreciation: he "[throws] himself precipitately into the arms of Rosara and Zavior," and he "expresses" to Zavior that without "his bounty, he should be destitute."[63]

In the melodrama, gesture relays "a charge of meaning that we might suspect to be in excess of what it can literally support."[64] The emphasis on gesture and its signifying excesses is important for several reasons: it serves as the primary form of melodramatic communication, at times very pronounced, making the action the central focus of the scene; it presents a visual complement to the sentimental signs created by the disabled body; and it produces moments where absence is made present. Theater historian Simon Shepherd maintains that withholding speech by the incorporation of gesture and movement creates apprehension, which results in "an understanding of one's imminent implication, real or supposed, in a series of events that are outside one's control."[65] In lieu of vocal speech, Myrtillo manufactures a type of palpable silence or gap that authorizes the able-bodied character to speak for the afflicted. This aperture is extended to the spectator, affording the same type of invitation to the able-bodied patron, implicating the audience member within the events of the mise-en-scène.

Myrtillo, like Julio, was a role performed by breeches actresses. In both cases, the actresses' femininity remained palpable despite their costuming. And in both cases, each character's disabilities are associated with feminized traits of weakness and passivity. The result is Myrtillo's complete reliance upon the benevolent male figure. His physical expressions invite spectators to assuage their anxiety at radical alterity by imaginatively and/or actually fulfilling their function as "(S)Zavior." The tenets of charity are not only successfully carried out, but they also ensure that it is paternal authority (over both the disabled person and the actress performing affliction) that brings about moral restoration. As affliction melodramas attempt to reorder a world turned chaotic by the presence of difference and immorality; they do so while also shoring up traditional attitudes about gender, class, and physicality.

The stylized gesture, sentimental rhetoric, and overwrought spectacle of suffering indicative of the affliction melodrama authorized a way of reading the disabled body that accorded with popular perceptions of affliction in the social sphere. Situated within this type of melodrama, the disabled subject became more than just the physical signifier of sentimentalism, but served as the conduit through which benevolence was realized. The demonstrative quality of theater, fused with its unique emotional and formal elements, functioned as an ideal medium to fully convey the tenets of the charitable relationship. The productive contrivances of theater helped to visually and emotionally code the moral and physical characteristics of the needy and the benevolent; reified the deferential dynamic critical to charitable intervention; and, most important, gave reformers a methodology for making their causes appealing. Institutional administrators borrowed from theatrical conventions and principles to execute public performances of their deaf/dumb and blind students, which showcased their inspiring talents and legitimized the need to publicly support reform for this disabled community.

"UNSTOP THE EARS OF THE DEAF AND CAUSE THE TONGUE OF THE DUMB TO SING": PUBLIC PERFORMANCES OF THE DEAF/DUMB AND BLIND[66]

The movement to aid deaf/dumb and blind individuals with education and rehabilitation rose alongside the creation of almshouses and workhouses in the nineteenth century. According to historian Christopher Lasch, institutions offered residence and labor opportunities to "a large number of like-situated individuals, cut off from the wider society for an appreciable period of time, [who] together lead an enclosed, formally administered kind of life."[67] Each type of facility provided a place beneficial for a variety of socially, economically, and physically disadvantaged types: the ill, infirm, or impoverished received care and attention, and the capable worker refined or learned his or her work ethic.[68] Though these institutions indiscriminately confined the destitute, the sick, the disabled, and the orphaned, they nevertheless gained public acceptance as a beneficial way to impose justice and order on unruly or undesirable elements of the public sphere.

Citizens recognized the multiple merits of the total institution and supported it as an attractive alternative to indiscriminate charitable activities, which often depleted resources and did little to help improve the status of the needy. The institution not only attempted to rehabilitate or restore people characterized in some way as "lacking", but it also acted as a policing agent, offering a convenient and relatively cheap means to segregate non-normative segments of the population. Lasch points out that this form of benevolent incarceration meshed with middle-class proclivities to maintain stricter class distinctions by insulating "themselves from the spectacle of suffering and depravity."[69] Additionally, the total institution reified the accepted antebellum beliefs that high ideals, self-reliance, and moral integrity comprised the model American character and by extension constituted an exemplary society. "Moral power" became the foundation for a superior civic and national government.[70] "The only way to perpetuate the new republic," argues historian Phyllis Valentine, "was to produce self-supporting, industrious citizens who would avoid corruption and recognize their civil obligations."[71] In this way, the asylum perpetuated a sense of nationhood synchronistic with beliefs about America's legacy as the privileged "city on a hill."

With educational asylums for deaf/dumb and blind people already established in London, Scotland, and France, Gallaudet traveled to Europe in 1815 to learn their pedagogical methods. In London, Gallaudet encountered the Abbé Sicard, the premier instructor of deaf/dumb subjects in France, and Sicard's two pupils, Laurent Clerc and Jean Massieu. After studying with Sicard and his students, Gallaudet invited Clerc to accompany him to Connecticut to assist him in building an American institution for deaf people. Two short years after his initial trip to Europe, Gallaudet's asylum became a reality, quickly attracting interest from neighboring states such as New York and Pennsylvania. By the late 1840s, schools for deaf/dumb pupils were erected across the country, from Maryland to California.[72] Fifteen years later, Samuel Gridley Howe, a New England physician, would follow in Gallaudet's footsteps, creating the New England Institution for the Education of the Blind in 1832 in Boston, Massachusetts.

The institution changed peoples' attitudes toward those who evidenced physical difference, sanctioning their social exclusion. More significantly, the concept of institutionalized benevolence effectively alleviated the need to foster a personalized relationship with the needy. The anonymity and distance fostered by the asylum fundamentally altered the production of charitable sentiment: citizens could demonstrate their benevolence simply by supporting the work of the institution. This, in turn, challenged asylum administrators to develop ways to solicit and maintain the public's emotional and monetary investment in the impersonal, clinical institution.

The call for assistance for these disabled people would persist over the course of the century, becoming a part of sustaining and expanding the many educational institutions generated in the wake of Gallaudet's pioneering efforts. By the mid-1800s, the nation was indoctrinated on these reform efforts, capable of recognizing the continued need to help improve the lives of the disabled community. Furthermore, the success of these various institutions, published in reports and showcased during public performances of students, erased any doubt of the moral and material benefits of this venture.

At the core of the perceived misfortune surrounding blind and deaf subjects was their inability to communicate with the able-bodied world and, more important, to receive the word of God. The disabled individual's separation from both the secular and the spiritual world was not only the true travesty of affliction, responsible for the misery and unhappiness befalling the person, but it also undergirded reformers' pleas for charitable intervention. In a piece published in the periodical the *Weekly Reader*, the writer directly enforces this logic:

> Now if the deaf and dumb in our country can by a proper course of instruction be fitted for useful and respectable employments in life; if they can have their minds opened to the reception of such intellectual and moral improvement as will render them comfortable and happy on this side the grave; above all, if they can be made acquainted with the revelation of God's mercy through Jesus Christ, who can hesitate to promote an object which is pregnant with so much good, and which addresses itself to the most enlarged views of Christian benevolence?[73]

Both the mortal and the immortal salvation of deaf individuals rests upon the ethically and morally superior able-bodied patron to fulfill his or her role as good citizen and potential savior. Gallaudet publicly touted his own educational asylum for the deaf/dumb as "a gate to heaven for those poor lambs of the flock who hitherto have been wandering in the path of ignorance."[74]

The call issued by this particular author indicts the general populace, challenging citizens to demonstrate their civic and Christian allegiance by facilitating, rather than denying, the afflicted individual's access to God. In doing so, the able-bodied patron achieves his own kind of spiritual and moral uplift. Disability operates within this process as a conduit through which to realize an ethically, civically, and spiritually superior world.[75] However, this type of appeal alone, infused with Christian ethos, remained an insufficient way to arouse the public's sympathies and provoke charitable action. In keeping with the doctrines of sentimental culture, the act of witnessing the display of both tragic suffering and glorious triumph was seminal to inciting citizens' emotional and social investment in this disadvantaged community.

Public exhibitions of deaf/dumb and blind pupils became a common practice throughout Europe and America as the first educational asylums launched their operations. Generally hosted or sponsored by institute administrators, these presentations were devised in order to showcase pupils' progress, to highlight the success and acumen of the educators, and to continue to generate support for the facility and its aims. With this in mind, these educational performances may be understood as precursors to the modern charity publicity event; they were manufactured occasions, artfully engineered and produced with the explicit purpose of publicly promoting the work of the institution. More important, public performances granted the opportunity to orchestrate a live encounter between the disabled and able-bodied communities, capitalizing on the provocative effects of this mediated proximity. Howe succinctly articulated the logic behind these events when he stated, "the sight and sound of the blind students would provide a more *immediate* and more *powerful stimulus* to the audience's feelings than could a written account."[76]

Mindful of the appeal and impact of theater, reformers incorporated the conventions of the stage in their exhibitions. Held in town halls, churches, auditoriums, or in some cases their own institutions, these occurrences took place in spaces consciously arranged to signal their designations as performances. A raised platform or other type of designated area demarcated the playing space from the rows of chairs, benches, or pews that formed the area for the audience. In many instances administrators publicized their events in periodicals, often selling tickets. The exhibition itself followed a fairly controlled, formatted structure. Because the purpose of the performance was to elucidate the pupils' and instructors' accomplishments, the event primarily consisted of the students exhibiting their knowledge through a series of rehearsed activities such as responding to math, geography, letters, and philosophy questions. In some cases, audience members were permitted to ask questions and encouraged to pose philosophical or spiritual problems to the students.

An account of an educational performance given in 1825 featured eight pupils from the Philadelphia Asylum for the Deaf and Dumb presented before sixteen hundred people in a local church. During the demonstration, one child answered grammatical questions, another responded to questions about geography, and a third "charmed every one by giving a history of LaFayette." All, the writer notes, "evinced a knowledge of the Bible" and could "write a sentence from any word given them."[77] Another exhibition, held in Paris at the National Institute for the Deaf and Dumb and recounted in the American periodical *The National Recorder*, pointed out the sophisticated nature of the students, who were able to respond to quantitative as well as philosophical questions.

During the Paris performance, when asked to discuss the difference between desire and hope, one of the students replied: "Desire is a tree bearing leaves, Hope a tree bearing flowers." Moved by this statement, the author wrote, "I may be deceived, but it appears to me that this last definition would have been admired had it been found in the writings of Locke or Condillac. . . . Their [the deaf/dumb] language, which may be called the language of ideas, is richer than ours."[78] Clearly capable of grasping rudimentary as well as difficult concepts, in this moment the deaf/dumb pupils are briefly aligned with the able-bodied spectators to the point of, in this writer's estimation, surpassing the speaking and hearing community with the robust nature of their language.

It is important to draw attention to these types of moments for the way they reveal disruptions to the carefully orchestrated perception of the disabled as less than able-bodied people. Here, the pupils, most likely without preconceived intention, push at the limits of the conceptual parameters assigned to them. In the course of performance, the chasm between able-bodied self and disabled Other is briefly breached, and these students occupy alternate subject positions that, unlike in the case of the melodrama, invite the spectator to empathize.

However, charitable paradigms hinge on the evocative manifestation of and belief in instability. Asylum administrators navigated a tenuous balance between highlighting progress, and by extension autonomy, and maintaining the necessity for assistance. Performance permitted administrators to mediate this tension by recreating the same type of sentimental dynamics evident in the melodrama. Witnessing their emotional performances in this way, spectators could, once again, affectively participate in the spectacle of need while also displaying their own sentimental fidelity. Likewise, the artificial nature of the event, the sense of students recast as authentic performers of their own disabilities, alleviated the contention brought about by a patron's identification with the deaf/dumb pupil to instead promote the same type of experience outlined by Smith: the spectator was helped to *imaginatively* associate with the person in need vis-à-vis theatrical devices yet remained aware of his or her own subject position as an able-bodied, unafflicted citizen.

A description of an early American educational performance, published in the *Philanthropist*, further elucidates this dynamic. The performance featured three boys and three girls from the Pennsylvania Institute of the Deaf and Dumb in 1821. The pupils, under the instruction of a Mr. Seixas, assembled at the House of Representatives in Harrisburg before what is described as "a considerable number of ladies and gentlemen."[79] An introduction of the institution's benevolent benefactor, Mr. Seixas, sets the tone of the event. Mr. Seixas first established the institution with personal funds, and when this became public knowledge, Philadelphia citizens raised four thousand dollars to assist with the building of the institution.[80] As in the case of the affliction melodramas, spectators are acquainted with Mr. Seixas's superior character, which elevates him morally and spiritually and also shores up his role as the dominant, paternal figure in the charitable relationship. This is further underscored by the writer's assessment that providing Seixas's background "had a most happy effect in preparing the minds of the audience for what was about to take place."[81]

What followed involved students displaying their "actual progress in writing, counting, and describing a variety of external objects." The disabled students' mastery of these skills, intended to improve their lives, temporarily undermines conventional views of the afflicted as helpless, positioning them within a normalizing discourse. Yet the same educational performance that makes this outcome viable concurrently allays it by reinstating the disabled to their role of grateful and needy recipient of charity. The writer illustrates this effect by concluding:

> And such was the resistless impression made upon their hearts and such the strong practical conviction forced upon their minds, of the great importance and utility of the institution for the deaf and dumb, that not a shadow of doubt remains with me of an act of incorporation and an approbation of a portion of the public funds for its aid.[82]

In other words, much like the melodramatic character that eventually remained dependent upon their benevolent patron, the deaf/dumb pupil's advancement remained contingent upon the institution and the public's continued benevolence to support its efforts.

While it was common practice for institutions to showcase their students separately, periodically administrators brought both their deaf/dumb and their blind pupils together in collaborative performances. One event, occurring at the Chatham St. Chapel in New York City and detailed in a report for the *New England Telegraph and Eclectic Review*, featured 140 members of this "unfortunate but exceedingly interesting class of individuals."[83] The writer attests that the spectacle of the "mutes" with their "eloquent countenances" seated in the orchestra "joined by the blind, feeling their way about, was a sight most beautiful and affecting."[84] In conjunction with the standard presentation of spelling words, answering arithmetic problems, and reading maps and globes, the students participated in a musical component. The blind girls' "sweet" voices, "joined with the clear notes of the boy who accompanied himself on the piano," resulted in tears drawn "from many an eye" in the house.[85]

The scene's ubiquitous sentimentalism, with its focus on disabled children collaborating in an art form also associated with high emotionalism, calls attention to the sentimental signs generated by the scene. The theatrical conventions framing this moment help to make this reading comprehensible, enabling audience members to present their affect and reaffirm their own virtuous characters. Focused on the "miraculous" event staged before them, patrons comprehend this moment less through the mechanics that accompany teaching the deaf/dumb and blind to sing and more through the emotion it produces. What becomes legible is an ethos that would attach itself to those with disabilities throughout the twentieth century: the cultural narrative of triumph over tragedy, brought about through the heroic efforts of deific reformers such as Gallaudet and Howe.

At the performance's climax, the deaf/dumb and blind pupils reveal their considerable capabilities by communicating with one another in an orchestrated display: "The blind girl held up her hand, the dumb watched every finger, every joint, every movement, and turning to their slates, wrote rapidly the words she had been spelling! Glorious triumph of humanity—the blind talking to the deaf."[86] This is repeated with the deaf girl offering her hand to sign as the blind girl feels along her fingers for the letters. The author states:

This double victory over insurmountable obstacles was truly beautiful, to witness the deaf who have no audible language, talking to the blind who can see none of their signs. We believe it has never before been attempted at any public exhibition, and the breathless silence which pervaded the church, the intense interest depicted on every face of that vast audience, showed how great was their interest and their delight.[87]

Part novelty exhibition and part seeming medical marvel, the demonstration presages the kind of display sensibilities as what would become the American sideshow. Here, the framework of educational and moral reform elevates these public performances to grant legitimacy to controlled voyeurism therefore also ameliorating critical questions of objectification and exploitation. This effect is further nuanced by the presentational aspects of the performance: the student/actors engage in a form of show for the express purposes of engaging the sensibilities of a sympathetic and absorbed audience. Enthralled by this showcase in all its beauty and moving tribute, audience members remain conscious of the fact that the students' acumen depends upon able-bodied support and instruction. This awareness not only facilitates the cultivation of charitable sentiment on the part of the audience, but it also diminishes the possibility that the disabled may transcend their role as charitable subjects. Simply put, educational performances artfully communicated the plight of disabled people as well as their eventual redemption and advancement. In the process they conflated the disabled with their sentimentalized signifiers in order to neutralize their perceived threat to a society rooted in ideologies of independence and autonomy, highlighting instead the agency and role of the benevolent patron.

The rubric of performance deployed by the definitive and authoritative parameters of the institution created an effect that would get replicated over the coming decades where the "complex embodiment" of the subject of charity becomes visible to push back on the conceptions of the Other. The public performances of Gallaudet's students, like their peers, the affliction melodramas, gave spectators a way to read the distressed body and respond in accord with their own benevolent fellow-feelings. But the same methodologies that code the disabled person (in this case, the deaf/dumb and blind) in terms of passive need are, ironically, the same ones that call attention to their multifaceted, infinitely more sophisticated subjectivity. Here the performance of ability supposedly loosened from the "shackles" of disability becomes the sly wink to a public who buys into a transformation that is not actually remarkable in any way, but is, rather, a witnessing to a lived subjectivity that has in reality always persisted.

In the first decades of the nineteenth century, the public participated in a shift from experiencing benevolence as a religious imperative to viewing it as a social practice bearing moral as well as material effects. The strategies reformers employed, taken from antebellum performance culture, to facilitate charity for "woefully afflicted" people also represent an emergent understanding in the ways in which benevolent fellow-feeling develops. Enlightenment philosophies about the machinations behind sentiment proved fertile ground for making correlations between theater and its principles and the charitable enterprise. In the process, the recipients of benevolence (in this case the disabled community) were *necessarily* marked and coded as needy; the more pitiful and compromised these individuals appeared, the greater the odds that the public would sympathize with them and imaginatively take on their suffering. The perpetuation of harmful stereotypes about the disabled and their roles in society, contributing to their objectification and historical effacement, became an acceptable trade off for the economic support facilitated by charity.

2 *Spectacular Benevolence*

Theatricalizing the War on Polio with the National Foundation for Infantile Paralysis, (NFIP), 1934–1945

On January 31, 1940, New York City's lavish Waldorf Astoria Hotel literally became a three-ring circus. The Saints and Sinners Club erected the "Society Circus" in the main ballroom, transforming the elegant event space into a massive circus tent featuring performers such as clowns, minstrels, and other circus acts. A highlight of the evening involved a mock circus trial against the popular vaudeville performers and stars of the 1938 musical *Hellzapoppin* Olsen and Johnson. Various performances spilled over into adjoining suites, including an authentic carnival sideshow and an equestrian show. "Hot dogs de luxe," served from a stand in the "silver corridor," rounded out the festive atmosphere.[1] Couched in the frivolity accompanying the comingling of lower-class diversions with upper-class sensibilities, the celebration belied a serious agenda: raising money to fight infantile paralysis, or polio.

The National Foundation for Infantile Paralysis (NFIP), established in 1937 by polio survivor President Franklin D. Roosevelt, revolutionized the approach to organized benevolence, indelibly altering American's attitudes toward charity. Ornate galas such as the one described above were common in the course of the NFIP's annual fundraising drives. From as early as 1934, prior to the foundation's creation, the delegation of individuals working to generate support for the nation's singular polio clinic, Warm Springs, distinguished their charitable endeavor from other ones by consciously positioning the conventions of play, performance, and spectacle at the center of their fundraising methodology. This strategic move marked a departure from previous ways that the public engaged with charitable sentiment, produced a means to control and manipulate public sensibilities regarding both the disease and the NFIP, and ultimately helped to galvanize the nation around a singular health cause.

The increase of public welfare organizations and other groups devoted to servicing the moral and civic ills of America in the early twentieth century indoctrinated citizens into a climate of reform and social responsibility. Like their nineteenth-century predecessors, these associations attempted to address specific problems identified as causing widespread social ills, such as tenement housing reform, urban planning, and child labor practices. The National Tuberculosis Association (NTA), created in 1907, poured its resources into curbing the spread of tuberculosis, established better medical care for those in need, and worked on finding a cure for the disease. One of the activities instituted by the NTA involved producing a specially designed Christmas seal or stamp, sold during the holidays, as a way to generate funds and promote awareness about this ongoing health issue.

Similarly, the American Red Cross, established in 1881 and formally recognized by Congress in 1900, devoted itself to providing education about first aid and water safety. During World War I, the Red Cross was the primary organization offering disaster relief as well as medical resources. During this time, the Red Cross introduced the notion of campaigning for "liberty bonds," funds that helped support both the association and the war effort. In this case, the Red Cross's efforts not only proved a lucrative tactic but also helped implement the precedent of yoking organized giving with national ideologies such as patriotism and civic obligation.[2] Both of these approaches ushered in the practice of attaching a product to a charitable cause. People could demonstrate their allegiance to a given charity through material goods, furthering the trend toward a culture beginning to recognize the merits of generating conspicuous compassion.

With few exceptions, the work of these and other organizations typically serviced niche populations categorized by need. Cultural beliefs about various social or health problems such as poverty, lung disease, or even heart disease associated these issues with moral or racial failings.[3] For those identified as white, middle class, and moralistically desirable, this logic produced a false sense of insulation from the country's troubling civic issues. Polio shattered this assumption. "Polio is no respecter of people," became the pervasive mantra instituted by the NFIP and reinforced consistently in all written and filmed materials; it struck indiscriminate of race, age, class, or geographic locale. Epidemics occurred almost annually, leaving the deceased and disabled in their wake. Moreover, polio lacked a known origin; often evaded early detection; and, most importantly, resisted cure. Polio remained a persistent, silent threat that affected *everyone.* Its most well-known victim, a virile young senator from New York named Franklin D. Roosevelt, existed as living proof that privilege, class, race, or moral integrity did little to protect from "the crippler."

With Roosevelt, a self-styled "cured cripple," driving the efforts behind the treatment and eventual cure of polio, the NFIP gained considerable momentum and recognition for its agenda. Performance culture provided fertile ground for the foundation's aims. Officials shaping the organization's annual campaigns applied public relations tactics to facilitate this charity's cause. Pageant performances, elaborately engineered spectaculars, and public service films existed as critical frameworks to communicate the polio crusade. These immersive theatrical vehicles appealed to individuals on sensory as well as intellectual levels, continuing the legacy of the types of experiences constructed by nineteenth-century reformers. The NFIP's endeavors offered provocative and attractive ways for the average person to, literally and symbolically, "play a role" within the larger cultural narrative of America's fight against disease.

Performance culture also allowed the NFIP to effectively exploit and productively manipulate activities not typically demarcated as theatrical but transformed into artfully contrived events vis-à-vis what theater historian Willmar Sauter identifies as recognizable "encoded actions." Sauter argues that in order for a situation to gain intelligibility as a theatrical operation, it must signify its artificiality in some way that spectators comprehend. "The type of encoding (e.g. gesture, speech, costume, or behaviors)," writes Sauter, "indicates . . . the type of performativity, which directs the spectator's expectations and ability to decode whatever happens from there."[4] The NFIP was the first organization to consciously reorganize charity initiatives around their performance potential. By reinscribing its activities within the rubric of theater, the foundation guided spectators' actions as well as expectations. A performance approach to the polio crusade set new precedents for fundraising campaigns, introduced enduring concepts such as the poster child phenomenon and the public service announcement for charity, and elucidated a controversial political dynamic of benevolence using the platform of public health to enforce discourses of nationhood.

STALKING THE CRIPPLER: POLIO AND THE PRESIDENT

A child, previously perfectly well, complains of a little stomach trouble or diarrhoea. It is feverish, restless, and irritable, and in the morning the mother finds that the child cannot stand, or, perhaps that it cannot move its arms. Some of the victims thus attacked die within a day or two from paralysis of respiration. Others ultimately escape death, but are more or less crippled for life.[5]

Grim, frightening, and alarmist descriptions such as the one above appeared regularly in the popular press throughout the summer months of 1916. A polio epidemic held the nation hostage as physicians and scientists worked diligently to provide answers to what appeared to be a mystifying illness. Outbreaks of the disease were first reported in early June in Brooklyn, New York, before spreading through the Bronx, Manhattan, and New Jersey. Health officials debated about leaving schools closed through September in an effort to curb outbreaks, movie houses closed, and physicians cautioned the public about holding large congregations in any kind of enclosed or confining spaces. Polio symptoms mirrored several other well-known diseases such as influenza and cholera, making diagnosis difficult until the patient had already experienced permanent or partial paralysis in the arms and legs. Children seemed particularly susceptible to the contagion. Dr. Simon Flexner, a leading physician researching polio for the Rockefeller Institute, noted, "according to all records, infantile paralysis [seems] to pick the strong and well children in preference to the weak."[6] These types of reports, combined with inflammatory headlines such as "Day Shows 12 Dead by Infant Paralysis," "Paralysis Cripple a Problem for the City," and "Oyster Bay Revolts over Poliomyelitis," contributed to the public's apprehension of the disease and its unpredictability.[7]

Scientists conducted research on the disease from as early as 1911; preliminary studies of the illness revealed that the inflammation of the gray matter surrounding the spinal cord was responsible for polio's debilitating effects. Doctors adopted the Greek word *poliomyelitis* to characterize the condition: *poliós* being the Greek term for "gray" and *myelós* referring to the anterior "matter" surrounding the spinal cord. Due to the high number of children infected with the disease, researchers used the terms *infantile paralysis* and *poliomyelitis* (polio) interchangeably.

In their early attempts to identify the source of polio, medical examiners circulated a range of hypotheses: some identified insects as plausible carriers of the contagion, and others speculated that dust, dirt, and unsanitary conditions were to blame.[8] New York City's Health Department worked with police and animal-control officers to gather and destroy stray cats and dogs feared to be polio carriers. Simultaneously, the city's health commissioner, Dr. Haven Emerson, authorized members of the Health Department to investigate the conditions of grocery stores, food markets, and other establishments that carried perishable items in and near infected districts.

Despite intimations from medical experts about the indiscriminate nature of polio, racial and class implications surrounding the disease became salient in mainstream news coverage. One news story insinuated that Italian immigrants brought the virus from Europe. In another account Emerson exacerbated this notion, remarking that since the middle of May, "90 immigrant Italians, including 24 children under the age of 10, had gone to live in Brooklyn, where the outbreak appeared."[9] A poem published in the *New York Times* at the height of the 1916 epidemic in July indicted the privileged for neglecting impoverished slum dwellers. The author describes the death of a "poor little lad with child-wise eyes" and asks:

> *Is he wondering now, if he sees*
> *Why life's as it is—*
> *Why in the Summer the rich house is bare.*
> *And the tenement packed to the stair?*
> *Is only surprise in his look,*
> *Or hurt in his pure little eye;*
> *"Was it because of the money,*
> *I had to die?"*[10]

Social historian Naomi Rogers argues that these types of racial slights were partly due to the inadequacies of health officials, who, failing to contain the disease, displaced their shortcomings onto the foreign Other, perceived as "guilty carriers."[11] Polio's racialized discourse amplified suspicions about the moral and physical integrity of foreign populations, adding a symbolic dimension to the disease. In her examination of illness and its metaphorical import, Susan Sontag argues that diseases that lack clear causality and resist effective or easily discernible treatment become overdetermined with meaning. "The subjects of deepest dread," writes Sontag, "[such as] corruption,

decay, pollution, etc. are identified with the disease."[12] The elements attributed to the nonnative individual—poverty, unhealthy living conditions, perceived ignorance about customs or behaviors—became synonymous with
polio, perpetuating negative stereotypes and confirming the misgivings of
some that the influx of foreign populations weakened America morally as
well as physically.[13]

During the outbreak of 1916, the nature of polio rapidly undermined
these assumptions. As the summer months progressed, numerous cases
involving white, middle-class men, women, and especially children were
reported across the country. Particularly susceptible to polio, children
replaced other communities as signifiers of the illness. Moreover, mandates
about sanitary practices and standards of hygiene proved particularly ineffective in curbing the spread of polio, dispelling the belief that the "unwashed
masses" from other countries perpetuated the epidemic. Published strictures
such as "Sweep floors only after they have been sprinkled with sawdust, old
tea leaves or bits of newspaper which have been thoroughly dampened" and
"Take a bath every day and see that all clothing which comes into contact
with the skin is clean" did little more than exacerbate anxieties around cleanliness.[14] According to a physician named Dr. Armstrong, not only did the
public's obsession with sanitation distract scientists from exploring more
probable causes for polio, but it also allowed for "certain private interests"
to "seize this opportunity to boost the sale of certain commodities, such as
tooth pastes, mouth washes, disinfection devices, etc."[15]

In the course of attempting to understand the disease and its origins,
polio inevitably became personalized. Illness attracts negative emotions,
theorizes Sontag, which are then grafted onto a pathogen to alter its significance and recast it back into the world.[16] Gruesome coverage that detailed
children's afflictions and deaths, editorials suggesting that the disease
evolved as "punishment" for citizens' laziness and lack of cleanliness, and
statements made by health officials that the disease was "beyond the control of science" all contributed to anthropomorphizing the contagion.[17] Polio
became reconfigured in the public's imagination and in social discourse as
a devastating menace or evildoer. The NFIP eventually dubbed polio "The
Crippler," declaring it a protean villain intent on robbing the nation of its
greatest resource and investment: the country's youth.

This cultural mindset toward understanding polio helped people clarify
its more mystifying aspects and became a way to account for its seemingly

arbitrary occurrences by likening it to a criminal that strikes at whim. It also figured into early efforts in raising awareness about the need for more resources to treat and care for polio patients. Sentimentalized depictions of suffering children, victimized by the diabolical polio interloper, appeared in many materials aimed at urging people to provide aid or relief to clinics, hospitals, and other facilities. For example, the Brooklyn Committee on Crippled Children, an association that serviced the needs of impaired children, emphasized the fate of young polio victims for fundraising purposes. One full-page newspaper ad bore the headline, "Who Will Care for the Little Cripples When They Leave the Hospitals?" The ad appeals to readers' sensibilities by stating that the "little sufferers will be lame or otherwise crippled" and "will have to go through life that way UNLESS THEY HAVE THE BEST AFTER CARE." "We must act at once," the ad urges, reminding the reader, "Who gives quickly gives doubly. WILL YOU HELP?"[18] Following America's acquaintance with its most famous polio survivor, FDR, these types of pleas gained additional impact. The emotional compulsion to contribute meant that individuals were assisting needy children while simultaneously fulfilling a civic and patriotic obligation as good citizens.

As fall approached and cooler temperatures fell over the region, the number of reported polio cases steadily declined, eventually leveling off in early October. Scientists and physicians maintained their intensive efforts to disclose the pathogen's origins and manufacture a serum to inoculate the public. The work of these medical pioneers, though initially unsuccessful, would eventually enable Jonas Salk to develop the polio vaccine in 1955. However, in 1916 the collective efforts of health officials, medical personnel, government agents, and ordinary citizens finally paid off, keeping the death toll to six thousand, with twenty-seven thousand left partially or permanently paralyzed.[19]

Americans witnessed polio's consistent cycles of attack and retreat throughout the next four decades. Health officials worked with relief organizations to offer care for polio victims but failed to produce adequate resources or facilities in the wake of escalating cases and diverse socioeconomic needs. It took Roosevelt's experience with the disease and his unique position as a public figure to bring renewed energy and urgency to the polio cause. Not only did Roosevelt's cultural narrative, which portrayed him as a triumphant victor over the enemy contagion, marshal the consolidated movement to address the full range of medical, research, and educational requirements necessary to successfully combat this illness, but it also solidi-fied his "triumph over tragedy" disability narrative as the most pervasive and powerful understanding of disability of the twentieth century.

Roosevelt contracted polio in 1921 at the age of thirty-nine while vaca-tioning with his wife and children at Campobello Island, a small island located off the coast of Maine; the disease left him permanently paralyzed in both legs. Prior to this, Roosevelt had enjoyed a burgeoning political career, first serving as a New York state senator and later as assistant secretary of the navy under President Woodrow Wilson. Those closest to Roosevelt understood the political and cultural implications of his situation. Louis Howe, one of Roosevelt's most trusted friends and advisors, remarked, "I'm not going to mention the word paralysis unless I have to. If it's printed, we're sunk. Franklin's career is *kaput*, finished."[20] The social perceptions about physical disability during this time in America's history, when "the body . . . did not contain the man; it was the man," attributed feminized qualities such as helplessness, passivity, and weakness to the bearer.[21] Consequently, physically disabled males also suffered from these emasculating discourses. The public viewed these individuals as lesser citizens due to their supposed inability to fully participate as earners in a capitalist society.

This combination of elements proved detrimental to an average per-son, let alone someone with aspirations to run for the highest office in the country. The need to convincingly convey uncompromised masculinity and exemplary health led Roosevelt to develop various, extensive physical and presentational strategies during his long seven-year recovery away from public scrutiny. Historical accounts of this time period document Roos-evelt's attitude and demeanor as seminal to relaunching his political career and refashioning his public self. Kathleen Black, Roosevelt's first physio-therapist, described FDR as "a wonderful patient, very cheerful," who "works awfully hard."[22] His ability to mask fear, doubt, and bouts of depression con-tributed to a newly emerging persona: a self-image characterized by "super-human powers of endurance" and newfound humility attributed to a deeply introspective journey through pain and suffering.[23]

In keeping with his progress toward health and plans to reenter public service, Roosevelt perfected another element vital to his self-presentation: he taught himself how to "walk." Roosevelt's ambulation involved a complicated process where Roosevelt swung his hips out and propelled his disabled legs forward, which enabled him to "walk" along with the aid of a cane and, usu-ally, one of his older sons. Roosevelt also taught himself to negotiate short flights of stairs in the event of emergency by adopting a method of sitting and "hitching" himself up, employing backward movements.[24] Later, during his time in the White House, Roosevelt brokered an unspoken mandate with the press to avoid photographing him in his wheelchair or in any similar situation construed as undesirable or politically harmful.[25] Despite his paralysis, Roosevelt's skillful body management, joined with his intelligence and charisma, helped win Americans' belief in his ability to lead. Furthermore, this forceful performance of self and the compelling narrative underlying it—overcoming significant challenges and ascending to success—drew attention to the polio problem while also serving as a powerful and inspiring model for disabled patients across the country.[26]

Three years into Roosevelt's recuperation he visited a small, failing resort in Georgia called Warm Springs. Located eighty miles southwest of Atlanta, Warm Springs earned its name from the many springs fed by hot, mineralized water that flowed from deep within nearby Pine Mountain and attracted vacationers from across the country.[27] Roosevelt learned of the small town from his friend the wealthy Wall Street banker George Foster Peabody. Peabody co-owned the town's Meriwether Inn and wrote to Roosevelt about a young boy afflicted with polio who, after swimming in the therapeutic waters of Warm Springs, regained the use of his legs enough to walk using only two canes.[28]

Warm Springs became the ideal place for Roosevelt to improve his health. Finding the experience particularly beneficial, Roosevelt expressed an interest to Peabody and co-owner Tom Loyless about renovating the dilapidated resort for fellow polio patients. News coverage of Roosevelt's stay and reports of his enthusiasm for the spa attracted others with the disease; prior to the hotel's reopening in the spring season, a small number of polio patients with resources and the ability to travel journeyed to the hotel in search of the restorative measures that aided the young politician.[29] This newfound notoriety for Warm Springs provided the impetus behind Roosevelt's efforts to utilize the facilities as both a vacation spa and a retreat for the polio patient.

By the following summer, Warm Springs hosted over twenty-five individuals with infantile paralysis in addition to able-bodied guests on holiday.[30] Roosevelt assumed responsibilities as director of operations, authorizing renovations and repairs to the property to make it fully accessible and outfitting the pool with the newest physical therapy devices. He also worked alongside fellow patients, educating them on the various muscle groups and teaching them how to record and track their progress.[31] Publicity about Roosevelt's efforts and affiliation spread quickly, making Warm Springs a sought-after destination for polio patients and their families searching for new methods to manage and potentially cure the disease.

In 1926, Roosevelt officially purchased Warm Springs, continuing his own rehabilitation along with his ambitious efforts to revitalize the resort. Shortly after he received control of the Meriwether Inn and its estate, Roosevelt solicited the endorsement of the American Orthopedic Association (AOA). Doctors and orthopedic specialists affiliated with the AOA visited the facility for evaluation from June to December in 1926. In their findings, the visiting physicians stressed that while Warm Springs offered no cure for the polio patient, it provided health management equivalent or preferable to clinical rehabilitation. The AOA's endorsement of Warm Springs as an official "hydrotherapeutic center" allowed Roosevelt to legally reconstitute the resort as a nonprofit organization entitled the Georgia Warm Springs Foundation. As a not-for-profit institution, Warm Springs became legally recognized by the New York State Board of Charities and thus eligible to receive grants and tax-free monetary "gifts."[32]

The cost of running Warm Springs was formidable. Consequently, Roosevelt sought outside funding in the form of private donations from associates and other wealthy philanthropists. While this proved initially effective, the stock-market crash of 1929 and ensuing economic depression significantly altered the landscape of private philanthropy. Between 1929 and 1932 donations to Warm Springs decreased from $369,000 to $30,000.[33] Roosevelt and his board of trustees, which included Louis Howe and Basil O'Connor, Roosevelt's longtime friend and law partner, realized that maintaining the facility required an enormous influx of revenue. In her research on the history of polio in America, historian Jane Smith summarizes Warm Springs' dire economic situation at this time: "What was left were debts, no endowment, and a need that grew more urgent as each summer's epidemics added the costs of caring for new polio survivors to the continuing expense of treating old ones. What was left was fundraising."[34]

POLIO AND PAGEANTRY: DISEASE AND NATIONAL DISCOURSE

In 1932, O'Connor and Howe turned their attention toward generating public support for the polio treatment center. Their ideas revolved around exploiting Roosevelt's popularity as a newly elected president and capitalizing on his image as a heroic man who overcame the disease to achieve great accomplishments. To many, staging an elaborate and ornamental gala in the midst of the country's financial turmoil may have appeared antithetical to the nation's needs, not to mention vaguely partisan in nature. However, journalist Victor Cohn testifies to Roosevelt's significance as a desperately needed symbol of hope for people during this time: "[Roosevelt] said, 'The only thing we have to fear is fear itself,' and the country believed it. People hung his picture in thousands of living rooms and storefronts. To most of them, he was more than president—he was a savior."[35] With this perception firmly entrenched in the public's consciousness, it seemed logical to strategically play upon the country's support for Roosevelt and, by extension, a polio-free future.

Warm Springs committee member Keith Morgan, a savvy insurance salesman with an extensive background in marketing, advertising, and public relations, along with fellow public relations guru Carl Byoir, proposed to make Roosevelt's birthday a day for the nation to recognize their president by helping to raise money for the facility. Byoir suggested capitalizing on the optimism of the early New Deal, extending it to resonate with Roosevelt's charitable cause.[36] As a result, the committee planned an elaborate Birthday Ball to celebrate Roosevelt, implicitly invoking his political feats vis-à-vis his explicit physical accomplishments.

Held at New York City's Waldorf-Astoria Hotel, the Birthday Ball was modeled after a typical society affair, with dining and entertainment forming the evening's primary activities. Along with the money generated from ticket sales, organizers encouraged Americans to get involved by holding their own ticketed Birthday Ball celebrations in their local communities, transforming town halls, school gymnasiums, or church basements into convivial, lucrative gatherings. The idea was met with resounding support and enthusiasm; regardless of their personal experience with or knowledge of polio, citizens could hardly resist coming together under such festive circumstances to pay respects to their president, the same man who had healed both himself and a nation, similarly "crippled" by the Great Depression.

An element that made the Birthday Balls distinctive from conventional dinner/dance affairs was the incorporation of pageant performance: incredibly sophisticated stage spectacles designed to pay homage to expansive historical events or dramatize esoteric ideas such as "freedom" and "truth." The years between 1905 and 1920 ushered in what some characterized as pageantry "madness," with hundreds of pageants performed by professional and amateur groups across the country. Manufactured for educational and tributary purposes, pageants brought entire communities together, often involving all members in the planning and execution of these large-scale events. American pageantry borrowed its format and style from European displays, which integrated revels and historical recreation during festivals and state occasions such as coronations. Folded into the charity event, pageant performance generated important meanings about disease, health, and most importantly nationhood. These theatrical events functioned as allegories meant to communicate and shore up distinctive American ideals, which, according to the pageant's rhetoric, depended upon polio's eradication for their realization.

First appearing as part of carnivals and parades, American pageants were initially dismissed as spectacular exhibitions that lacked civic utility and held little more than entertainment value. European revels, morality plays, and historical recreation events eventually influenced the style and format of American pageants; no longer a product of gratuitous show, pageants were reshaped to inform individuals of local and national legacies, affirm a collective identity, and instruct a future generation of citizens on maintaining a traditional belief system.[37] Pageantry, as historian David Glassberg surmises, attempted to engender community participation with a level of artistic integrity necessary to revision American history, vital to "the transmission of proper values and ideals."[38]

Schools, church sects, local historical societies, and women's groups were only a few of the different organizations that developed and produced pageants for their communities. The creation of the American Pageant Association (APA) in 1913 offered materials and guidelines designed to help standardize pageant performances and help organizers receive training and resources. Typical "how-to" pageantry instruction divided the production into three formats depending on the site of the show and its principle purpose: there were parade-style types of exhibitions consisting of floats depicting various scenes, marching companies, or equestrian troops; outdoor performances in stadiums, courtyards, commons, or amphitheaters, where spectators might watch a narrative of a particular historical event; and indoor entertainments in church halls, gymnasiums, auditoriums, or other conventional performance settings, where pageantry unfolded through singular scenes (often tableaux vivant) related to a specific topic or source.[39]

Despite these designations, many pageants were often intermixed with other types of events such as fairs that contained both stationary exhibitions and live entertainment or forums featuring individuals who participated in historical re-creation.

Most pageants involved scripts, music, pantomime, or all three, making them an appealing form of drama for novice groups that might utilize and showcase a range of talents or skills. In a helpful pageant primer published in 1912 by Esther Willard Bates, she recommends the length for an average pageant at "2 1/2 to 3 hours" consisting of "8–10 episodes."[40] However, more elaborate pageants might take place over the course of days or weeks. In one case, a pageant constructed to commemorate both the history of Peterborough, New Hampshire, and one of its most revered citizens, renowned composer Edward A. MacDowell, lasted for three days.[41] Likewise, in the nation's first missionary exposition, held in Boston, Massachusetts, and aptly titled "The World in Boston," thousands of men and women performed for a week, "serving in relays of a few hours."[42] Pageants not only attracted large groups of spectators for their entertainment quotient, providing an activity that appealed to middle-class families, but they also functioned to assist citizens in reaffirming shared beliefs and ideas about the community's historical legacy. According to Glassberg, this process facilitated the collective rejection of an imperfect present for an idealized past.[43]

Early on, pageants were valued as political and social tools, instruments that aided activists and reformers. The National Association for the Advancement of Colored People (NAACP), for example, used pageantry performance in 1913 as part of its fiftieth-anniversary commemoration of the Emancipation Proclamation. The NAACP employed this art form to issue a critique of racism and its continuing impact on the nation. The Patterson Strike Pageant, produced the same year, was also a response to America's current political and economic system, its underlying message a call for reform.[44] Suffragettes were another group to seize upon pageantry in one of the most coordinated and visible efforts associated with the pageant movement. Mobilizing their attempts to provoke criticism and scrutiny of the many gender inequities that failed to adequately account for women's inability to vote, suffragettes developed pageants that dramatically and spectacularly broadcast their political message.

By appropriating pageantry to further the aims of social causes, pageant organizers revised notions about the cultural and political efficacy of these events. The ideas, concepts, and historical images put forth in pageantry, many believed or hoped, might then translate into some form of civic action. A similar logic prevailed in the pageants staged in the Birthday Balls. Only in this case, promoting civic action was replaced with raising social consciousness about instilling and enforcing American values such as health, abundance, and cultural superiority.

The Birthday Ball pageants were intended to entertain while spectacularly conveying unambiguous American principles. Despite a lack of innovation or even originality, these pageants nevertheless possessed the capacity to both instruct and transfigure: by suturing a glorious past to a triumphant future, these performances symbolically altered the realities of disease and economic hardship facing many citizens into a commemoration of utopic nationhood, metonymically actualized through its female performers.

The first President's Birthday Ball, held on January 30, 1934, attracted over five thousand people and generated over $100,000 dollars for Warm Springs. Attendees included local and national political figures such as New York's mayor Fiorello LaGuardia and former first lady Edith Wilson, as well as others in the upper echelons of American society. As previously noted, committee officials urged people to hold their own celebrations, offsetting the obvious class and economic disparities that arose from setting the ball in such a lavish and exclusive venue. One news story expounded on the ways in which the event would bring together "rich and poor, old and young, city man and farmer, Republican and Democrat, conservative and radical, employer and employee, Catholic and Protestant, Jew and Gentile, white man and Negro, the Indian on his reservation."[45]

This veritable homage to diversity elucidates the strategic positioning of the Birthday Balls. Not only were they conceived of in the hopes of accruing massive support for Warm Springs, but they were also meant to highlight polio as a universal threat, indiscriminately impacting across race, class, or gender. Even with this mindset in place, the first Birthday Ball necessarily excluded many of the aforementioned communities due to economic as well as prejudicial constraints. The representations produced in the course of the ball exacerbated the politics of omission even as the committee attempted to create consensus around this worthy *American* cause.

Along with live music and dancing, the evening included spectacular tributes to Roosevelt, including the presentation of the guard mount by "members of the old Seventh, wearing their familiar full dress with tall black shakos, gray jackets, and white trousers," and medleys of the president's favorite songs.[46] The evening culminated in a series of theatrical displays described as a pageant. The thematic or narrative cohesiveness of this performance remains unclear, but the event included ballet dancers and a collection of concepts such as "freedom," "tolerance," "courage," and "truth," embodied by local debutantes and socialites.

The pageant's climax involved the presentation of Roosevelt's fifteen-foot birthday cake, accompanied by fifty-two debutantes "in long gowns of shimmering white satin, with huge ruffles of white chiffon about their shoulders [and] with towering satin covered hats shaped like triple-tiered birthday cakes upon their heads [who] formed themselves into the shape of a birthday cake, holding candles straight up over their heads and lighting them from concealed electric batteries."[47] Near the close of the gala, "sixteen debutantes, wearing costumes of red, white, and blue, with star-shaped headdresses," carried pieces of a picture that, when assembled, depicted the president in his sailing togs, on his boat during his vacation last summer.[48]

The messages of patriotism and robust masculinity are inescapable in this tribute. Instead of peddling pity or even the suggestion of illness, Birthday Ball organizers used these ornamental presentations to manufacture and emphasize principles such as physical health, productivity, prosperity, and independence, critical to the American character and ironically embodied through a president who was physically disabled. Pageant display helped to elide this notion, refocusing attention on the proposed implications of building an idealized nation. Roosevelt reiterated this underlying premise in his radio address, broadcast around the country at the close of the ball. "Let us remember," Roosevelt intoned, "that every child, and indeed every person, who is restored to useful citizenship is an asset to the country and is enabled to 'pull his own weight behind the boat.' In the long run, by helping this work, we are not contributing to charity, but we are contributing to the building up of a sound nation."[49] Benevolence becomes realigned with civic responsibility, vital to the proliferation of America's future in both the makeup of its populace and in the maintenance of its core beliefs.

The economic and popular success of the first ball prompted organizers to expand its scope and content the following year. In 1935 more than two hundred celebrations were held in the New York metropolitan area alone and over seventy-five hundred fetes nationwide. Reports of events taking place in locations such as Manila and Little America (Antarctica), home to the

Byrd expedition, reveal the influence of this occasion and testify to people's interest in participating. The Waldorf's smaller ballrooms held floorshows featuring prominent dance troupes, radio personalities, opera singers, and stage performers, with the evening's main event the highly wrought "Pageant of America." In it, America's most precious resources were celebrated and embodied through the ostentatious display of female performers, capitalizing on the public's appetite for this gendered form of spectacular exhibition. Within pageantry conventions, these natural and manufactured resources became legible as symbolic narratives interchangeable with discourses of national identity and civic obligation that had little to do with the economic, health, or industrial realities unfolding in the public sphere.

Over three hundred New York society matrons, debutantes, and leading actresses of the stage and screen appeared within the course of the pageant. Women representing the Atlantic and Pacific oceans at the opening of the pageant were "linked by the Isthmus of Panama," accompanied by performers designated as seaweed, waves, and coral reefs.[50] Precious metals symbolizing material prosperity such as gold and silver were featured alongside other materials such as oil and silk. Agriculture and its promise of physical and economic fulfillment also figured prominently. For example, Miss Irene Rich, a prominent screen actress, appeared as the Spirit of Corn, wearing a "yellow velvet costume with a towering ear of corn."

What proceeded involved a panoply of America's assets anthropomorphized through detailed and decadent costumes, exposing the bodies of the performers in a way that unmistakably grafted overt, though contained, sexuality onto the markers of American identity. Adorned in lavish gowns meant to accentuate and reveal the contours of their bodies, these women exhibit their femininity alongside nationalistic ideals such as abundance and economic ease, coded within their respective resources. The pageant presents competing images and ideas: spectators oscillate between visually consuming the performers as sanctioned, mitigated sexualized objects and as dramatic, symbolic metaphors for the values of the commonwealth.

The sophisticated nature of these representations, the attempt to create verisimilitude through ornate costuming and accessories, amplified a feminized spectacle that anesthetized the material and political relationships between items such as silk and oil. In this sense, pageant performance conveyed the message not only that the country's past, present, and imagined future were pervaded by white advantage and health, but that the qualities associated with this exclusive identity excised any material or symbolic signifiers connected with physical, financial, or racial difference. This was accentuated by the performers themselves: the republic's resources, responsible for its overall prowess and wealth, were spectacularly revealed through the bodies of attractive, young, white women of a conspicuous class and social background.

Subsequent pageants continued in this tradition. They dramatized properties and values to produce what Glassberg identifies as "communal transformation," which in turn created a "renewed sense of citizenship" by displacing illness and hardship with the images of an idyllic union.[51] The 1936 pageant "Health, Wealth, and Happiness" incorporated elements such as food, sports, and exercise and portrayed domains such as art/culture and commerce. This performance borrowed aspects of conventional pageantry in its inclusion of classical figures such as Mercury, representing travel, an "outgrowth of wealth," along with Venus and three graces portraying love under the rubric of "happiness." In this pageant, a young debutante named Donna Maria Torlonia portrayed "wealth" wearing a long white, Greek-style tunic and sporting a massive headdress made of gold coins. Two handmaids dressed in similar Greek-style tunics formed her escorts. Apart from Miss Torlonia's headdress, there is little to denote wealth or its qualities. Instead, femininity, race, and class become the dominant discourses generated through the performers' bodies and their symbolic approximation to the legacies of antiquity, notions of high art, and perceptions about women's social status. Personified as passive, statuesque objects, these women literally embody what Laura Mulvey, writing on film decades later, characterized as "to-be-looked-at-ness."[52] Offered within the context of the pageant, with its connotations of art, entertainment, and the play of performance, their objectification becomes permissible and unproblematic. The performers and their symbolic significance are instead reread within the logic of this specific performance mode, predicated upon the pleasurable and, in some instances, visually titillating amalgamation of the emblematic and the literal. This collision fostered a new way to present the motivation for benevolence: buying into the cause at hand without having to grapple directly with the complications of the present and its political, social, and ideological complications, ultimately meant buying into a utopic future.

The Birthday Balls' successes presented a novel formula for fundraising that openly embraced decadence, excitement, fun, and civic pride. Iron lungs, braces and crutches, and polio's grim reality persisted in the public sphere, but over the course of a day, Americans could amicably deflect this actuality by performing a better present and, by extension, future. A precedent emerged through these earliest fundraising efforts that helped to set the parameters for future endeavors as the committee for Warm Springs outgrew its purpose and became the National Foundation for Infantile Paralysis in 1937. With a greater population to serve and more funds needed for an eventual cure, the NFIP expanded its activities in both extent and offering. O'Connor and others on the NFIP board understood that other emotions such as civic pride, veneration for the nation and its leader, and patriotic duty were equally as powerful as pity, if not more so, and just as economically viable.

GREETINGS FROM DIMES SQUARE! SPECTACLE AND MEDIA

Though Birthday Balls continued to prove lucrative, the need for increased resources as well as funds for medical research outpaced the committee's efforts. On September 23, 1937, Roosevelt issued a statement officially recognizing the creation of the National Foundation for Infantile Paralysis. The foundation's general purpose, Roosevelt asserted, was "to lead, direct, and unify the fight on every phase of infantile paralysis." According to Roosevelt, this required involvement in each phase of the disease:

> from scientific research, through epidemic first aid, through dissemination of knowledge of care and treatment, through the provision of funds to centers where the disease may be combated through the most enlightened method and practice, to help men and women and especially children in every part of the land.[53]

The NFIP's administrative structure reflected its commitment to service the areas Roosevelt outlined as well as brokered a novel format that would become the model for America's future charitable organizations. O'Connor acted as the foundation's president, overseeing a group of various powerful and influential men such as Edsel Ford, Marshall Field, and Thomas Watson, serving on a Board of Trustees. A General Advisory Committee made up of medical officials worked with subcommittees to address the areas of scientific research, public health policies, education, and treatment of after-effects. Medical and scientific research became the priority of the NFIP; panels of medical experts were established to review grant proposals and other medical policy-related matters.[54] Elsewhere professional publicists, journalists, fundraisers, and sales people comprised the NFIP's labor force, "peddling polio the same way they could have sold cars or corsets or annuities."[55]

Another factor that made the NFIP unique was its dependence on volunteerism to oversee and distribute critical resources. Local committees were established in communities across the country charged with allocating funds for braces, wheelchairs, casts, and other therapeutic aids. The foundation, O'Connor explained, was a "neighborly" organization. This neighborhood, broadly conceptualized, consisted of the American public, urged to contribute money, time, and effort toward a common cause. O'Connor stressed at the outset of the NFIP that the organization intended to "fund to the fullest extent possible" the cost of patient treatment.[56] People received financial assistance on the basis of need, which made it possible for even the most destitute individuals to access treatment.[57]

The foundation's organizational structure and approach facilitated effective and efficient ways to provide all citizens with the medical attention and aid they required. In the process, polio remained at the fore of the public's consciousness. The foundation's presence and sustained activities reminded Americans to stay vigilant against polio's persistent threat. Most important, framing the NFIP as a communal entity instilled a sense of culpability and responsibility among Americans. As O'Connor emphasized in a 1941 radio broadcast, "The National Foundation for Infantile Paralysis is your national foundation—supported by you. You have demanded that infantile paralysis be conquered, and it is being conquered slowly."[58] He went on to assure the public that "we are no remote government agency. Our chapters are made up of the people, serving with only the compensation that comes from knowing that a worthy task is being properly performed."[59] This brought the activities as well as the driving mission behind the NFIP to the level of the ordinary citizen, who might take assurance in knowing that should polio strike them, mitigating measures were in place. Consequently, the NFIP accrued crucial funds, and the American people acquired a sense of empowerment over an unseen, elusive enemy that threatened the stability of the nation's future.

Within a short period after Roosevelt's announcement, requests for aid and treatment poured into the foundation's New York headquarters. Between 1938 and 1945 the NFIP experienced tremendous growth and momentum, implementing many of the policies and practices that sustained it through the critical years of vaccine trials. Smith credits the organization's accomplishments to O'Connor's ingenuity and his ability to surround himself with the "right" people. She writes, "If he wanted a thinker, he recruited one, and then hired another person to catch the bright ideas and put them in circulation, and a third to make sure the world was well informed about the wonderful show the NFIP was putting on."[60]

Smith's language alludes to the NFIP's deliberate deployment of methodology indebted to performance culture for its critical impact. Another way the foundation distinguished itself from other charities organized around disease or social problems was by structuring its efforts in the form of a cohesive narrative, communicated to the public in polarizing, easily comprehensible terms. Polio, the NFIP consistently reiterated, constituted a mysterious and deadly agent imperiling the health and well-being of ordinary Americans; polio touched "folks like you," went the implicit and sometimes explicit rhetoric. The foundation used this imperative address to call people to action, enlisting their help and participation as important agents in an unfolding social drama.

Anthropologist Victor Turner extracts the notion of social drama from occurrences in cultural systems where citizens experience a "public breach" that unsettles the normal workings of the society. What follows is a series of stages from crisis to redress to eventual reconciliation. Oppositional factions emerge during this process, caste distinctions become more pronounced, and eventually different means of redress that provide ways to "assess social behavior" and its consequences unfold.[61] Theater offers a particularly salient and useful way to facilitate redress in social drama. "Performances," Turner states, "probe a community's weaknesses, call its leaders to account, desacrilize its most cherished values and beliefs, portray its characteristic conflicts and suggest remedies for them, and generally take stock of its current situation in the known world."[62] According to Turner, theatrical practices support more than a re-presentation of an event or experience; they afford transformation and cultural critique.

The NFIP's war on polio followed a format analogous to a social drama in the way it concisely articulated the crisis, drew distinct boundaries around supporting and opposing factions, and used performance culture to provide the vehicle for redress. As previously discussed, pageantry illuminated American ideals and shored up a cultural narrative about progress, autonomy, and prosperity during a social period characterized by economic uncertainty. The version of America generated through pageant performance functioned as the symbolic, promised antidote to the destruction wrought by polio.

In a similar fashion, spectacular public events engineered as part of the annual "Dime Drives" and the narratives created for the NFIP's film and television campaigns articulated the polio crisis message in compelling terms that made participating in the fight against the disease attractive, socially palatable, and fun. The foundation brought coherence to its crusade and generated a comprehensible model of benevolence due, in large part, to its use of performance culture conventions. Performance not only presented a way to theoretically manage and solve the polio problem; it explicated discourses of embodiment and national identity.

In 1938 discussion turned to soliciting Americans to send money directly to Roosevelt at the White House during a designated week. Eddie Cantor, a popular radio personality and vaudeville entertainer, greatly admired Roosevelt. His support for Roosevelt went back to an acquaintance the two men made during Roosevelt's formative years as a young politician and lawyer.[63] Cantor was an ideal match for the foundation. At a campaign meeting, the entertainer proposed appealing to the public by terming the event the "march of dimes," punning on the well-known, contemporary newsreel *The March of Time*, and urging people to send their money directly to Roosevelt at the White House through his radio broadcast.

At first officials resisted the idea, arguing that it chafed against their desire to slowly distance Roosevelt from the NFIP's endeavors in order to avoid calling attention to the president's disability. Cantor's influence and reach prevailed, and Roosevelt agreed to participate. Other entertainers, such as the Lone Ranger, Bing Crosby, Jack Benny, and Edgar Bergen, joined in, taking advantage of radio's capacity to reach the masses and capitalizing on their own iconic status to encourage citizens' involvement. Though the initial response was dangerously slow, by midweek 30,000 letters had arrived, an increase from the average 5,000 letters the White House typically received on a given day. By the end of the drive over 150,000 letters had reached the White House, making total donations exceed $200,000.[64]

This lucrative gimmick became central to the foundation's fundraising agenda. Each dime drive ran for several weeks prior to the end of January, culminating in the climactic Birthday Ball. The popularity of this particular tradition only served to exponentially increase the number of parties, galas, balls, and elaborate gatherings in cities and towns across the country.[65] Mainstream newspapers and magazines donated free space to advertise the dime drive, along with foundation news. Together with the individual letters containing dimes sent to the White House, the fundraising committee created special cards that could hold up to ten dimes, making it even easier for people to send larger amounts of money. Cards were available virtually everywhere, and everyone from the very young to the elderly were strongly persuaded to fill up their cards for Roosevelt and the thousands of children depending on the public's donations.

As part of this mass-marketing-type push, "Mile 'O Dime" booths were constructed in public spaces in cities across the country. These simple booths contained grooved surfaces that measured an approximate "one mile." Throughout the day, people were encouraged to deposit their change to fill the "mile." A filled booth totaled approximately $8,987.00. Instructive fundraising pamphlets and guides created by the foundation and distributed to local chapters aided in helping organizers run an effective campaign. Tips included urging local chapters to recruit reliable volunteers and to choose busy, well-trafficked public locations. NFIP officials also suggested incorporating a "milk bottle stunt," in which bottles or jars labeled with the names of states were also placed on the stands. The logic followed that people could enjoy contributing to the NFIP by showing their state affiliation.[66]

Other ideas included featuring a guest speaker; creating a cardboard "wishing well" for the collection of dimes; and enlisting the help of women, who had "the time, energy, and enthusiasm" for the fight against polio. As one guide stated "They [women] want to help. It is a cause close to their hearts."[67] The foundation also promoted giving away lapel buttons bearing slogans such as "Give a Dime" to each person, noting that "people seem to expect something upon placing their dimes on the line, and the use of the button has proved helpful."[68] This particular detail highlights the foundation's understanding of the nascent "give to get" logic that would significantly impact contemporary charity practices.

Distributing pins and other products was not the only innovation implemented by the NFIP. The nature of its fundraising events resembled carnivals and festivals, completely revising the way people understood charity.

Fig. 1. Franklin D. Roosevelt and Basil O'Connor, President of NFIP, counting dimes at the White House, 1943. March of Dimes Archive.

DETAIL OF MILE O'DIMES STAND

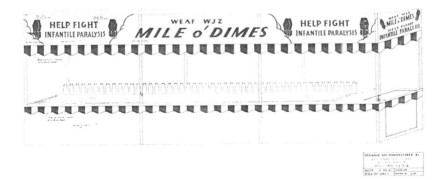

Fig. 2. Model for a Mile O'Dimes Stand, a booth used in the dime drives where individuals could deposit coins in designated jars or slots. From *A Mile O'Dimes Fundraising Guide* booklet, ca. 1942. March of Dimes Archive.

For example, the 1942 fundraising began with a large gathering in Times Square that included current and former paralysis patients with a fifty-piece band; appearances by entertainers; a "parade, an outdoor ice show, and athletic exhibitions"; and a speech by Governor Alfred Smith.[69] The *New York Times* reported on a surprise performance that took place in Times Square as part of the year's charity drive:

> Jack Oakie told the crowd to "kick in" with their dimes; then Sabu, the young Indian film star, mounted the rostrum to appeal to the crowd.... Jimmy Dorsey and his orchestra played some jitterbug tunes. Other entertainers included Dean Murphy, imitating President Roosevelt's voice in an appeal for contributions; Benny Fields, Broadway minstrel, who sang "Brother Can You Spare a Dime," and Gene Krupa, the lightning drummer and band leader.[70]

These events, orchestrated and executed on a large scale, encouraged spectators to sympathize through celebration, to demonstrate their conspicuous compassion by aligning with Roosevelt and his famous supporters in his polio crusade.

This presentational gestalt became a customary feature of NFIP endeavors, contributing to the organization's brand. Organizers for the 1945 campaign once again took over Times Square to transform it into Dimes Square, a charity playing space. An enormous replica of a movie theater's facade occupied the center of the square, a reference to the Motion Picture Industry's efforts and collaboration in the drive. Movie theaters across the country became prime donation sites. Ushers were trained to make a direct appeal and take up a collection before the main feature. When the NFIP created its Radio Division in 1943, exclusively devoted to producing radio and film promotions for yearly drives, audiences typically viewed an NFIP short starring a popular entertainer who spoke movingly about the importance of the foundation and of the public's support. These cinematic petitions primed spectators and facilitated donation collections.

Oversized posters depicting the face of an adorable little girl, gazing out at spectators, flanked the structure in "Dimes Square" to visually echo the campaign slogan, "Give in the name of your child." Behind the movie theater an enormous birthday cake dwarfed the entire scene. In the midst of the festivities, the actor and comedian Jack Benny "collected dimes in a four-foot

Fig. 3. Dimes Square, 1945. In one of the NFIP's largest fundraising drives, organizers took over Times Square, the popular hub of New York City's movie, entertainment, and tourist sector, to transform it into the visual and performance locus of the 1945 dime drive. March of Dimes Archive.

papier-mâché fiddle," while just prior to the unveiling a special trolley car and conga line "tied up Broadway." A press release from the foundation reports: "Riding in the car was Ole Olsen and fifty members of the Olsen and John-son 'Laffing Room Only' Company. Olsen and his show girls jumped on and off the car all along Broadway, 'sticking up' the people on Broadway for funds with the aid of blank cartridges fired from regular pistols."[71]

Theater historian John MacAloon characterizes spectacle as having a "common spatiotemporal location" marked by an "expressive theme, affective style, and ideological intention or social function."[72] He describes the work of spectacle as dependent upon the actions of participants to transcend the superficial nature of these presentations. In taking action, spectators move beyond the spectacle's images, its larger-than-life exhibitions, to access the meanings embedded within the event.[73] This phenomenon is similar to what Victor Turner outlines as belonging to "liminal spaces." For Turner, liminal arenas support new community formations and facilitate plural meanings.[74] Dimes Square constitutes the locus where such formations take place and where multiple and seemingly contradictory meanings exist. The signifiers of the charity plea—the image of the child encoded as needy, the symbolic representation of health and FDR's triumph over tragedy in the form of the birthday cake, the urban environment with its markers of capitalism and commodity—coalesce in the performance of comedians, musicians, and dancers.

These seemingly disparate elements become legible, not as discourses competing with sympathy but as amusements that matter, as critical vehicles through which to experience and demonstrate benevolence. It is important to note the absence of material signifiers to suggest disability, disease, or corporeal difference. Just as in the Birthday Balls, this type of diversity was expunged. The competing narratives produced by actual polio patients or images documenting the realities of the disease remain safely relegated to medical literature and news stories. Similar to a pageant, this event was meant to evoke an idyllic past and utopic future, a dynamic maintained through citizens' participation and their willingness to affirm the vision of a nation untouched by disease or disparity. The display and activities coloniz-ing Times Square to transform it into a staging arena for the war on polio supposedly enabled citizens across class, racial, and age lines to experience collective benevolence in a newly conceived ritual marked by pleasure, celebration, and play. United by their consensus to eradicate polio, spectators participating in this event consolidated their diversity to collectively affirm belief in the triumph of American ingenuity over conflict.

HELP ME WALK AGAIN: POSTER CHILDREN AND PSAS

With their successful methodological structure both yielding positive results and producing brand recognition (the foundation essentially trained Americans to recognize dime cards, wishing wells, and drive booths as properties of the polio crusade in general and as the operations of the NFIP in particular), foundation officials devoted attention to remaking another important component of their campaigns: sentiment. Unlike prior charity campaigns that trafficked in excessive or overwrought emotionalism, the NFIP revised affective structures, linking them to a patriotic ethos, as well as to discourses of health and individualism. In the process, the foundation exploited and capitalized on the figure of the child as an icon that denoted polio's greatest casualty. By focusing on children, the organization endowed the polio crisis with additional gravity, making it difficult for people to deny their willingness to help. A pledge during the annual dime drive was not just a pledge to Roosevelt, but a commitment to aid the nation's children and preserve America's future.

The foundation's Radio and Motion Picture Department, created in 1943, was largely responsible for the NFIP's new, more emotionally nuanced appeals. Board members hired Howard London, a public relations executive with extensive contacts in the entertainment industry, to run the department. London overhauled the foundation's publicity ideology and tactics. In an unpublished manuscript about the history of the Radio and Motion Picture Department, writer Christopher Lasch noted that part of what made London's efforts successful was his model of the "average listener": an individual of average intelligence who used simple words and possessed little patience. "He [the average listener] wanted to be diverted, not informed," stated London. "The Foundation should therefore be careful to mix information with diversion, to present the former in the guise of the latter." More important, London firmly believed that the ordinary citizen responded to and identified with sentiment. He mandated that all visual or print materials should "appeal directly to the emotions. That is the basis of all advertising." He added, "And mention children. All the colorful writing in the world won't help if the emotional appeal is left out."[75]

While images of children regularly appeared in foundation literature, they typically functioned to complement campaign materials. For instance, the 1942 fundraising campaign, organized around the president's "Diamond Jubilee Birthday," featured posters with a smiling, cheerful-looking boy and girl urging the public to "enlist in our national defense against infantile paralysis" by participating in the Birthday Ball celebration. Children occupied a symbolic function, connoting qualities such as innocence, vulnerability, and moral integrity. From as early as the nineteenth century, children had been characterized in highly sentimental terms. They were portrayed as little souls who deserved "the right to dream and play" and warranted people's pity and compassion due to their helplessness and (in some cases) victimization in a cruel world.[76] Polio, the NFIP implied, robbed children of these basic rights. Without the nation's future, the preservation of American ideals of self-reliance and prosperity hung in the balance.

The NFIP indelibly changed the relationship between children and charity "advertising," most notably with the involvement of Donald Anderson, the nation's first "poster child," in the NFIP's 1946 campaign. Hospitalized for polio in a Shriner's Hospital in Portland, Oregon, Anderson was discovered in a manner similar to the way film directors plucked obscure women from their dull lives to make them Hollywood starlets. Volunteers from the local NFIP chapter encountered Anderson during a visit to the polio ward, photographing the child in his crib. An account of that meeting is described in an archived press release: "His wistful look and enormous eyes peering over the top of his hospital crib attracted their [the volunteers'] attention. Photographs published in a local newspaper caused such a significant stir that the National Foundation decided to make Anderson their poster boy."[77]

Anderson set the precedent for all proceeding poster children for the NFIP, as well as for future charity organizations, exhibiting the appropriate mixture of attractiveness and tragedy. These posters depicted Anderson in "before" and "after" modes. In one shot, Anderson appeared propped up against his crib, wearing a neck brace and staring dolefully out at the camera. The juxtaposed frame portrayed Anderson dressed in casual clothes, striding purposefully and happily toward the viewer. Ghosted footprints follow Anderson's literal and symbolic progression to complement the slogan "Your

Fig. 4. Promotional poster for FDR's Diamond Jubilee Birthday Party, 1942. From a fundraising campaign booklet. March of Dimes Archive.

dimes did this for me!" appearing on the poster's right-hand corner. The visual and textual elements in the poster's design work together to graphically dramatize the plight of the polio child and concurrently facilitate an imagined connection between the subject and spectator.

Strategically positioned in print campaigns to garner the kind of emotional appeal London insisted upon, poster children embodied the ideological and material threat posed by polio. They also functioned as symbolic conduits between a troubled present and a utopic (i.e., disease- and disability-free) future, between able-bodied and disabled citizens. Margaret Drury, the foundation's 1947 poster child, was presented in a manner analogous to Anderson. Her poster shows Drury using her walker, with a pair of crutches visibly hanging off its back. Like Anderson, she confronts the

Fig. 5. Donald Anderson, 1946 March of Dimes Poster Child. March of Dimes Archive.

camera, gazing at the envisioned patron, her right hand open and extended, inviting the viewer's intervention.

This type of sentimental solicitation became a hallmark of other NFIP poster children. Terry Tullos, Drury's successor in 1948, appeared on his poster in a more simplified composition: he faces the camera to display his full body, his black leg braces contrasting with the flesh of his small legs. His hand reaches out in a now-familiar gesture. Performing their roles as pseudo-celebrities, with their sentimentalized images circulating across the nation, these children occupied unique roles and contributed to a complex structure of meanings. On the one hand, poster children were objectified through the manufactured style of charity advertisements. These posters conveyed a very specific but limited narrative about disability, namely that it followed the model put into play by FDR: disability is a condition that with hard work

Fig. 6. Margaret Drury, 1948 March of Dimes Poster Child. March of Dimes Archive.

and treatment may be overcome. This is evident in all the poster media that portray the children in various stages of mobility and recovery. On the other hand, with the exception of Anderson, who appears to be walking and thus restored to normalcy, the children evoke embodied hybridity, showing the traces of both disability and able-bodiedness. As a result, these charity posters become provocative texts that force the viewer to become aware of the various material and ideological contradictions in play.

It is worth noting that able-bodied children also fulfilled important functions in the scope of the NFIP's endeavors. Accounts of children participating in the dime drives and fundraising activities accentuated their seemingly inherent purity and unselfishness. A piece published in the *National Foundation News* elucidates the figurative and literal utility of entreating other children to take up the charitable crusade. The story recounts the generosity of Sharon Flynn, a three-year-old who learned about polio from the "little girl next door who wore a nice, shiny brace." When Sharon's mother explained to her child that the brace helped strengthen the girl's legs, Sharon "went to her special piggy bank from which she shook $10.06, her 'life savings.'"[78] The

Fig. 7. Terry Tullos, 1947 March of Dimes Poster Child. March of Dimes Archive.

photograph accompanying the article accords with the affective tone of the writing.

Sharon smiles broadly, clutching her piggy bank. In the background, a large NFIP poster depicts a young polio patient at home with her family, beginning to walk without crutches. The poster's inspirational imagery brokers an explicit correlation between Sharon's charity and its positive effects. Visually, Sharon's position in relation to the little girl featured on the poster provides a contrast between healthy bodies and sick bodies, a distinction dependent upon every American's participation in advancing a polio cure.

Despite many critics who charged the NFIP with gross manipulation and exploitation of its subjects, decrying the "promotional raid on the mind, heart, and pocketbook" of Americans, the foundation continued to follow London's strategies.[79] In doing so, the NFIP became particularly adept at manipulating its campaigns in innovative ways that enhanced and reinforced

Fig. 8. Sharon Flynn, an ordinary little girl from Niagara Falls, gained attention from the NFIP for her "fundraising" efforts. The NFIP often showcased the activism of regular citizens and called special attention to the involvement of the nation's children. *National Foundation News*, 4.4. (Feb. 1945), 15.

the parameters of this American social drama. For example, the 1945 campaign featured child actress Margaret O'Brien as a celebrity child ambassador. A letter written to Mrs. Roosevelt from public relations consultant Dorothy Ducas describes a publicity gimmick involving O'Brien and the president's dog, Fala. According to Ducas, O'Brien had expressed great enthusiasm to meet the president and Fala in an earlier press appearance. Ducas writes: "We thought that we might possibly use this to the advantage of the Infantile Paralysis Appeal by having her greet Fala at the entrance to the White House, for the benefit of photographers, and present him with a March of Dimes collar which she is already getting ready."[80]

London not only understood the effects of engineering the right kind of appeal using distinctive elements to form a cohesive and compelling narrative; he also recognized the importance of using the right mode of communication. With expansive connections in the Hollywood film industry, London identified the importance of the film medium. According to Lasch, London's experience with film and radio "made him more sensitive to auditory and visual images than written ones. Impressions meant more to him than ideas."[81] London helped to create films arranged in a conventional, cinematic narrative style that, like narrative film, entreated the spectator's absorption in the film story but also reinforced the viewer's role as a public servant in the fight against polio. The foundation's film work strove to compel spectators' participation by essentially inviting them to be a part of the narrative.

Public service announcements (PSAs) emerged during the foundation's formative years, in the early 1940s, introduced by advertising consultant James Webb Young. He suggested that advertisers enhance their public identities by generating ads for good causes and disseminating information about important current social issues. PSAs used inventive, creative "sloganeering" and persuasive rhetoric or images to raise public awareness.[82] Sociologists Richard Bagozzi and David Moore identify two main types of PSAs: those aimed at people in direct need of assistance and those created to instigate public intervention. Their findings suggest that in the latter case, the appeal is indirect, as if to intimate that "the threat in such ads is not of danger to the message recipient, per se, but rather to someone else."[83] The NFIP deftly wove both types of public service approaches into their charity advertising, highlighting the plight of the polio patient, while implicitly indicting the spectator as a potential polio target.

Many PSA trailers were screened in movie theaters across the country. Partnering with the NFIP in 1939, the Motion Picture Association of America (MPAA) enlisted the assistance of movie theater managers and personnel to run PSA films and coordinate theaters as additional donation sites. In a campaign strategy booklet circulated to movie theater managers, the foundation suggests setting up "wishing wells," smaller dime booths, and even ornate displays using mannequins to portray fundraising efforts in the lobbies of theaters to promote donations. "Dramatize the presentation of your trailer and collection," suggests the writer. "Give it atmosphere."[84] Primed for an evening of entertainment at movies featuring well-known Hollywood celebrities, spectators accepted the PSA appeals of stars such as Greer Garson or Mickey Rooney as a proscribed extension of the cinematic discourse that attempted to breach the distance between the star and the ordinary citizen.

One of the NFIP's most widely known public service films, *In Daily Battle* (1945), set the tone and style for proceeding media works. It also introduced the seminal phrase "the Crippler" as anthropomorphized shorthand for polio. The film opens with a wide shot of children playing outside. A shadow appears, superimposed over the children; an outline of a crutch is discernible near the shady form. Stage and film actor Orson Welles provides the voiceover for the menacing "star" of the movie: "My name's polio. I consider myself an artist; I specialize in grotesques, twisting and deforming human bodies."[85] The scene dissolves to a rural farm, with a young boy helping his father. "Ahh, here we are," the voice intones as the shadow settles over the young boy, who suddenly clutches his stomach in pain, exhibiting signs of weakness and fatigue. The scene dissolves a third time, to an urban street. "It's easy to scare city folk," the voice states. "I have many disguises to fool people; you can call them symptoms." This time, the shadow starts to overwhelm a group of African American adolescents playing near a brownstone stoop. "I'm very fond of children," states the voice, using the same intonation as a leering predator.

The film highlights three polio patients—two young children and an older man—reinforcing its indiscriminate nature. It goes on to depict NFIP chapters working in a streamlined fashion to mitigate the Crippler's devastating effects. A different voiceover accompanies footage of busy and efficient chapter volunteers and staff coordinating with medical personnel to get people medical attention: "The National Foundation posted a death warrant for infantile paralysis—a criminal still at large. Your chapter is constantly on alert." Montage segments show nurses ministering to patients; physical therapists treating patients; and volunteers canvassing for support, telling people who balk at taking the foundation's "charity" that "the National Foundation is a trust fund to help people like yourself." By the film's conclusion, each polio patient has received adequate medical attention, and a series of shots depicts the same group of children from the film's opening, running, skipping, and playing together.[86]

In Daily Battle illustrates the NFIP's unique film aesthetic, which elegantly unites the same kind of immersive properties found in classic Hollywood cinema with an educational or documentary influence. The film conveyed a story, presented in a way that made it easily identifiable and relatable to Americans experiencing this epidemic. By presenting polio as a villainous character in this film, the foundation converted the disease into a stock type, similar to the evil antagonist popularized in melodrama. The menacing tone and presence created by Welles's voiceover work gives way to representations of health, treatment, and the progress contained in the promise of medicine and science. *In Daily Battle* does not elide depictions of people with disabilities, but it certainly deflects the realities of these individuals' lives by focusing the spectator's attention on remaining alert and proactive. As such, the foundation was able to contain people's fears about polio through implicitly reiterating the American ideal made famous by Roosevelt: triumph over tragedy.

Using this approach, the NFIP concisely and evocatively communicated the nature of the disease to both foreign and domestic individuals. Additionally, *In Daily Battle* presented a morally polarizing perspective of the epidemic, reiterating the viewer's ethical and civic responsibility to make it nearly impossible for people to refuse to contribute to the foundation. Narrative films such as *In Daily Battle* secured the individual's allegiance to the NFIP by graphically demonstrating the merits of the foundation; provocatively illustrating the consequences of withholding support; and enforcing public culpability by reiterating that the NFIP functioned as a kind of massive insurance entity, ready to provide for you should you become ill.

Since its inception, the NFIP had relied upon a fair amount of star power to help promote its cause. When it came to films and PSAs, Hollywood figures like Margaret O'Brien and Judy Garland, among others, readily lent their celebrity to the foundation. Theater historian Robert C. Allen states that "the overall ideological function of the movie star is to help preserve the status quo and thereby the power of the dominant ideology."[87] Women such as O'Brien and Garland most definitely fulfilled this requisite: their wholesome, squarely American images spoke for the dominant ideology that the NFIP sought to create and maintain: the ideology of robust youth and the realization of the American dream.

In her PSA, Judy Garland appears with fellow star Mickey Rooney. The segment opens with a shot of the two buying ice cream. They are at once "ordinary" people (i.e., just like you) who happen to be actors and private citizens and glamorous movie stars (i.e., people you aspire to be). Rooney makes a point of putting his extra dimes in an envelope marked for Roosevelt and the March of Dimes. As the two walk along the street, the following exchange unfolds:

> JUDY GARLAND: Gee Mickey, we don't know how lucky we are and how much we have to be thankful for our health and happiness. Can I put a dime in your envelope?

MICKEY ROONEY: Sure you can! (Turns to face the camera) And that's what every good American should do! Join the March of Dimes![88]

The direct-address technique became a staple of the NFIP's film work. It solidified a connection with the imagined spectator, again breaching that gap between the fetishized celebrity and the "real" citizen. At the same time, the direct appeal broke the piece's cinematic narrative, disrupting the viewer's absorption. The 1946 PSA campaign featuring Margaret O'Brien depicts the actress preparing for a day of shooting at the MGM movie studios, ostensibly showing her performing the role of "child actress Margaret O'Brien." O'Brien appears sad and forlorn, listlessly greeting costars such as Spencer Tracy. Eventually a stagehand named Tom notices her unhappiness and inquires about her melancholy. She responds, "A friend of mine is sick . . . mighty sick." She goes on to say, "It's infantile paralysis and do you know that might have happened to me." In the script, the stage directions read: "Margaret now looks away from Tom . . . straight into the eyes of the audience . . . and she continues—'or to your little boy or girl.'"[89]

Viewers experience sympathetic identification with these celebrities as they reveal themselves to be "average" Americans. Their affective pleas for assistance underscore this connection in the way that the famous advocates emphasize the tenuous disjunction between self and suffering Other. The NFIP ideologically positions the star to signify coveted values, social responsibility, and familiarity with the common person. At the same time, the celebrity maintains his or her remove from the general populace, elevated by cultural status but, more important, spared from the effects of polio by virtue of good health and proactive efforts (i.e., donating to the public health trust fund: the NFIP).

A 1954 PSA featuring Lucille Ball and Desi Arnaz perfectly encapsulates this consciously proscribed effect. In it, Lucy and Desi invite the viewer into their home to meet their young children, Lucy Desiree and little Desi, playing contentedly in the couple's living room. Desi addresses the viewer, stating, "We're awfully proud of our children, just as you are of yours, and we're thankful to God for their health and happiness." As he and Lucy take turns speaking on behalf of the NFIP, the camera cuts between close-ups of the two actors, so that their respective faces fill the frame. "A lot of people's children are healthy and happy now," Lucy remarks pointedly, "but who live in fear, I know I do; the fear, my friends, is polio—infantile paralysis."[90] The segment continues with the couple outlining how to donate to the March of

Dimes to help fund polio vaccine trials, urging the public to "help wipe out the Crippler in our time."

The piece functions to convey familiarity and a sense of intimacy with the celebrity television duo. In the process, it announces itself as explicitly manufactured through the stars' direct address and camera work, which frames the family in a tableau meant to signify idyllic domesticity. The play between the real (the fundraising campaign) and the artificial (the setting of Lucy and Desi's house and the staging of their young children) promotes an effect similar to the one created in live performance: though the spectator recognizes and understands the mechanisms supporting the fictional aspects of the performance, she chooses to suspend her disbelief and uphold the event's constructed reality. In the case of the NFIP's PSA campaigns, this approach transformed the spectator's feelings of solidarity with the celebrity as a "friend" or confidante into action. Essentially, the pitches operated to first absorb the viewer into the PSA's narrative structure and then to break this investment by restoring the spectator back to his or her crucial role as a social actor.

Through the vaccine trials in the early 1950s to the successful creation and deployment of the Salk vaccine in 1955, the NFIP honed its aggressive and astonishing promotional strategies. Television provided an increasingly important medium for the NFIP. PSAs about foundation fundraising and, later, vaccine inoculations found their way onto popular shows such as *The Howdy Doody Show* and *The Lone Ranger*. Television not only reached a mass audience; it carried a cultural caché at the time that made it additionally appealing to the general public. In a word, television was exciting, and its stars were part of a nascent industry invested in encapsulating the American experience at its most superlative. This included helping to envision a world where children remained healthy and free to grow into prosperous, "good" American adults. People who demonstrated their benevolence for the NFIP bought into this idealized vision of the nation as much as they bought into a collective insurance conglomerate against polio.

Inarguably, the foundation's legacy of its generative years was setting into motion the research and resources that would lead to the Salk vaccine. However, the impacts of the NFIP's methodology produced an additional legacy that deserves historical prominence: the vaccine trials and their eventual success would not have been possible without the foundation's impressive representational, ideological, economical, and social machinery. The

NFIP's activities realized various operations underpinning the creation of charitable sentiment from the nineteenth century forward: the theatrical aspects of the cultural performance, the power and influence of emotionally laden rhetoric conveyed through the star body, and the politics of representation in visual culture. These materials and practices provided new ways to approach the twentieth-century need for charity, issuing innovations that inarguably altered Americans' understanding of and appetite for spectacular benevolence.

3   *Wheelchairs and One-Liners*
Televising Need in the Charity Telethon

It is hour fourteen in the 1976 twenty-four-hour *Jerry Lewis MDA Labor Day Telethon*, broadcast from Las Vegas, Nevada, the glittering city turned perpetual slot machine and bastion to late capitalism. For the past thirteen hours telethon host comedian Jerry Lewis has sung, danced, and performed all his best comic bits and characters. He has also played best-guy pal to a slew of America's celebrity royalty, including Frank Sinatra and Sammy Davis Jr., in the name of raising money to help people with muscular dystrophy. "Jerry's Kids" are the people with muscular dystrophy whom Lewis aims to save, a goal he incessantly parrots throughout the telethon's punishing broadcast. Cruising into hour fourteen, however, Lewis is anything but his comically elastic, ebullient self. To state it bluntly: Jerry Lewis is *pissed*. He paces in front of the camera, edging up to a rant. "I have a lot of work to do," he grouses. "We really have to get cooking now; we've had fun and some of you have been a little lazy." He pauses briefly to fix the camera with an accusing stare as if to say, yes, *you*, Mrs. Goldberg from Queens, I'm talking to *you*.

He begins again: "You've had time to check us out and I've been placating for too long, been too passive. You have to go to the phone." His breathing becomes labored; he is feeling his righteous indignation all the way down to his gills. "If you can just sit there and have all this stuff coming to you for free, can still sit there and do nothing—I feel really sorry for you. We have given an awful lot of stuff free; we've given emotion, love, feelings for humanity." Lewis breaks off in midscold. He shakes his head as if seized by a magnificent idea: Why wait for Mrs. Goldberg from Queens to put down her knitting and her bowl of Farina to go to the phone and call in a donation? Why not go right to the source? Under Lewis's calculating gaze, the studio audience morphs into a cartoon field of dollar signs and spinning gold coins.

Less agitated and more energized, Lewis mutters that he "should have thought of this hours ago." He approaches one of the many stage managers standing in the shadows and asks him for a bucket. Who is this union-bound stage manager to refuse Lewis, especially when he has worked himself into this frenzy rife with a combustible amalgamation of ego and pathos? Similarly, who is this audience, held transfixed in the spectacle unfolding before them, to deny Lewis's unabashed and more than a little frightening rendition of passing around the collection plate at a Sunday church service?

With his bucket glistening a shiny fire-alarm red in the stage lights, he rushes into the audience. "You've been sitting here all night having a helluva time, dig it out. Put it in there! We can get a lot of money, stick it in there." Lewis instructs others on his crew to grab buckets and follow his lead. He stalks the aisles while people nervously fish around in their pockets and bags to the tune of his semipornographic exhortations: "Yeah! That's it baby! Stick it in there! Get it up!" The band starts to play, providing a festive aural backdrop for this overt and ecstatic display of raw capital solicitation. Lewis, with his bucket nearly full, winds up on the studio floor, dancing around in his money-fueled climax, yelling to no one in particular, "Yeah! Yeah! It stimulates them!" A camera cut-away to a local "Love Network" station raising money in its own community mercifully interrupts Lewis's monetary coitus, releasing the studio and home audiences from this perversely engaging telethon moment.[1]

Lewis's involvement with the MDA and his seemingly unabashed performances, like the one executed on the 1976 annual charity telethon, are legendary. He is a critical and polarizing figure for the MDA, drawing both admirers of his selfless benevolence and fierce detractors of what many characterize as offensive and lewd behaviors that perpetuate negative perceptions of disabled individuals. Despite the distaste or accolades Lewis merits, he is practically enshrined as an icon who redefined the relationship between the celebrity body and the charity industry.

The NFIP's incorporation of many different entertainers in its annual charity drives highlighted the utility of these broad appeals. Through the foundation's annual campaigns, America's performance community became perceived as a united front, working together to benefit the common good. Their participation not only emphasized the notion that polio impacted everyone, regardless of social standing; it also capitalized on the paradox and the appeal that stars are both "ordinary and extraordinary" people.[2] Conversely, the MDA's partnership with Jerry Lewis produced other effects. It sutured Lewis to the MDA in such a way that Lewis became a type of brand for the charity organization; it unequivocally bolstered Lewis's national visibility during a time when his film and television career was declining; and it ignited the telethon phenomenon, a performance text seminal to the late-twentieth-century charity industry and critical for Lewis's celebrity self-image.

Whereas previous work on telethons focus on their representational practices and economic significance, this chapter examines the MDA in its seminal and most influential years from 1976 to the early 1990s to reframe the MDA telethon as a performance text in order to deepen understanding about how and why its representational politics remain especially effective. Film historian Jeremy Butler characterizes performance texts as "a collection of signifiers (bodies, visual images, technology, verbal and written rhetoric, etc.), patterned into structures that have meaning for the spectator."[3] The MDA telethon is one such performance text, consisting of highly stylized, meticulously controlled, and mediated components of signifiers that present proscribed real and cinematic encounters with disabled individuals explicitly produced to generate a cultural narrative around muscular dystrophy in a way similar to the NFIP's strategies to theatricalize the polio threat. Every detail—from the adorably heartbreaking pleas for donations from the year's current poster child; to former cohost Ed McMahon's measured call for a timpani drum roll to announce telethon tallies; to Lewis's infamous, sob-wracked rendition of the song "You'll Never Walk Alone," from the 1945 Rodgers and Hammerstein musical *Carousel*—signals its reliance on and allegiance to performance culture to produce its desired affective and charitable effects. Complicating this finely made play of televisual angst and prospective redemption is Lewis himself, whose bombastic telethon persona nearly overtakes the event as he vies for spectators' love and sympathy alongside his cherished kids.

Lewis made his career as an intensely physical comic, playing the uncontrollable dimwit to partner Dean Martin's suave, poised straight man. When the duo split, Lewis continued to hone this comedic character in a number of successful films. With a daunting number of hours in which to sustain viewers' interest and a platform that gave him free creative reign, Lewis found a second home for his outlandish comedic machinations on the telethon. As evidenced by the occurrence at the 1976 telethon, Lewis often created bizarre, disturbing, and at times inappropriate performance moments throughout the show that seemed to have little in common with the community of disabled people he claimed to love and support. "Jerry Lewis himself," writes disability studies historian Beth Haller, "makes an intertextual statement about disability through his comedic role as a 'moronic' oddball and misfit."[4] Other critics voice similar concerns, distilling Lewis's prominence in the MDA and on the telethon into a narcissistic venture cloaked in benevolence run amok. Writing for the *Washington Post* about the telethon in 1997, entertainment critic Tom Shales remarked, "If you took a poll of 100 Americans, you'd certainly hear from some who'd like to find a cure for Jerry Lewis as well as a cure for the neuromuscular diseases covered by the fund-raising."[5]

Indeed, it is tempting to file Lewis's telethon performance under the category of "in truly bad taste" or to relegate him to the status of fading celebrity icon attempting to recapture his Hollywood heyday. However, to do so would be to misunderstand the symbiotic relationship between Lewis and the telethon, as well as to willfully ignore the necessary work that his telethon involvement accomplishes. Lewis's interjections disrupt spectators' absorption in the telethon's melodramatic and sentimentalized spectacle of need, releasing the individual from overidentification with the distressed Other to facilitate critical action. More than a form of "comic relief," the behaviors Lewis engages in during the course of the broadcast activate spectators' awareness of their responses to looking at difference and what it means for those embodying that difference to look back.

Because Lewis traffics in the arena of slapstick comedy, his performance gestalt is unapologetically physical and visual. Consequently, his idiosyncratic demonstrations hijack viewers' attention, prompting them to experience what Garland-Thomson understands as the charge of surprise produced by the permission to stare at the novel and unusual.[6] In this moment, spectators must shift their attention to accommodate a new meaning-making schema that organizes Lewis's manic performance within the telethon's larger narrative. The inability of the individual to achieve a satisfactory sense of orientation with respect to Lewis temporarily arrests spectators' sensibilities and enlarges the consciousness around the different acts of looking and their implications courted by the telethon. That is to say, Lewis's ungovernable body not only supplies temporary discharge from the scene of physical difference but also relieves the spectator from contemplating the return of the disabled person's look.

Lewis may have propelled the MDA and its telethon into national prominence, but this would not have been possible without the organization's early recognition of television's attraction and power. What the NFIP began with its use of television to air public service announcements, the telethon event continued by using the medium to concentrate and massively disseminate its message. Along the way, it also modified the way the public encountered physical disability. Contained within the sanctioned, contrived space of a television broadcast, the telethon granted people the experience of sentimental identification with and pathos for the physically disabled at a reassuring distance. In this respect, the telethon was also evocative of the nineteenth-century melodramas of affliction: both types of performances bring disabled figures into a mitigated proximity with spectators, and both events use theatrical tenets to urge patrons to imaginatively cast themselves in the place of the Other. Garland-Thomson eloquently encapsulates the effects of such engagement: "When we do see the usually concealed sight of the disability writ boldly on others, we stare in fascinated disbelief and uneasy identification [asking] 'How can this person look so much like and yet so different from me?'"[7] Television became a convenient way to participate in the charitable process, insulating the person from actual interactions with the needy through its alienating technology.

The NFIP's successful fundraising and organizational strategies evolved into standard practice for charity associations operating in the latter half of the twentieth century, including the MDA. Organizations such as the United Way (1949) and United Cerebral Palsy (1949) followed the foundation's publicity and administrative model. They brought together visual media (i.e., posters, print advertisements, and eventually television) with rhetorical techniques to recreate the sense of urgency, community, and intimacy perfected by the NFIP's campaigns.[8] Furthermore, as one of the first major charities created to address the problems of a highly specific illness, the NFIP reinforced the notion that cure was the dominant goal and the association's ability to dispense assistance merely a means to that end. The MDA would pick up on and take advantage of this stance to defend its sometimes questionable representational practices. In a 1993 interview with Lewis published in *Vanity Fair*, writer Leslie Bennetts asked him to account for the charge from disabled rights activist groups that the telethon was offensive and disparaging to disabled people. Lewis dismissed his detractors, saying, "I don't give a good goddamn what they call it; I am giving doctors money so that your new baby and my new baby never have to deal with this."[9]

Another byproduct of the NFIP's influence and its singular focus on disease eradication was, as Lewis's quote highlights, the emphasis on revenue. Those organizations that concentrated their efforts on health concerns, such as United Cerebral Palsy or later St. Jude's Children's Research Hospital, made capital drives a priority, which in turn blurred the distinctions around volunteerism and donations as equally prized demonstrations of benevolence. The industry-wide shift toward more aggressively pursuing funds meant that more organizations were competing for fewer private and public dollars. The MDA drove innovation in this newly defined social landscape by openly courting corporate sponsors and more explicitly yoking consumer goods with support for the charitable cause.

Disability historian Paul Longmore describes this burgeoning trend in the charity industry as a cultural turn toward showing benevolence through "conspicuous contribution."[10] A much stronger "give to get" mentality prevailed than what had previously been evident in the NFIP's era, due in part to the proliferation of goods and services connected to any number of charity associations and to the public's penchant for exercising their consumer freedom. Longmore notes the shortcomings of this mindset: "Many Americans fear that, getting and spending, buying and consuming, they have become takers," states Longmore, "severed from any authentic community by an insatiable, self-centered pursuit of material possessions."[11] However, in the guise of the twentieth century's mindset around conspicuous contribution, charity ironically offered a way to ameliorate the corrosive effects of this capital ethos. People could "feel good" about their consumer habits, knowing those trends helped to sustain an ethically stable society, a collective attitude media critic David Thomson cynically characterizes as "credit card salvation."[12]

This new accent on capital, coupled with the increased visibility and participation of corporate entities, formed the social backdrop of the MDA's populist ascent in the late-twentieth-century charity industry. The ritualistic nature of the telethon, combined with Lewis's stance as a self-appointed paternal savior and entertainment host, ushered in a new way for citizens to comprehend and relate to charitable practices. Moreover, this zeitgeist moment in the organized benevolence movement helped to unsettle conventional attitudes about the physically disabled community and to facilitate an evolving disability rights enclave that used the often exploitative television medium to their political advantage.

THE MDA AND THE EMERGENCE OF THE TELETHON EVENT

The Muscular Dystrophy Association began in the early 1950s as a grass-roots effort instigated by a dystrophic man named Paul Cohen and a group of parents whose children were similarly diagnosed. At the time, scientists and physicians knew little about muscular dystrophy, other than that it was a condition that weakened nearly all aspects of the muscular system, from arms and legs to heart and lungs, reducing the individual's mobility. Cohen and his cohort mobilized to launch fundraising that would further medical research and help acquire resources for those living with the disease. The organization toiled in relative obscurity until a chance encounter with a stage manager for the NBC-produced *Colgate Comedy Hour*, starring singer/actor Dean Martin and comedian Jerry Lewis, catapulted the MDA into America's consciousness.

The unlikely entertainment pair had begun working together informally at the Havana-Madrid nightclub in New York City in 1946.[13] Their act emerged from improvised moments between one another's sets; Martin and Lewis traded sorties back and forth, interrupting one another with different types of comedic business. Martin traditionally played the "straight" man to Lewis's physical and verbal acrobatics, maintaining his sophisticated veneer, acting as a "foil [to] Jerry's supersonic delivery."[14] Their off-the-cuff performances gained critical attention and public popularity. A review in *Billboard* described the unusual act balanced in nuanced incongruity: "[The] boys play straight for each other, deliberately step on each other's lines, mug and raise general bedlam. It's a toss-up who walks off with the biggest mitt. Lewis' double-takes, throw-aways, mugging, and deliberate over-acting are sensational. Martin's slow takes, ad-libs and under-acting make him an ideal fall guy."[15]

Martin and Lewis's novel comic chemistry marked a departure from the style of earlier entertainment pairs, such as Bob Hope and Bing Crosby or George Burns and Gracie Allen. Groomed from vaudeville, silent film, and radio, these performers engaged in wordplay, song-and-dance numbers, or conventional joke-telling routines. Martin and Lewis drew upon these conventions, adding elements of exaggerated physicality or the brutal exertions of slapstick for comedic effect. The pair's style, marked by unpredictability and playful chaos, tapped into a subversive atmosphere underlying American culture, in the process of slowly extricating itself from the tragedies of war and balanced on the cusp of a period known for its conformity and conservatism.[16] Martin and Lewis's increasing fame and popularity translated into a large consumer base that consistently turned out in significant numbers for the duo's latest project, whether film, television show, or charity telethon.

The Colgate Comedy Hour marked a high point in the team's career. The program, a musical variety–style show that brought together the biggest stars in radio, film, theater, and vaudeville, hosted by a rotating schedule of comedians, gave Martin and Lewis expansive visibility.[17] The two men became acquainted with the MDA and its efforts through one of the show's stage managers, Bud Yorkin. Yorkin's nephew suffered from the mysterious, debilitating illness that doctors had failed to explain or treat. The stage manager implored Lewis to make a "plug" for the newly created MDA, asking the public to make a donation (no matter how large or small) to the organization in order to help fund research.[18] In his autobiography, Lewis recalls:

> [It started in] December 1950 on the Colgate show, clowning around filling time at the end of the program, when suddenly I ad-libbed a pitch to the video audience: "Will you people out there each send us two dollars? One for Dean and one for me." Wow, the sponsor really got hot over that, but meanwhile the money came in all week long, and we turned over about two thousand dollars to the MDA research fund.[19]

Following this initial plea for funds, "end-of-the-show MDA spots" became standard practice. According to Lewis's biographer Shawn Levy, the performers made their pitch "even when guest acts had to be cut because the show was running over its time allotment. Jerry would briefly step out of character just before the closing credits and make his pitch, using his natural voice for the first time all evening."[20] In November 1953, Martin and Lewis brought this momentum to a peak in their first foray into the telethon format, hosting a sixteen-hour event billed as *Dean Martin and Jerry Lewis's Radio and T.V. Party for Muscular Dystrophy.*

The telethon phenomenon emerged in the late 1940s as a pop-culture trend. It spoke to the public's preoccupation with unique events such as the all-night dance contest, flagpole-sitting competitions, roller derbies, and the radiothon. Continuity and endurance comprised the most attractive features of these quirky stunts, which usually involved some competitive aspect and were often sponsored by radio stations or other local businesses. These unusual acts, sustained over long periods of time, generated excitement and heightened suspense among spectators. Telethons traded on longevity with the sole aim of raising a large amount of money in a compressed time period. They helped contain audience members, both in the studio and at home, thus bolstering the television station's market share, while also adding a dimension of interaction to the televisual experience: over the course of the broadcast, viewers were constantly solicited and encouraged to "get involved" or to "help make a difference" by calling or sending in a monetary donation to the charity.

Television was an ideal vehicle for this new fundraising and entertainment spectacle; it fulfilled the function of a "public service apparatus," broadcasting entertainment and information that reached a significant amount of people simultaneously.[21] Under the skillful manipulation of various charity organizations, television helped these associations infiltrate American homes with the urgent call for benevolent intervention, cautioning the mass culture against failing to perform its ethical responsibilities. Additionally, television offered established programming foundational to the telethon's general aesthetic: the variety show.

Based on the vaudeville performance circuit, where spectators paid for an evening of acts that ranged from song-and-dance numbers to comedic performance to jugglers, acrobats, or puppetry, the televised variety show provided a new kind of legibility and artistic sensibility to this type of offering. Media theorist Lynn Spigel describes the variety show as a "schizophrenic mix of vaudeo," a vaudeville style of performance reconfigured and represented through the mediatized space of television, mixing artistic sensibilities while troubling the boundaries of taste and conceptions of highbrow and lowbrow.[22]

When producers appropriated the vaudeville arrangement for television under the rubric of variety or comedy shows (e.g., *The Colgate Comedy Hour, The Texaco Star Theatre, The Ed Sullivan Show*, etc.), spectators recognized the pastiche of entertainment for its distinctiveness, allowing for programming that supported eclecticism and surprise rather than proscribed dogma.

The charity appeal, factored into this arrangement, operated within rather than antithetical to the telethon's flow of performances. The variety show schema not only supported the telethon's entertainment model (a revolving door of performances) but also allowed for seemingly natural breaks or pauses to facilitate the periodic insinuation of the charity plea. Within this format, disruptions to the variety structure, where spectators were reminded of the underlying purpose of the broadcast, became effectively marbleized into the telethon's competing spectacles of entertainment and frivolity.

Milton Berle hosted one of the nation's first recognized telethons in 1949, in honor of the Damon Runyon Memorial Cancer Fund. Runyan, a recognizable author, had lost his battle with throat cancer earlier that year, prompting his friend Walter Winchell to create a fund in Runyan's memory for the research and treatment of the disease. Winchell organized a television fundraising event loosely based on the marathon concept, enlisting NBC to carry the broadcast. In order to promote the event, NBC publicized it as a "telethon," hyping Berle as its emcee and promising some of the largest names in show business. Fifteen stations in the greater New York area carried the telethon, which lasted for sixteen hours and generated $1.1 million dollars for the Runyon fund.[23]

The Runyan telethon introduced the public to this unique brand of fundraising and created a generic structural template for producing telethons. For example, Berle's role as host established the precedent of employing one or more celebrities or well-known figures to preside over the broadcast. In the case of Berle and later Lewis, the telethon host often performed during the telethon, showcasing the star's talent to add an extra entertainment feature. Elsewhere, the host's chief responsibilities included guiding the telethon's program trajectory, ensuring smooth transitions between entertainers and other guests, reminding spectators to pledge donations, and acting as the telethon's motivating emotional and physical force by projecting energy and enthusiasm.

Martin and Lewis followed Berle's lead, producing a lucrative and popular program that benefited the MDA as well as the duo's careers. *The Dean Martin and Jerry Lewis's Radio and T.V. Party for Muscular Dystrophy* coincided with a major fundraising initiative sponsored by the Letter Carriers' Association of America (LCAA). Households across the nation received envelopes specifically designated for the MDA; the LCAA encouraged citizens to make a contribution, which letter carriers collected after their regular route shifts. The telethon platform enabled Martin and Lewis to expand their variety show format, giving the public over ten hours of nearly uninterrupted programming of the popular team to benefit a good cause.

The first telethon closely resembled a typical week's edition of *The Colgate Comedy Hour*; muscular dystrophy, along with the individuals impacted by the disease, remained conspicuously absent. It is useful to briefly examine a few moments from the broadcast that illustrate Lewis's approach to the charity event, a tactic that permitted the comic to put his talents in the spotlight rather than taking time to highlight the nature of the disease.

The broadcast opens with an appearance by radio and film personality Eddie Cantor, asking the public's assistance and giving a nod to Martin and Lewis, "who have taken this cause to heart by making the public aware of this dread disease, muscular dystrophy." The camera widens to show Martin standing by a grand piano, smiling graciously at the applause. In contrast, Lewis launches himself onstage, nearly crashing into his performance partner. He turns to the seventy-piece orchestra assembled behind Martin and performs an exaggerated double take, as if noticing the musicians for the first time. "Hi-ya fellas!" Lewis shrieks in his infamously shrill voice, gawking at the audience and camera. Abruptly he turns to the orchestra and proceeds to conduct the musicians by flailing his arms. He instructs the players to rise and sit in a visually and aurally syncopated pattern that quickly unravels in confusion and chaos. He turns to Martin, beaming with obvious glee.[24]

Later on in the broadcast a stage manager instructs Martin and Lewis to fill time before a station break. The orchestra begins to play the song "Gypsy," and Lewis begins to dance. He jerks his body on the stage in movements resembling those of a duck or chicken, bobbing his head back and forth rhythmically. In the next instant he twirls around gracefully, performing a lazy gliding motion that morphs into a style reminiscent of the frenetic Charleston style of dancing popularized in the 1920s. Lewis flings his legs and arms wildly from side to side. Careening around the stage, he catches his arm through a trombone slide held by Martin, becoming temporarily entangled. He bops over to the orchestra with his back to the audience. When he turns to face the audience he has placed two conductor batons on either side of his mouth, simulating animal tusks; Lewis continues dancing with his tusks, miming seal-like clapping. As the song concludes, a stage manager informs the pair there are thirty seconds remaining until the end of the station break. Lewis abruptly begins a soft-shoe tap dance. He turns to the audience and says, "Well, when all else fails," and in one swift movement propels his body into the air in a devastating pratfall. Martin helps his disoriented partner to his feet, and Lewis grins stupidly and eagerly, apparently pleased with the audience's laughter and applause.

The pair's performance, a traditional comedic format showcasing incongruity and subversion (i.e., Martin's handsome, composed figure juxtaposed with Lewis's gangly appearance and frenetic energy), becomes the focus of the show. Celebrities such as actress Dinah Shore and opera singer Anna Maria Alberghetti make sincere pleas for individuals to donate money to the MDA, periodically breaking up the segments of entertainment provided by Martin and Lewis and their other performing guests. Despite these moments and because actual individuals with muscular dystrophy are excised from the telethon, the show's template seems to advance the escapism of performance and the pleasure of the comically histrionic to ironically distract from the reality of disease, the primary motive for the telethon event.

In these early telethons, issues of taste or appropriateness were neutralized by the cultural fascination with watching individuals expend themselves in real time. The goal of performing, essentially uninterrupted, for ten hours became as important as raising money for the MDA. For Lewis, this also meant pushing himself and his novel type of comedy in a way that not only announced a change in the public's comic sensibilities but also established a performance style that Lewis incessantly returned to and relied upon in his film and charity work, making both inextricably connected.

In contrast with previous comic traditions based on formulaic joke structures meant to establish logical patterns, which are eventually overturned in the punch line, Lewis's comic style relies on his ability to physically and verbally improvise in the same way jazz musicians generate sequences of notes that often have no intrinsic association with the original piece. He often eschews organic intelligibility, challenges notions of rationality, and privileges performance form over content. Understood in these terms, Lewis's physical comedy shares traces of the absurdist tradition in Western theater. Theater historian Martin Esslin describes absurdist drama as divorced from logical motivation, preventing the spectator from deriving the "full meaning of these strange patterns of events."[25] Lewis's humor, predicated on verbal nonsense, physical hyperbole, and irregular thought patterns, illuminates the irrational nature of humankind and its ordering structures.[26]

The effects of this aesthetic include pleasure, discomfort, and estrangement. Unable to identify with Lewis due to his bizarre, often nonsensical
comic performance, spectators remain aware of their distinctness from the
display. Esslin describes a similar effect achieved by the theater of the absurd:
"It is impossible to identify oneself with characters one does not understand
or whose motives remain a closed book. . . . Emotional identification with
the characters is replaced by a puzzled, critical attention."[27] Lewis's comic
essence, which may accrue its own intelligibility within the mise-en-scène
of a film or sketch, acquires different significance when presented within the
context of later telethon broadcasts. Within this atmosphere, his comedy
facilitates breaks in the programming array of sentimentalized images and
charity rhetoric to foster what Esslin terms "critical distance," which ultimately promotes spectators' benevolent intervention.

Following the public dissolution of their professional relationship in
1956, Martin dropped out of view, while Lewis maintained sporadic activity
with the MDA. Along with hosting telethons in 1957, 1959, and 1961, Lewis
participated in filmed PSAs. He also permitted the MDA to use his name
and image to promote the organization and to generate support for other
community and nationwide fundraising events.[28] Apart from these limited
engagements, Lewis took a significant hiatus from his charity work.[29] Levy
notes Lewis's ambivalence toward his role in the charity organization during these years. "On the one hand," writes Levy, "[Lewis] had for all intents
and purposes built the organization by adopting it as his personal cause; on
the other, he seemed to want to keep some distance between himself and an
organization that, in the minds of many, had been synonymous with Martin
and Lewis."[30] Lewis's professional schedule also restricted his involvement
with the MDA, a factor that seemed to increase his demand as a celebrity
spokesman.

Though Lewis thrived as a solo performer into the first half of the 1960s,
his film and television career slowly waned in the wake of several critically
dismissed projects.[31] Film historians speculate that Lewis's revitalized partnership with the MDA in the mid-1960s came about as a direct result of this
professional decline and growing personal obscurity. "The fight against muscular dystrophy seemed to have become [Lewis's] life's work," notes Levy.
"And ironically, while his film, TV, and stage projects floundered and even
dried up, his philanthropic career burgeoned."[32] In his biography of Jerry
Lewis, film historian Frank Krutnik makes a similar assessment: "Following

the slide of his cinematic career, the [telethon] also represented a personal triumph for its star-presenter at a time when his confidence was at [a] low ebb."[33] Faced with declining stardom, decreased opportunities for performance, and the possibility of fading from cultural memory, Lewis reinvented his career through the annual MDA telethon.

In 1965, Lewis received a letter from Bob Ross, the current MDA executive director, outlining the dire need to reanimate the MDA's public image and rally support for its cause. He writes, "We really need a major telethon this November or early December—or even in January. Your devoted fans here in New York comprise the ideal audience for your 'return.' What do you think?"[34] A year later, Lewis assumed his duties as host of the then titled *Jerry Lewis Labor Day Telethon*. The show was broadcast in the New York area only, raising a little over one million dollars. For the next four years the telethon's grand total rose steadily as it became broadcast more widely throughout the country and even in Canada, eventually surpassing two million dollars in donations by 1969. The annual telethons afforded Lewis over twenty hours of airtime to fill, artistic control, and massive public exposure. As Levy succinctly states, "[Lewis] was the star of a hit show—a hit for which [citizens] not only dropped all else on a summer holiday weekend but actually opened [their] wallets, to staggering results."[35] Additionally, the charitable aspect to the event elevated Lewis's cultural status. As telethon host, Lewis not only fulfilled his job as an entertainer but performed what many (himself included) characterized as a "labor of love" on behalf of his "kids." This new iteration of Lewis's public persona produced a composite identity that blurred the private and professional: Lewis became part slick entertainer, part charming "idiot," part benevolent patriarch, and part messianic hero.

By 1976 the telethon proved itself a formidable revenue generator for the MDA and an irresistible vehicle for Lewis. Outgrowing its studio location in New York City, the telethon relocated to Las Vegas. This move signaled an alteration in the charity industry's understanding of the scope and conception of fundraising campaigns. With the MDA's embrace of the glitzy, gaudy, show-business aesthetic came celebrated acceptance of its concomitant economic possibilities. Lewis took over the helm of telethon operations; he dictated the style, format, and sensibility that would provide a model for all other proceeding telethons. His affiliation garnered viewers and attracted the most iconic and popular names in the entertainment industry, significantly bolstering the telethon's success and reputation as an event worthy of any all-star Hollywood vehicle.

TELEMONIALS: PATHOS, PITY, AND MADE-FOR-TELEVISION DRAMAS

The telethon reemerged in the late twentieth century as more than a novelty event or a glorified variety show peppered with genteel reminders to assist those with disease or disability. It was first and foremost a significant revenue-generating opportunity, providing a means to broaden the MDA's resources, enhance and publicize the organization's reputation, and essentially brand the association within the charity industry. The MDA telethon effectively cornered the market on this platform, but this did not make the organization immune to competition from other charities also pursuing their aims with an equal amount of zeal. Sensitive to this climate, telethon producers worked to make the show engaging, exciting, and, most important, emotionally compelling.

Unlike previous broadcasts in the late 1950s and early 1960s, where images of disability were as scarce as Lewis's humility, late-twentieth-century telethons deliberately courted disabled individuals to participate in the broadcast. While television afforded expansive visibility to the MDA and to people living with muscular dystrophy, streamlining fundraising to reach a large number of consolidated individuals, it did so by presenting experiences, people, and narratives at a considerable remove. Indebted to the same content and format as live theater (i.e., re-presenting a narrative), television attempted to engender a commensurate live experience, but as Spigel points out, it failed to achieve this analogous communal dynamic. She writes:

> The spectator was now physically isolated from the crowd, and the fantasy was now one of imaginary unity with "absent" others. According to popular wisdom, television had to recreate the sense of social proximity that the public theater offered; it had to make the viewer feel as if he or she were taking part in a public event. At the same time, however, it had to maintain the necessary distance between the public sphere and private individual on which middle-class ideals of reception were based.[36]

In an effort to bridge this distance for the home viewer, and bring the emotionally potent encounter with the disabled individual into proximity with the spectator, the MDA telethon created highly stylized segments that represented the experiences of people with muscular dystrophy as engrossing, sentimentalized narratives.

One particularly revealing case involves a serial that ran within the 1976 telethon characterized as the "Clown Spots." These vignettes offered an opportunity for the telethon to breach the distance manufactured by the television medium to suture an authentic connection between the viewer and, in this case, the disabled individual. The segments featured Lewis and an unidentified actress, made up in an Emmet Kelley style as the tragic clown figure. Aired strategically throughout the broadcast, the "Clown Spots" relay the story, told in pantomime, of Mr. and Mrs. Clown. The first piece depicts the Clowns in their cozy, middle-class-looking domestic sphere, watching the MDA telethon. Lewis's voiceover implores those at home to call in a donation, and Mr. Clown dutifully and amiably performs his role, making his pledge while conspicuously patting his wife's rounded stomach.

The second half of the story takes place on Christmas Eve, when, following a comically large and jovial meal, the Clowns exchange gifts. Mrs. Clown delights in her gift; Mr. Clown beams lovingly at his wife over his gift. The festive atmosphere of the gathering changes as Mr. Clown places a large box in front of his son, seated in a high chair. The infant actor lacks makeup, which may be the result of health concerns for the child actor but nevertheless stresses his physical difference. Mr. Clown gazes morosely at the package, reluctant to remove the wrapping. He eventually opens the box for his son, and the camera slowly pans down to reveal its contents: a large, metal leg brace. The camera pans back up to Mr. and Mrs. Clown, who have moved away from the table and stand together, clutching one another in grief and sadness over the fate of their dystrophic child.[37]

This overwrought melodrama plays upon spectators' fears of a future where the resources for those with muscular dystrophy are unavailable and where life-threatening limitations for the nation's children exist. In the process, this dramatized telenovella also heightens the sense of urgency and responsibility placed on the public to donate. Lewis's grotesque pantomime speaks to his shrewd grasp of the more exploitative properties of advertising and unearths ethical questions about unapologetically employing what many social and popular critics cite as a "pity approach" to eliciting benevolence.

With historical precedents established by nineteenth-century sentimen-tal culture, pity has played a significant role in manufacturing a conceptual framework around the disabled community; unfortunately, it is a formative and widely accepted agent in charity campaigns. In an interview given in 2001 Lewis made this mindset completely transparent, stating: "If it's pity, we'll get money. I'm just giving you the facts."[38] Disability historian David Hevey expands on this to draw an analogy between the methodology of charity organizations and commercial advertising agencies. Both entities, Hevey points out, are invested in selling. Whereas commercial advertising sells products and services predicated on desire and attractiveness, charity organizations sell a cause, producing images that ascribe social and symbolic identities to the impairment or problem. Subsequently, "charity advertising sells fear."[39] The impetus to donate as a way of alleviating this fear and in the process avoiding the same fate as those with muscular dystrophy underpins the "pity approach."

Each year telethon organizers seemed to make the most of the "pity approach" as a permissible practice. The success of the NFIP's incorpora-tion of poster children made their involvement an acceptable and desirable component of modern organized benevolence.[40] Though neuromuscular disease affects both adolescents and adults, for over twenty years of telethon broadcasts the MDA almost exclusively utilized images of afflicted children. Following the baby boom of the 1950s, the child once again occupied a place of importance as the vessel of peace and prosperity in the wake of global turmoil. According to historian Ellen Barton, the "nuclear family," a concept associated with middle-class bourgeois life, placed the child at the center of a value system concerned with preserving the fundamental tenets of health, morality, and a sense of "normalcy."[41] A child physically impacted by the effects of disability posed an implicit threat to the material and symbolic integrity of the family, as well as the civic body.

The 1976 campaign solidified this approach in its coining of the slogan "Jerry's kids." During this fundraising drive the MDA partnered with the convenience store chain 7-11. Patrons were encouraged to donate money or extra change in collection cans located at store counters. A special television jingle accompanied advertisements for the initiative that depicted Lewis proudly waving a can and crooning, "lend a hand, and if you can / let me keep the change for my kids."[42] The neologism "Jerry's kids" was born. More than a fundraising slogan, and later fodder for critical protest, "Jerry's kids"

A Million thanks for helping MDA make good things happen for "my Kids".
Jerry

Fig. 9. Publicity still of Lisa Cagle, the 1976 poster child, and Jerry Lewis. These types of publicity shots were standard issue in press materials from the MDA that were disseminated to media outlets as well as local chapters throughout the country. New Hampshire Muscular Dystrophy Association, Media Files.

distinguished the MDA from its competitors as not just another impersonal health organization, but as a family unit, with Lewis fulfilling the role of benevolent paternal figure. Under this model, the American public became extended kin with personal stakes in the crusade against neuromuscular disease.

The MDA built on the iconography of the adorably pitiful child already established by previous charity associations to make the figure of the child essential. In 1952 it followed in the wake of the popular NFIP campaigns and instituted a poster child to represent the organization. The typical MDA poster child was under ten years old and fit a generic model: "curly haired, crippled, and cute."[43] Additionally, Lewis featured prominently in the medical materials of the designated child, which yoked ideas of paternalism and benevolence to the campaign. Along with the national organization, each local chapter designated its own poster child, whose tasks entailed making public appearances on behalf of the MDA; participating in interviews or the creation of other press materials; and, for the national poster child, attending the annual telethon as Lewis's special guest.

When criticism against the telethon become more pronounced in the latter half of the century, many former poster children began to speak openly about the negative effects of serving as ambassadors to the MDA. Disability rights activist Laura Hershey characterizes her experience with the MDA as demeaning and hurtful. She describes herself as a "cheerful victim" when it came to representing the MDA: "I became a prop in the TV studio." Brother and sister Mike Ervin and Cris Matthews, also former poster children, became strident opponents of the telethon's use of children to play on the sentiments of the public. Their activism would eventually result in the creation of a national protest group titled "Jerry's Orphans."[44]

However, other poster children testify to their positive experiences serving as national spokespeople for the organization. Matthew Brown, poster child from 1977 to 1978, remarked on his tenure: "It made me feel proud, because I knew I was making a difference. And to be so good at it that I was selected as national poster child was one of the proudest moments in my life." Holly Schmidt, the poster child for the 1968–69 campaign, discussed how her involvement with the MDA helped her to foster community with other disabled individuals. "I didn't really have a connection with other disabled people," Schmidt notes. "I didn't know any when I was younger. Then, when I started working for MDA, that gave me the opportunity to meet other disabled people and realize I wasn't the only one."[45] Though most who served in this capacity testify to hard work and intense physical and emotional commitment, they also acknowledge the benefits of undertaking the responsibility, particularly as it related to the more glamorous facets of the MDA. In addition to getting the opportunity to meet with Lewis, whom many lauded as a hero, these children met with such high-profile celebrity and public figures as Elvis Presley, Sylvester Stallone, and even President and Mrs. Kennedy. Through their involvement with the MDA and on the telethon, poster children experienced the elation and allure that accompanied being treated like a "minicelebrity" in their own right.

A typical telethon encounter between Lewis and the poster child involved Lewis introducing the youngster by paying homage to him or her in a song. In the case of the 1989 poster child, Ashley Antolak, Lewis serenaded the young girl with lyrics emphasizing her charm and innocence:

Wait till you see her, lovely and bright
Learning and playing her games
Once you've seen the courage, the fight
You'll never be the same
Precious and dear, whenever she's near
Wait till you see that smile![46]

During these performances, the camera typically cuts away from Lewis to closeups of the child. In some cases, the images are simultaneously projected on a large screen behind Lewis. The camera also captured footage of the individual's parents, seated in the first row, smiling proudly.[47] Following the song or a similar preface, Lewis introduces the youth to spectators as a particularly "special," "terrific," or "courageous" child. Children who retain mobility appear unaided to stand alongside Lewis; his arm is laid protectively over a shoulder or rests lightly on the child's head. Other children using wheelchairs or walkers and sometimes assisted by their parents or an attendant pose next to Lewis, who generally remains standing, periodically stroking the child's hair or face.

The visual and rhetorical coding of this scene is clear: Lewis represents the paternal guardian; his body is the site of health and energy, juxtaposed with the lovably tragic figure of the child with muscular dystrophy. Following the song and brief business where Lewis might ask the child's age and if they have any brothers or sisters, Lewis inevitably inquires, "Do you love me?" At this moment, the comedian often leans down for a hug or kiss, shoring up the parent/child dynamic. Whether the child reciprocates verbally or looks shyly out at the audience, Lewis takes both cues as an affirmative, stating, "I love you too."

It is important to note that these exchanges rarely feel overly scripted. Rather, part of their emotional effectiveness comes from the sense that both Lewis and the child are acting in the moment, moved by their affection for one another and for the cause binding them together. The "natural" appearance of charitable sentiment is particularly crucial in order to undercut the reality that the telethon is a mediated, meticulously plotted event. In turn, the poster child dutifully performs what former poster child and disability rights activist Laura Hershey identifies as "the cute-and-grateful act." The individual upholds the public's perception of youth and innocence, while also illuminating the adult's responsibility as benevolent intermediary.[48] In this moment, the child's physical appearance on the telethon reinvigorates the spectator's emotional investment in the charitable enterprise, calling attention to the lived effects of disability on actual people.

Filmed narratives of those impacted by neuromuscular diseases, shown throughout the broadcast, form another important representational and ideological component to the telethon. The MDA began supplementing live guest appearances with prefilmed vignettes of ordinary families affected by muscular dystrophy beginning in 1980. They follow a sequential arc from diagnosis, through acceptance, and culminating in an expression of hope and belief in the MDA's charitable work, entreating spectators to voyeuristi-cally experience these life stories as if they might be their own.

The MDA refers to these segments as "patient profiles," which speaks to a medical model of disability that reinforces a pathological binary between sick and healthy bodies. A more appropriate characterization for these pieces is "telemonials," for their resemblance to spiritual testimonials. These narratives are scripted, filmed stories that recapitulate the individual's jour-ney from despair and hopelessness to eventual salvation, from personal trag-edy to a state of grace. Telemonials resemble documentary film shorts that incorporate cinematic devices and digital techniques to convey and enhance the narrative of disability. Musical cues, different types of film edits such as dissolves and fades, the use of varied camera shots and angles, and time-lapse enhancements are all conventions that generate the graphic aesthetics informing the vignette's narrative and affective content. In most instances, the individual testifies to a generic perception of the disabled experience that turns on loss and limitation, followed by dependence on others for survival. The implicit moral of each story remains consistent: muscular dystrophy affects individuals "just like you"; your benevolence (i.e., your donation) ensures/insures a brighter future for all citizens.

Many critics of the telethon deplore the telemonial, arguing that it exploits and objectifies the disabled. Telemonials, they argue, utilize sensa-tionalism to create "melodramatic spectacles" or "stories packaged as prod-ucts, rather than truth."[49] There is validity to these critiques. Inarguably, the media conventions present in these segments operate to manipulate the perceptions of these individuals, converting them into sentimental signifiers of qualities such as lack and passivity. Yet telemonials are necessary perfor-mance structures. Telemonials create perceived intimacy with the disabled individual; they attempt to temporarily undermine the alienation produced by television and the estrangement engendered by physical difference.

One typical example of a telemonial from the 1989 telethon features the story of five-year-old Justin and his family. The piece begins by establishing shots of the factory where Justin's father works; a montage of scenes foregrounds the mechanisms of industry: assembly lines filled with products ritualistically pass in and out of the frame, workers heft enormous crates onto trucks from the loading docks, and a close shot reveals Justin's father powering a forklift. Most telemonials incorporate a conventional voiceover technique. In many cases an able-bodied spouse or family member provides the primary perspective in this initial framing device. Justin's father performs the voiceover, in which he introduces himself and his family as ordinary, middle-class Americans: he testifies to his modest but proud life as an industrial-plant worker with a wife who devotes herself to raising their son, Justin.

The next shot consists of Justin's parents, seated together in their living room. The domestic space provides the main location in these telemonials, establishing another set of visual and scenic principles. Spigel persuasively argues that the portrayal of family rooms, living rooms, or other familial spaces on television engenders a communal relationship between viewer and televised spectacle. Television, Spigel posits, reproduces social relations such as friendships and kinships, "shared between the home audience and the television image," that result from television's inclusion in the domestic sphere.[50] The setting in this telemonial functions in a similar way. Bringing viewers into Justin's home, and vice versa, promotes visual and emotional identification, with the at-home viewer perhaps tuning into the telethon from his or her own living room. An additional set of codes emerges in the choice of this backdrop for Justin's story; the space connotes the feminized activities of nurture, care, and community, qualities historically associated with women and the domestic realm.

The actual testimonial portion unfolds in an interview style, with the participants speaking candidly to an imagined subject situated behind the camera. As the parents begin to tell their story, they speak about and for Justin. They describe detecting a change in Justin's motor skills as an infant. During this conversation Justin's parents become visibly upset. His mother dabs her eyes; his father's voice cracks when he recounts hearing the diagnosis of Justin's dystrophy. Soft flute and piano music plays underneath the parents' narrative, heightening the scene's sentimental quality. Justin does not appear until more than one minute into the telemonial, filmed outside the house on the public space of the playground.

Oscillating between long and close shots, the camera depicts an idyllic scene of familial leisure and play; Justin laughs as his parents take turns pushing him on a swing. This moment establishes a contrast between the labor practices evinced in the opening scene attributed to the able-bodied and the nonlabor associated with children. It also emphasizes the disparity between youth and maturity to situate Justin in a precarious position: the fate of both his adolescence and his adulthood remains uncertain. The final scene of Justin's parents in their living room reinforces this notion. A close shot of Justin's mother fills the frame as she speaks poignantly about what lies in store for Justin and her family, which is largely unknowable. She advances the need for the MDA to find a cure so "other parents won't have to go through this." Music continues to play softly, building to a slight crescendo before the scene fades to black.[51] By maintaining focus on the family unit, the telemonial presents an idealized representation of domesticity that appeals to able-bodied adults. At the same time, Justin's dystrophy (though not yet fully visually discernible) becomes an implicit threat to the family's cohesiveness and stability.

Rather than simply permitting spectators to "project their worst fears onto people with muscular dystrophy," as Hershey contends, the telemonial's cinematic remove allows for the potential that the viewer will recycle this anxiety into benevolent action.[52] In other words, the same types of artful contrivances that give the telemonial its intelligibility as a cohesive narrative, inviting sympathetic identification with the disabled person, concomitantly offer remove from the spectacle of distress. Rather than being rendered inert by grief and emotion, spectators may utilize the disconnections present in the telemonial to become critically engaged and intervene.

Telemonials supplement the distraction engendered by the telethon's other performance and spectacle components to engineer a dynamic that accommodates the public's appetite for ocularcentrism. Whereas commercial cinema uses the film apparatus to make its framing and viewing of subjects naturalized within the scope of the mise-en-scène, telemonials are necessarily overt in the ways they control and filter the spectator's gaze. One telemonial, for instance, featured in the 1987 telethon, recounts the story of Jim, a middle-aged firefighter diagnosed with amyotrophic lateral sclerosis

(ALS). Visual cues augment verbal ones so that when Jim's daughter talks about her father's difficulty in transitioning to a wheelchair, the sound of two timpani drum beats accompany a quick cut to a closeup of an empty wheelchair. This trope is repeated when his daughter discusses the way her father lost his ability to use a knife and fork. Here, two timpani drumbeats precede closeup shots of Jim's firemen boots, the signifiers of labor, juxtaposed with his daughter's narrative of loss.[53] This telemonial unmistakably trains the spectator where to look. The accompanying cues—dramatic music, the use of cuts rather than dissolves or fades—instruct the viewer *how* to look at this model of embodied difference.

The melodramatic, sensationalistic telemonial elements were gradually softened and redesigned to align with cultural tastes in the last decade of the twentieth century and in the first decade of the new millennium. Narratives featuring young children, adolescents, and adults living with neuromuscular disease became more prevalent. Disabled individuals also acquired a larger, autonomous presence within the telemonial, telling their own stories in their own words, which made the presentational style more conversational. This transition also allowed producers to play with direct address to the camera and by extension to the televised or live audience. In another noticeable rhetorical and visual development, telemonials began to emphasize the person's accomplishments, demonstrating progress and momentum rather than the messages of tragedy and hopelessness that pervaded earlier telemonials. In 2000 a telemonial aired portraying a seventeen-year-old man named Shawn Dover. The piece depicted the teen driving, receiving scholarship awards, and discussing his plans to "gain more independence" and attend college.[54]

Even with the persistent trappings of sentimentalism accompanying these telemonials, their willingness to entertain alternate depictions of embodied difference makes room for the viewer to access multiple, contradictory representations of the disability experience. For the purposes of the charity plea, which depends on making need intelligible cognitively and emotionally, the subversive potential of disrupting the sentimentalized "pity approach" is typically contained within the telemonial itself. The representations that focus on similarities between a person like Shawn Dover and an able-bodied spectator are offset by his mother's tearful interview discussing her devastation at learning of Shawn's diagnosis or by footage depicting Shawn in his motorized wheelchair, using enhanced computer technology to do his schoolwork or read a book. The emphasis on difference, redeployed through dramatic and film conventions, persists in order to call attention to the underlying need for assistance, not necessarily to celebrate the mechanics of physical difference.

Telemonials act as cinematic artifacts that provide members of a seemingly anonymous community (the disabled) with visibility and identity. The telemonial renders muscular dystrophy in sentimental and theatrical terms, placing it in relation to personal narratives designed and configured to induce an affective response. In the process, telemonials reassure the public that neuromuscular disease remains a worthy cause; that real lives are indelibly impacted; and that, despite evidence to suggest otherwise, the fate of people with muscular dystrophy depends upon spectators' benevolence.

WHEELCHAIRS AND ONE-LINERS: LEWIS'S COMIC ANARCHY

If it were not for the MDA telethon's spectacular host, it might have diminished alongside telethons produced by United Cerebral Palsy, March of Dimes, and St. Jude's Children's Research Hospital. After all, those telethons conformed to a similar format, mixing live entertainment with appearances by corporate sponsors or civic groups making large donations and showcasing the people most impacted by disease or impairment. Likewise, these other telethons incorporated well-known hosts, such as actor/singer Danny Thomas, who also counted on the influence of their star power in their sincere bids for the public's assistance, much like Lewis. The difference between Lewis and other celebrity telethon hosts involves his unapologetic and novel performance persona. As evidenced in his earliest telethon work, Lewis is always already the boyish, playful, hyperactive, kinetically startling, and sometimes brash or offensive comic performer, a persona that earned him critical accolades. Whether viewed in positive or negative terms, this comic act, rendered in pronounced, periodically shockingly, inappropriate moments, remains a seminal part of the telethon's revenue-generating agenda.

Writing for the British publication *Sight and Sound* in 1952, journalist Daniel Farson acknowledged the tangled mass of contradictions and discrepancies that became Lewis's signature comedic style early in his career:

[Lewis] can neither sing nor dance, and does so continually. His laugh is hideously shrill, his voice an ear-splitting whine; his face contorts like wet plastic, his eyes are strangely mobile; and his favorite phrases—"Is this for real?"; "For this we should pay?"—suggest that he has only recently encountered the English language. He is a "mistake," yet he is rather nice for we can feel superior to him, while furtively sympathizing with his petulant, childish defiance of convention. He is unathletic, but successful sexually. His naivety disarms; his infantile behavior suggests the awful child that will never grow up.[55]

Lewis's deft ability to exemplify a range of comic incongruities—he appears simultaneously masculinized and feminized, mature and infantile, in control and yet prone to manipulation—produced pleasurable deviance that appealed to the public in its apparent harmlessness and fun.

Other responses to Lewis substantiate a more critically negative view of the comic and his generative work as part of the Martin and Lewis performing team. British writer Milton Shulman lamented the popularity of Martin and Lewis, stating of Lewis in particular that "in more enlightened times it would be considered impolite, almost indecent, to be amused by such ugliness, lunacy, and deformity."[56] Similarly, film critic Robert Kass excoriated Lewis and his comedic style; Kass charged Lewis with embodying characters that were "profoundly anti-human and anti-life," adding, "[Lewis] is a Pied Piper of escapism, bleating an empty-headed tune which attracts millions."[57]

Others simply dismissed Lewis as an "idiot" who mindlessly "aped" for attention. "He appears to have the mentality of a child of six," stated critic Raymond Durgnat, "but a six-year-old primed to explode into every emotion which he has been suppressing since he was one."[58] Writing about these types of responses to Lewis, sociologist Murray Pomerance points out, "The apparent extremity of [Lewis's] performance specifically references the stance from which it is measured as such, in this case the unexpressive meter of bourgeois life."[59] The cultural anxiety surrounding Lewis's peculiar brand of comic performance accords with mainstream critics' apprehension over the loss of corporeal and social control, the inversion of social norms, and the confrontation with physical and ethnic difference. During the telethon, Lewis's performing body becomes the site where these analogous fears are exorcised. His comic persona becomes an acceptable vehicle for spectators to divest themselves of the anxiety produced by the presence of disability to instead neutralize their unease in the release provided by the spectacle of Lewis's comedic absurdity.

Vaudeville and burlesque were key influences for Lewis. Vaudeville's format privileged the performer's virtuosity, challenging entertainers to perpetually redevelop their material and presentation. Theater historian Henry Jenkins describes the vaudeville dynamic:

> Vaudeville's player centered mode of production resulted in a constant foregrounding of the performer's status as an entertainer; variety audiences valued attempts to command the spotlight and produce a strong impression. The vaudevillian, as master of the act from conception to execution, sought material tailored to particular performance skills. Performers were never subservient to the script; rather, narrative, where it existed at all, facilitated their familiar tricks.[60]

This type of creative autonomy suited Lewis; it gave him liberty to experiment with the comic genre and showcase his considerable talents as an entertainer, and most significantly, it helped him nurture and refine his unique comic mode. Physical comedy became Lewis's performance operandi at the start of his career, with his gangly, malleable physique serving as the locus where the contradictions and incongruities central to the comedic art were manifest and played out to the delight of live and film audiences.

Both vaudeville and burlesque featured aggressive, action-oriented comic business, incorporating pratfalls, gimmicky spectacle, and physical play. These elements also gained widespread use in comedy cinema throughout the 1920s and well into the 1930s, especially in the films of the Marx Brothers, Charlie Chaplin, and later the Three Stooges. Physical comedy, often consolidated under the rubric "slapstick comedy," subverts spectators' expectations by exploiting incongruity and exaggeration, heightening material or visual discrepancies through the performer's physicality.[61] By inverting the norms associated with society and the body, physical comedy challenges dignity, authority, and cultural notions of decency and taste.[62]

Jenkins recognizes a commensurate impulse in physical comedy, or what he identifies as "anarchistic comedy." According to Jenkins, "anarchistic comedy addresses a desire to break free from restraint, to enjoy an abundance of energy and spontaneity, to challenge authorities who restrain our creative potential, and to negate the logical order."[63] Anarchistic comedy is grounded in the clown figure, a character representing liminality, existing within the lower orders of the social hierarchy, and typically performing antics that disrupt or unsettle the dominant social order. The clown's anarchistic presence within the social structure threatens to expose the hypocrisy and ridiculousness of the culture's value and power systems. Moreover, the clown retains a powerful position as the pivotal point of physical comedy. Film historian Alan Dale points out that the clown "suffers humiliation for us," adding that "the clown's martyrdom becomes the good time the audience is having."[64] This characterization is evident in all of Lewis's work, including his telethon appearances.

In attempting to make the aesthetic and kinetic properties of Lewis's comedic work accessible, Durgnat offers this helpful description:

> Like all great impressionists, he thinks with his body, and translates the soul's impulses into a semaphor of spastic acrobacy; he stutters with his feet, he trips over his tongue, squints with his kneecaps and turns the simple act of crossing his legs into a bout of cat's cradle. His strabismus, quite devoid of the peaceful blankness of Ben Turpin's of yore, startles the spectator, like a klaxon; I wasn't surprised when a friend complained that watching our hero in *Artists and Models* made him feel seasick.[65]

Other critics observe similar properties: media theorist Scott Bukatman defines Lewis as "paralysis in motion"; film critic Kass writes that Lewis exhibits "supercharged lunacy" and "unconfined exhibitionism."[66] These assessments do more than characterize the comic's physical style of play; they evidence a visceral and physical response to the *experience* wrought by Lewis's comedy. Wallowing in physical humiliation, Lewis unabashedly represents social and embodied nonconformity, blatantly illustrating the futility of struggling against natural or material forces and taking the spectator along with him in the process.

Lewis's films showcase this most explicitly. In *The Nutty Professor* (1963), one of his best-known and most popular films, Lewis plays Julian Kelp, an introverted weakling in search of love and acceptance. In one of his many attempts to boost his self-esteem and physical appeal, Kelp joins a gym. The sequence that follows pits Lewis against the machines, twisting and transforming his body into a cartoonish caricature of itself. At one point his arms become grotesquely elongated, stretching out on the floor in front of him like two great rubbery reams. The obvious artifice in this sequence heightens the absurdity and grotesqueness of Kelp's physical alteration, permitting spectators to laugh from a neutral distance. Yet Lewis's portrayal of the hapless "goof," lovable misfit, or bumbling fool invites sympathy from the spectator, who identifies with Lewis's beleaguered everyman through the humility of physical comedy.

Countless films feature Lewis spastically dancing or hurling his body through the cinematic mise-en-scène, entangled in vacuum cleaner or telephone chords or subjected to endless fumbling with chairs, coats, and other household items. The body's phenomenology and its failure to cope with the world's materiality becomes the primary focus, producing responses that range from pure pleasure to discomfort in witnessing the body's subversion in a world suddenly and irrationally turned chaotic. The overt artifice involved in many of his films supports moments that permit Lewis to acknowledge, along with spectators, the pleasurable incongruity between reality and art. During such times, Lewis implicitly assures the audience that he, the actor and private citizen, remains intact underneath these schizophrenic characters.[67] When this same disruptive spectacle bleeds through the telethon event, without the self-conscious wink to the audience signaling contrivance or play, the effects and responses become significantly more complex. Lewis's comic machinations, made impossibly but permissively unreal on screen, become embarrassingly distressing on stage to undermine the oppressive spectacle of need and physical compromise presented throughout the telethon.[68]

During the course of the telethon, Lewis seizes moments, many of which are improvised and unrehearsed, to echo his earlier work in film and on stage. He trades comically suggestive, often questionable exchanges with telethon guests. In 1990, producers aired a prefilmed segment that portrayed Lewis frantically visiting various famous celebrities and entertainers to garner their participation in the telethon. The film shows Lewis outside the dressing room of actress Shirley MacLaine, who is in the middle of preparing for the opening of her one-woman Broadway show. Before entering, Lewis giggles outside the door, using the high-pitched nasal whine of his "kid" persona to call out to the actress. The following dialogue takes place:

MACLAINE [feigning exasperation]: Hi. Jerry. Look, I know why you're here. You want me to do your show. Fine. I'd love to, yes, great.
LEWIS (elicits a goofy laugh): Oh boy! That's terrific, Shirley!
MACLAINE [smiling]: Okay, okay. Now scoot. I've got to get dressed.

LEWIS: The audience would like it if you didn't.
MACLAINE: Didn't what?
LEWIS: Get dressed![69]

Elsewhere, Lewis brings this dynamic to live moments; he openly flirts with entertainment reporter Leeza Gibbons; he playfully gropes a Rockette; his face lights up as two attractive young cheerleaders featured in the opening number allow themselves to receive a kiss from the aging comedian.

One of the most risqué exchanges to date occurred on the 2000 telethon with Latina dancer and singer Charo. Sitting behind a desk like a talk show host, Lewis interviewed the Latina icon, making playful, marginally inappropriate comments about her physique. In an attempt to gain control of the segment, Charo begins:

CHARO: I would like to be serious now.
LEWIS: I'm about as serious as I'm going to get [glancing down at his lap]. Get down there, goddamnit [addressing his lap]. [He takes a beat and says to the audience by way of explanation]) My dog is under under there. Eddie! Sit still![70]

Though essentially harmless, if not tasteless in content, the sexually infused play of these instances introduces a subversive element into the telethon that temporarily redirects the spectator's attention away from the sentimental images of the broadcast to the pleasure, fun, and comic relief offered by Lewis's humorous performance.[71]

Lewis also brings a high degree of physical comedy to his hosting duties, earning him notoriety for the way his hyperkinetic body functions in contrast to the bodies of individuals with neuromuscular disease, who appear restricted in their range of movement. His body becomes the site of continuous disruption in its own topical transformations, but also in the way that Lewis insinuates himself between performers and the materiality of the television studio. "[His] body," writes Shaviro, "is less an integral object than a zone of passive but intensely heightened sensitivity to the pulls and pressures of the social and political environment."[72]

Throughout the telethon, Lewis trades on the types of physical acrobatics that propelled him to stardom in the first decades of his career. Microphone stands, utility chords, and even golf clubs seem to take on a life of their own, entangling the helpless comedian; the camera serves as a prop for Lewis, who peers into the lens so that his distorted face fills the screen; a trumpet proves his archnemesis, dangling ludicrously from his mouth after his tongue becomes fused to the mouthpiece.[73] Lewis submits to the lawlessness of imbalance and uncoordinated action, allowing these and other material objects to function as extensions of his own elastic physicality. Lacking any narrative coherence (i.e., they do not exist as part of a film or sketch), these moments exist in a purity all their own. They are discordant ejaculations of absurdity that interject outlandish incongruity and exaggeration into an event that, without these outrageous moments, would risk collapsing under the weight of its own emotionalism.

His other type of body work operates in similar ways to intervene and offset the telethon's sober representations of disability. Lewis takes advantage of sharing the stage, remaining perpetually on for the telethon's duration. At any moment, while a celebrity guest espouses Lewis's good works or while Lewis accepts a check from a service group or sponsor, the comedian might spontaneously contort his face, crossing his eyes, wiggling his eyebrows, or letting his tongue loll from his mouth. For instance, during the 1986 telethon, as guest host Leeza Gibbons began talking about many of the corporate sponsors involved in the telethon, Lewis stood slightly behind her forming grotesque faces and farcically miming her speech.[74]

During a number featuring a Vegas-style female chorus line, Lewis inexplicably jogs into the middle of their formation. He attempts to mimic their complicated kicks and dance steps, throwing his body into wild spasms only to be jostled and knocked about in a flurry of sequins and large feather headdresses.[75] In another segment, taken from the 1985 broadcast, digital music begins to play over an empty stage. Lewis first steps tentatively onto center stage, looking around furtively. He starts to spontaneously dance to the synthesized beats and chords, meant as an intro for a group of professional break-dancers. Lewis's movements suggest the involuntary convulsions of those who suffer seizures as he violently shoots his legs in front of him, punches the air with his arms, throws his head forward and backward, and weaves his whole body with precarious instability. When the dancers bound onto the stage, Lewis scrunches his shoulders sheepishly as if caught engaged in something taboo and quickly jogs out of sight, pumping his legs outlandishly high for comedic effect.[76]

For many, Lewis's comedic performance appears in dubious taste and indicates a high level of self-indulgence that is both inappropriate and out of place given the nature of the telethon. Yet the comedic nature of these disturbances, specifically their hyperbolic style and pronounced execution, helps to facilitate an atmosphere of emotional and cognizant discord determined as productive to the telethon's larger aims. Lewis's antics produce the type of comic anarchy that, according to Jenkins, "allows the audience to experience a similar albeit vicarious escape from emotional restraint through its *stylistic* excesses and energetic performances."[77]

The type of escape Jenkins describes is analogous to what Garland-Thomson locates as the "thrill of surprise" produced by the sight of something unusual. In her theoretical exploration of staring, Garland-Thomson argues that novelty, especially visual novelty, results in a rush of dopamine, the chemical associated with pleasure, from the brain. The laughter and even shock generated by Lewis's comedy may cause this type of pleasure surge even as it also makes the spectator uncomfortable. Garland-Thomson describes the effects: "Ironically, at the root of our craving for novelty is an anxious drive to be rid of it so that we can sink into a calmer world where nothing startles or demands our visual attention."[78] Within the context of the telethon it becomes impossible to look elsewhere in order to restore the type of dynamic Garland-Thomson identifies. Instead, spectators can only be aware of their responses to Lewis and of the outrageous and therefore extremely artificial nature of his performance.

This produces an effect described by literary theorist Kenneth Burke where the "comic frame of reference" exposes the distinction among acts, motives, and operations, "enabling people *to be observers of themselves, while acting. Its ultimate would not be passiveness, but maximum consciousness.*"[79] Lewis's comedy, steadily erupting throughout the telethon and seemingly antithetical to the telethon's main focus, actually works in tandem with the telemonials and other performative elements of the broadcast to promote productive dissociation from the spectacle of need. Charity depends upon the ability to foster emotional identification with the suffering individual while upholding the diversity between self and Other; this gap enables the individual to remain alienated from emotional absorption and, in Burke's assessment, retain "maximum consciousness," which may result in benevolent action.

The emphasis on Lewis's materiality creates another, equally important effect worth explicating: it brings awareness to the workings of the imperfect, seemingly uncontrollable, volatile body that resists clear categorization and provokes unease in onlookers. More than changing tastes, age is the enemy of the physical comic, and Lewis has not escaped immunity from the natural aging process. By the late 1980s and into the early 1990s, the comic could be seen sweating profusely, with labored breathing, after song, dance, and other physical numbers. In these same years, Lewis also spent large amounts of his hosting time seated behind a desk a la Johnny Carson or at a podium. But perhaps the most startling alteration to Lewis's telethon persona occurred in 2002, when a severely bloated, nearly unrecognizable Lewis kicked off the telethon by assuaging people's fears and concerns about his own health.

Press reports documenting the comic's dealings with numerous health issues, including diabetes, heart disease, addiction to painkillers, and even prostrate cancer, circulated at different intervals in the latter half of Lewis's career. In the year leading up to the 2002 telethon, Lewis had undergone treatment for pulmonary fibrosis, a scarring of the lung tissue. To treat this condition, doctors prescribed the powerful anti-inflammatory steroid prednisone, which caused Lewis's severe weight gain. The weight gain put additional pressure on Lewis's spine, further aggravating a host of old back injuries he had incurred during his days taking comedic falls on and off stage. The result: stultifying depression and suicidal thoughts.

Eventually Lewis had a type of "pain pacemaker" implanted in his spine that helped mitigate the pain through electromagnetic pulses. Initially, his health issues threatened to keep him from his duties as telethon host. "My staff, the doctors, everybody thought I shouldn't do it," said Lewis. "They were afraid I would turn people off by looking ill." Lewis dismissed their concerns, responding, "Can anyone please tell me when I said, 'I will only help these children as long as I look good'?"[80]

Despite Lewis's reassurances to his team and MDA personnel, he devoted several minutes of precious airtime at the start of the telethon, airtime typically dedicated to an over-the-top song-and-dance number, to account for his physical state, what he termed "the cosmetics of this condition," effectively denying that his body had been negatively effected by the fibrosis. "Don't feel sorry for me," Lewis directed, contradicting the imperatives put forth by the telethon to pity the disabled children and adults presented through the broadcast. He closed by reiterating that "I've never lost my commitment to my kids" and that he looked forward to putting this health scare behind him "in order to get back to normal."[81]

In this particular telethon, Lewis's embodiment, in its nonperforming status, warrants attention for the way it complicates the images and messages about disability that the telethon attempts to make salient. His insistence on a conventional understanding of "good health" (i.e., able-bodiedness) exists at odds with the visual depiction of his body, which evidences physical limitation, a trait (erroneously or not) associated with disability. Spectators are asked to confront Lewis's body as a corporeal vehicle first and as a celebrity icon second, or, as Thomson states: "When bodies begin to malfunction or look unexpected, we become aware of them as bodies rather than as tools of our intentionality."[82] For many in the disability rights community watching the 2000 broadcast, the irony of Lewis's word choices was not lost. His awkward insistence on his ableness reifies the unsettling dichotomy between able-bodied "saviors" and disabled "victims." Yet the spectacle of his own diverse body, combined with images of disabled people that confound easy categorization, blunts the ideological force of his statements.

JERRY'S KIDS MEET JERRY'S ORPHANS: THE ACTIVIST RESPONSE TO THE TELETHON

As early as 1980, a shift in pubic tastes for visual, media, and literary materials relating to minority populations became palpable. Shortly before the 1981 telethon, an editorial appeared in the *New York Times* written by Evan Kemp, a disabled individual and executive director of the Disability Rights Center in Washington, DC, that leveled stinging criticism at the MDA in general and the telethon in particular. Kemp made the case that the telethon's approach "equate[d] the handicapped with total hopelessness," adding, "When a telethon makes disabling conditions seem overwhelmingly destructive, it intensifies the awkward embarrassment that the able-bodied feel around the disabled people."[83] Initially the MDA dismissed Kemp's criticisms, but other detractors followed Kemp's lead, eventually forcing the MDA to adjust some of its presentational techniques.[84] Telemonials, as previously mentioned, began to feature adults and emphasized productivity and accomplishment rather than despair and victimization. By the late 1990s, the poster-child neologism was replaced with the title "Goodwill Ambassador," and more disabled adults and children appeared live throughout the broadcast to speak on their own behalf.

Another element that shaped more contemporary telethon broadcasts involved greater concern over the rise of the charity conglomerate and its allocation of funds. With a trend toward running the charity organization based on a business model, replete with perks and benefits for its chairperson and board members, public interest groups began to demand greater accountability of the MDA's balance sheets. Organizations sought to maintain the notion that giving was connected with an intrinsic desire to help a less fortunate individual, but the scope and economic influence of entities such as the MDA and other associations made it impossible to ignore the bottom line: money improves the lives of disabled individuals, not just caring or concern. As such, telethon broadcasts beginning in 1990 contained additional segments designed exclusively to provide detailed accounts of the programs and resources funded by the public's telethon dollars.[85]

Despite these format changes, dissent persisted. In 1991, Mike Ervin and his sister Cris Matthews, two former poster children from Chicago turned disability rights activists, launched the first large-scale telethon protest. Mobilized with others who shared their views that the telethon was outdated, with Lewis as its most offensive component, the duo formed the group Jerry's Orphans. Ervin and Matthews, along with their supporters, stationed themselves at the front entrance to the television studios of WGN, the local Chicago affiliate broadcasting the telethon. Other protests occurred simultaneously in Boston, Detroit, Los Angeles, Minneapolis, and Las Vegas.[86] Hershey, for example, organized her own protest in Denver in 1991 under the slogan "Tune Out Jerry." Protesters wore signs attached to their wheelchairs that read "No Pity" or "This Kid Is All Grown Up."

The activist initiative failed to weaken Lewis's fierce support and advocacy for "his kids." Nor did it deter the aging entertainer from reiterating his position that without him, the dystrophic children of the world would be in dire straits. However, the increased presence of people resistant to the telethon thrust the discussion of this fundraising vehicle, Lewis, and the ethics of the entire enterprise into national debate. Following the first round of protests in 1991, Robert Jones, a reporter for the *Los Angeles Times*, wrote:

> As long as the emotional currency translates into the real currency of cash, who cares? Before [the 1991 telethon] was all over, the final tote board had hit $45,071,857, and the corporate contributions just about matched that. Figure roughly $80 million for the day's work. That's a chunk. Let's ask this last question of the marchers who would like to see Lewis drummed out of the telethon:

Just who is going to keep this cash machine going? Who is going to stand on that stage for 21½ hours, maintain emotional correctness, never indulge in cashable pity, and still pull in $80 million for muscular dystrophy?[87]

In one of the many letters written in support of Lewis and published by the MDA, a parent echoed this sentiment: "If you have to beg, borrow, or steal, make people cry or shake their heads, too bad! Our kids need everything you get for them!"[88]

Lewis himself was eventually interviewed regarding the protest activities. In a piece that aired on the news magazine television show *Primetime Live,* Lewis spoke candidly to journalist Chris Wallace about what he perceived as his humanitarian work. "I am so right," Lewis insists, "because my heart and my gut steers me." He adds, "I do very good work. No one can tell me otherwise." Later on in the piece came the following exchange:

WALLACE: Some of your kids have now turned against you and are calling themselves Jerry's Orphans. Forget the issues. Personally, what does that do to you?

LEWIS: Why didn't they call us anything when we bought them the wheelchairs, Chris? Why wasn't I terrible man when we bought them the wheelchairs that are getting them around?[89]

The disconnection between Lewis and the population he purported to be selflessly serving became transparent in that broadcast. For Lewis, the issue would always revolve around questions of his sincerity and integrity as a surrogate father figure and savior to his kids, a typology lifted from the pages of a Holcroft melodrama. In another portion of the interview he compares himself to the legendary Babe Ruth, who supposedly gave a dying little boy the will to live by promising to hit a home run in his honor.

Ironically, the megalomaniac stance that gave Lewis his confidence and swagger was the same one that continued to polarize discourse about the telethon and his role as host. His refusal to acknowledge anything but love and pride for "his kids" and for the way he conducted himself as a benevolent figure has served to keep protests of the telethon relevant and has inspired a new generation of disability rights critics to emerge. As recently as 2007, individuals have taken to cyberspace to encourage people to boycott and/or speak out against the telethon. A blogger with the moniker "Cripchick" posts information about the derogatory practices implemented by the telethon and even features a "Letter to the Editor" template that anyone may copy, personalize, and send to their local medial outlets.[90] Protesters in Charlestown, South Carolina, have maintained their activist presence against the telethon consistently for the last twenty years, and Hershey continues to speak, write, and draw attention to the pejorative aspects of the fundraising event each year.[91]

The early efforts of "Jerry's Orphans" and the contributions of other individuals and collectives brokered competing perceptions of disabled people that chaffed against the model of the telethon as a massive welfare machine. Disability rights activists called for engagement with and understanding of the disabled community as the foundation for benevolence, not what they charged amounted to handouts motivated by paternalism. Moreover, the activist involvement in the telethon highlighted the disabled as a community of individuals capable of speaking back to, in the view of Lennard J. Davis, "essentialist claims" of modernism "that identity is written on and rooted to the body."[92] Their resistance further called into question the contrivance of the telethon itself and in the process explicated the disability identity as multifaceted and fluid.

These sentiments encapsulate the primary dichotomy underlying all charitable enterprises that involve, for better or worse, a permissible amount of emotional exploitation, coupled with the spectacle of distress, which is both desired and necessary. Performance culture feeds this appetite for display and exposure, even if it is at the subject's expense, and provides a legible structure for both the givers and the receivers of charity to fully participate in a number of ways. With this in mind, performance culture then also serves as a mutable framework for individuals to intervene in, conform to, resist, and reshape critical attitudes and behaviors.

CODA: IS AN MDA TELETHON WITHOUT JERRY LEWIS STILL AN MDA TELETHON?

It was not about financial crisis or environmental disaster, but the 2011 *Huffington Post* headline arrested readers' attention nonetheless: "Jerry Lewis Retiring from MDA Telethon."[93] The man who had shaped the MDA's charity brand and undeniably informed the telethon format announced that the 2011 telethon would be his last as host. In the report circulated widely among news and web outlets, Lewis wrote: "As a labor of love, I've hosted the annual Telethon since 1966 and I'll be making my final appearance on the show this year by performing my signature song, 'You'll Never Walk Alone.'" The release went on to note that Lewis would remain in his post as MDA chairman, quoting the comic as saying, "I'll never desert the MDA and my kids."[94]

People responded to the news with a combination of surprise and resignation that a new era in telethon broadcasts was well under way. Many posted comments on the web wishing the comic well and thanking him for his decades of humanitarian service. Other individuals echoed sentiments that those in the disability rights activist community had vocalized for years: it was past time for Lewis to let go of his antiquated and narrow-minded approach to servicing disabled men, women, *and* kids. Perhaps the work of "Jerry's Orphans" had finally prevailed.

Nearly three months after Lewis announced his retirement came another shock in the form of a terse statement released by the MDA that Lewis would not be returning as telethon host or serving as the organization's national chairman. "Jerry Lewis is a world-class humanitarian," wrote MDA's chairman of the board, R. Rodney Howell. "We're forever grateful to him for his more than half century of generous service to the MDA."[95] Replacing Lewis would be an ensemble effort made up of four hosts: Nygel Lythgoe, executive producer of *American Idol* and judge on the show *So You Think You Can Dance?*, and entertainment reporters Nancy O'Dell, Jann Carl, and Alison Sweeney. The telethon itself would run for only six hours, astringently truncated from its historical twenty-one-and-a-half-hour limit.

Another wave of dismay, this time mingled with outrage, surged through the webosphere. Fellow comics expressed indignation and disgust at the way they perceived Lewis's firing. People speculated that Lewis's often charged and controversial comments in the popular press, about everything from his unapologetic views of his "kids" to his open contempt for the state of young entertainment, had finally caught up with him. Television writer Mary Elizabeth Williams offered a more tempered assessment. She conceded that despite Lewis's comic ingenuity, the changing tides of tastes and methods in the charity industry were too strong for the MDA to resist. "There are other ways to use charity to fight disease now," wrote Williams. "There are even more efficient ones."[96] Even with this cultural mindset, telethon supporters remained anxious about the impact of Lewis's absence, articulating a question similar to the infamous philosophical query, "If a tree falls in the forest and no one is around to hear it, does it still make a sound?" If an MDA telethon runs without Jerry Lewis, is it still an MDA telethon?

The answer turned out to be both yes and no. Lewis remained physically exempt from the telethon but was invoked throughout the broadcast by Lythgoe and other celebrity guests who wished the comic well and thanked him for his efforts. Near the close of the show, producers ran a two-minute montage that paid tribute to Lewis throughout his long tenure as telethon host. Footage highlighted his inexhaustible telethon performance: singing, dancing, comically bumbling around the stage, chatting with entertainers, and interacting with his disabled guests. A choir made up of seventy children from a Las Vegas choral group and featuring pop stars such as Jordin Sparks and Jon Secada performed a medley of patriotic songs to close the broadcast.

Lewis clearly left an aesthetic vacuum: gone were his physically elastic machinations and his many unscripted cringe-inducing moments that critics identified as "schmaltzy" and that others decried as simply offensive. What the MDA made up for in terms of notions of taste they lacked in the organic unpredictability and expected disruption that Lewis provided. Confronted with this vacancy, the producers had to more carefully and deliberately engineer telethon segments to flow in such a way as to allocate sanctioned, mediated, *appropriate* breaks from the show's cloying affect.

A telethon without Jerry Lewis is still a telethon. It is simply a different type of telethon, aligned with contemporary sensibilities that dictate a willingness to engage with physical difference that is presented free from its arbitrary and unknowable nature. Unwittingly, Lewis's performance highlighted the randomness of physical disability, which contributes to its designation as a politicized identity impacting across race, class, and sexual orientation. Lewis's display of embodied difference left little room for nuance in the telethon's characterization of disability. In his absence, producers could mitigate the variability of embodied difference with a scientifically influenced model of disability as a temporary location that is distinctive in its manifestation. This in turn meant that viewers had to negotiate a new, more complicated relationship to the spectacle of difference that obfuscated the dichotomy between identifying with and separating from the Other.

One example of this can be found in the appearance of Abbey Umali, the

MDA "tween" Goodwill Ambassador. Umali is a twelve-year-old California native who lives with Charcot-Marie Tooth disease, a weakening of the muscles as a result of myelin deficiency. Umali, a petite, brown-haired little girl who loves to sing and dance, did not signify her disability through any material markers on the telethon broadcast (in a press release on the MDA website, Umali mentions using leg braces to help her mobility). Her self-presentation exuded an amalgam of qualities that might be characterized as "normal," while her designation and involvement in the telethon brought attention to her subjectivity as a disabled child. Viewers must process and make sense of these dueling images with all of their ideological baggage, eventually forcing them to exercise a greater degree of self-awareness and self-reflexiveness about why and how to respond to Umali and others like her on the telethon.[97]

With or without Lewis, that response ultimately translated into collective benevolence, demonstrated through a staggering $6.5 million raised in the course of six hours. The MDA proudly proclaimed the telethon a huge success, pointing out that this was the highest tally since 2008, when the global recession set in. Critics proclaimed on the telethon's total as well, noting that it was $2 million more than Lewis had netted in 2010, during what turned out to be the entertainer's final broadcast.

Acts of Conspicuous Compassion

Charity in the Reality TV Era: *Extreme Makeover:
Home Edition*

The twenty-first-century charity imperative begins with a long camera shot
that captures the outline of a stark, rugged Montana mountain range cut
out against a supernova sunrise washed in orange, pink, and magenta hues.
A closeup of wheat, the proverbial "amber waves of grain," shivering in the
breeze fills the frame. A rolling piano provides accompaniment to this idyllic scene, seemingly plucked out of the pages of *National Geographic*. An
overhead shot pans down on a lone man, outfitted in hip waders, fly-fishing
from the middle of a small, rocky island set into a crystalline stream, careening around his ankles. The figure is not an ordinary fisherman or even a
casual tourist enjoying the pristine wilderness on a perfect, fall morning.
He is Ty Pennington, host of the ABC-produced show *Extreme Makeover:
Home Edition*, a reality-based program in the big and trendy business of
transformation reality shows. Each week, one deserving family becomes
the recipients of extreme charity with an extraordinary and fantastic home
renovation. As the transformation unfolds, the lives of the family members
undergo incalculable change in front of millions of viewers watching around
the globe.

On this perfect day in America's heartland, Pennington makes the Montana landscape, with its sweeping grandeur and seemingly limitless boundaries, the backdrop to a compelling and heart-wrenching narrative starring
the Carter family from Billings, Montana. Julie Carter and her daughter suffer from a hereditary condition that shrinks the individual's skull, making it
too small for the brain. Neurological material eventually slides into the person's spinal column. Julie has started a grassroots support group designed
to help educate patients and families with the same disease. Her coworkers
and volunteers describe her as a "healer." The humble family shoulders their

medical challenges and burdens from the confines of their home, a shabbily renovated chicken coop. Parts of the house bear evidence of its former owners, as the design crew notes, with concrete dividers and chicken detritus littering the walls and floors.[1]

Relayed anywhere else, the Carter family's troubles sound like the kind of pulp fiction found in the pages of women's magazines and sensationalized supermarket serials from a bygone era. In the realm of the salacious, spectacle-driven vehicle of reality TV, however, their story is not only the norm but less extreme or extraordinary than many of the other narratives presented on the program. Since its premier episode in December 2003, the show's participants have included a family with six children, five of whom suffer from rare and multiple forms of autism and experience extreme sensitivity to their environment; a family living on a Navaho reservation in a cramped mobile home without heat, running water, or electricity; a couple whose dozen foster children, several with special needs, are battling lead poisoning from their old, deteriorating house; the family of a little girl whose left leg was amputated when she saved her five-year-old sister from an oncoming truck; the Sharrock family, whose son, Patrick, has brittle bone disease and who broke both of his legs before he was born, kicking in the womb; and the Hassalls from Kentucky, with two adopted children, one of whom is a special-needs child from China with a cleft palette. Brian Hassall is a seventeen-year veteran of the local police force, recently shot on duty and working the night shift. Brian suffers from severe migraines, brought on by sunlight. Consequently, he sleeps in the family's dark, dank, mildew- and mold-infested basement. His wife, Michelle, has a rare blood disorder and was diagnosed with lymphoma cancer, making it impossible for her to spend time with her husband in the basement.[2]

These types of scenarios are not novel additions to the reality programming that populates network and cable television. *Extreme Makeover* is a twenty-first-century update of earlier shows such as *Queen for a Day* (1956), *Strike It Rich* (1950), and *It Could Be You* (1956), where contestants competed for rewards based on their ability to relay their most pathetic, miserable, heart-tugging stories. Popularized during the quiz- and game-show craze of midcentury, these shows introduced an element of the supposedly unscripted and real into television programming. They also appealed to the public's proclivity for witnessing the spectacle of distress only to be released from such exhibitions by charitable intervention, either their own or the goodwill of another. On many of these early television shows, benevolence came in the form of consumer products (i.e., a luxury vacation, a new appliance, a shopping spree, etc.), demonstrating a more pronounced way to suture charity to the healing balm administered through capitalism.

Extreme Makeover: Home Edition is one of a new breed of reality TV shows, a trend coined as "do-goodism" television that has raised the stakes in terms of content and payoff for this nascent genre.[3] A description of the program on its web site describes it as a "a race against time on a project that would ordinarily take at least four months to achieve, involving a team of designers, contractors and several hundred workers who all have just seven days to totally rebuild an entire house—every single room, plus the exterior and landscaping."[4] The project is an extensive rebuild for a worthy family. Executive producer Conrad Ricketts credits himself with factoring in the notion of helping distressed families, which was not part of the show's original pitch when ABC gave the project the green light. In an article for *New York Times Magazine*, Ricketts recounts to writer Jake Halpern how he hit upon the idea central to the show's current incarnation:

> Ricketts was driving around Santa Clara, California when he came upon a small, ramshackle house. Standing in front of this house was a woman and her daughter, the "cutest little blonde that you have ever seen in your life." When Ricketts asked the woman why she had the "nastiest" house on the block, she replied: "Mr. Ricketts, our little girl has been fighting leukemia for four years, and every dime we have has gone to help her, and we have no money to fix the house." Ricketts said, "And I knew, at that minute, this was the soul of our TV show."[5]

Ricketts's epiphany, instigated by the woman's adorable young daughter, gestures back to the NFIP's discovery of Donald Anderson and attests to the longstanding visual and emotional appeal of needy children. Ricketts's recognition that the depiction of suffering and domestic redemption would factor significantly in the show is also revealing. It announces his understanding of television's most evocative powers and also signals his sense of the kind of spectacle that would most enthrall a large number of television viewers.

With such massive tasks to accomplish in a limited time frame, *Extreme Makeover: Home Edition* relies on thousands of volunteers from local and regional communities for labor and resources. Community businesses also donate thousands of dollars' worth of materials. In some cases, the owners receive recognition for their generosity in the form of on-camera appearances and/or advertising during the broadcast and on the show's web site. In later seasons, other entities. such as small banks and mortgage lenders, have also donated services and products to help defray the family's enormous new financial burden. Celebrity and sports icons have also figured prominently into the program as surprise guests. The 2009 season brought an additional element of excitement and glamour when producers invited different celebrities to actively participate in the design and construction of the new house. Popular television and music personalities have included actor David Duchovny, country music star Clint Black, and R&B artist Mary J. Blige.

The program's emphasis on the relationship between the task at hand and the time allotted to complete the job borrows from the telethon's essential time-compression element to heighten excitement and anxiety. This approach also accentuates one of the program's foundational ideologies: the nature of transformation. The act of undergoing, and in turn bearing witness to, extraordinary alteration underlies all charity initiatives since the nineteenth century. *Extreme Makeover: Home Edition* promises the transcendent, and according to media historian Gareth Palmer "magical," transformation of the hard-luck but resilient family. In the process, the alchemy extends to the cast and crew, thousands of volunteers, and the average spectator, watching from his or her own sheltered space of privilege and distance. "By undergoing this transformation," writes Palmer, "the [families] go from being objects of our pity to ones of our envy."[6] This becomes doubly evident in the show's promotional language: "Viewers witness not only the unbelievable transformation of the house, but during the final and emotional reveal, they see how the home makeover has impacted the lives of the deserving families."[7] The result is a seamless and highly ecstatic journey that charts the elevation of the distressed via communal benevolence, aided by the deliberately mystified forces of capitalism and consumer culture.

Additionally, the performance aesthetics germane to reality TV— its use of documentary-film-style camera shots and editing techniques to provide the veneer of the unscripted and spontaneous—allot producers the ability to manipulate representations and still maintain claims to the "real." As a result, viewers become emotionally invested in the weekly narratives (despite their inevitable, predictable, and formulaic outcomes), virtually if not literally. Spectators participate in the uplift and conversion of an "average" family, repositioned on the television show to symbolize a vision of America rescued from a failed welfare state and restored through a new kind of spectacular benevolence in which the conventional give-to-get mentality underpinning charity becomes a secondary motivating factor. In its place arises an atmosphere of conspicuous compassion, fueled by twenty-first-century celebreality culture that elevates voyeurism and spectacle and rewards a give-to-get-seen imperative.

GOING PUBLIC: REALITY TV

Emergent scholarship on reality TV places it in relation to a number of transitions taking place within television programming, as well as within the larger sphere of the broadcasting industry. Shows that contained elements of the documentary-film aesthetic or trafficked in the candid style were evident in programs such as *Candid Camera* in the 1940s and later, in the 1970s, with the twelve-part PBS series *An American Family*. However, the breakout popularity of MTV's *The Real World*, a show that filmed the improvised experiences of a group of young people living together in New York City, in 1992 marked a new entry into cable TV offerings. By the turn of the century reality shows were staples of regular programming schedules.[8] In both America and the United Kingdom, reality TV accounts for over 30 percent of television's market share, with programs such as CBS's *Survivor* and ABC's *Dancing with the Stars* attracting anywhere from ten to twenty million viewers during a single episode.[9]

The rising expenses of television production, coupled with changes made to the syndication rules in the last decade, are only a couple of factors influencing the increase in reality TV programming across networks. Media historian Anita Hill writes, "Local stations provided a significant revenue source for independent producers who would sell programmes made specifically for local stations and/or programmes that had been aired previously for network stations."[10] Fewer time slots allotted to independently produced shows meant a lack of nonnetwork, traditionally scripted shows available to viewers. Additionally, many participants on reality TV are supposedly nonunion actors. Because they are not entitled to the same wage scale and benefits as union actors, creators can keep the cost of production low. Indeed, overall budget costs for reality TV programming tends to be significantly lower than for conventionally shot and scripted shows, making them easy to reproduce so that the network may run the equivalent of two seasons of a reality show within the span of one calendar year.

The steady infiltration of reality programming amid scripted shows also signaled a change both in viewer's tastes and in their relationship to the television-viewing experience. Reality TV announces itself from other modes in its "self-conscious claim to the discourse of the real."[11] Spectators appear privy to unrehearsed action and events presented as unfolding in real time. In the course of the broadcast, viewers transcend their roles as passive viewers to become active observers of the scenes of drama, heartbreak, competition, or transformation taking place. This dynamic is further explored in many programs that invite spectators to call or text-message information to the show. Competition shows such as FOX's *American Idol* and ABC's *Dancing with the Stars* employ this approach, basing the outcomes of their contests on viewers' votes. Other shows, such as AMC's *Top Chef,* solicit spectators' input on the most popular or least popular figures, posting a poll and asking viewers to text-message their choices.

At the heart of reality TV exists a sense of intimacy, immediacy, and voyeuristic fascination with taking average people and placing them in unusual circumstances. The cultural and ideological implications of this television mode reach beyond escapist fantasy or debased entertainment. Media historians Anita Biressi and Heather Nunn argue that reality TV aims to reveal "social, psychological, political and historical truths and to depict the rhythms and structures of everyday life with the least recourse possible to dramatization and artifice."[12] Issues of class, race, sexuality, and gender figure just as prominently in reality shows as they do in their scripted counterparts. By virtue of its assertion of realness, this television genre houses rich sites of interrogation and fertile places to enlarge the public dialogue around social, political, and economic inequities.

What is most significant to its influence on benevolence is the way reality TV capitalizes on many powerful personal and cultural metanarratives, such as searching for true love (ABC's *The Bachelor/Bachelorette* franchise, FOX's *Joe Millionaire,* VH-1's *Rock of Love, I Love New York,* and *New Chance at Love*); undergoing radical personal or lifestyle transformation (ABC's *Extreme Makeover: Home Edition,* HGTV's *Trading Spaces,* NBC's *The Biggest Loser,* Lifetime's *How to Look Good Naked,* FOX's *Bridalplasty*);

or winning a competition (CBS's *Survivor*, ABC's *The Amazing Race* and *Dancing with the Stars*, NBC's *The Voice*, FOX's *American Idol*, Bravo's *Top Chef*, Lifetime's *Project Runway*). Within these programs, larger issues unfold that range from the maintenance of heteronormative attitudes, the exploitation of racial stereotypes, and the erosion of the American nuclear family, to the cultural obsession with health and bodily perfection. *Extreme Makeover: Home Edition* is no exception. It also engages with problems of class, embodiment, and economic disparity. Unfortunately, the solutions to these challenges offered by *Extreme Makeover: Home Edition* and other shows have less to do with political motivation than with providing instant gratification, fantastic rewards, and extravagant acts of charity conferred upon a small group of chosen individuals.

As theorists Susan Murray and Laurie Ouellette surmise, reality TV demonstrates an "ability to more fully provide viewers an unmediated, voyeuristic, and yet often playful look into what might be called the 'entertaining real.'"[13] It achieves this result by drawing together diverse aesthetic and cinematic devices and borrowing from a variety of narrative genres that range from soap operas and crime dramas to game shows and melodramas. Most notably, reality TV traffics in what many have observed to be a style influenced by various iterations of documentary film.

The interest in documenting subjects through film in the early 1920s and 1930s produced work that prized verisimilitude and "actuality" as distinctive modes. The British filmmaker John Grierson has been credited as one of the figures responsible for propelling documentary film into the public's consciousness. Taking social issues as his main film subjects, Grierson used cinema to inform and educate rather than entertain. For Grierson, the film apparatus allowed him to involve spectators in the "social process." The working-class subjects of his documentary films became humanized as heroes or victims rather than presented as objects of curiosity or pity.[14]

The sense of intimacy between the filmed subject and the spectator generated through documentary film is perhaps one of its most potent impacts. Spectators are transported to the environment of the film scene in a way that discourages the kind of escapism or fantasy pervading narrative cinema. Similarly, documentary film also attempts to re-present real situations and scenes with a kind of objective integrity supposedly excised from narrative, commercially generated cinema. The technology implemented by documentary filmmakers aids their capacity to capture aspects of reality. More portable and smaller film equipment makes location captures easier and more accessible. Techniques used to record ambient sound and unfiltered noise, and then layer voiceover commentary onto the finished product, all add to the unpolished, raw, present look and feel of documentaries. These elements figure prominently into contemporary reality TV programming and are responsible for its subtle and seductive play between actuality and artifice.

One key aspect of documentary film that is most readily available in reality TV is the personal-interview trope. In a typical interview captured within a documentary film, the subject may respond to questions presented by the interviewer, who does not appear on camera. This not only permits the subject to speak in his or her own words but also sets up a direct-address dynamic, as if the person were speaking to a specific spectator. Most reality shows include a "confessional" element, pioneered by MTV's *The Real World*. Periodically throughout the show, cast members retreat to a designated room known as a "confessional booth" to extemporize their uncensored thoughts, feelings, and opinions.

In the context of the reality show, the interview convention is fraught with an overt self-awareness that does not necessarily permeate the documentary film. These types of "confessional" interviews are ostensibly performed for a range of purposes: they exacerbate the show's climate of exhibitionism; they supposedly provide insight into the participant's character; and, most important, they close the gap between spectator and reality TV performer by simulating intimacy. It is hard to believe, given the tenuous distinction between authenticity and contrivance evidenced in these types of programs, that the subject is unaware of his or her self-presentation. In this respect, reality TV facilitates a system of knowledge about self-display in relation to the fabricated, insulated world of reality television that influences perceptions of the signifying self in the public sphere.[15]

The similarities between reality TV and documentary film are based in tools and conventions. As many media scholars point out, documentary film is often connected to explicitly political and social aims. That is to say, many documentarians are interested in using the medium to expose inequalities, examine political injustices, and explore trends that impact humanitarian efforts. Documentaries also invite a multiplicity of perspectives in an effort to obtain an aura of objectivity. Most reality TV shows do not promote social welfare as their primary aims. The exceptions are "do-goodism" programs like *Extreme Makeover: Home Edition*, *The Biggest Loser*, and the self-help-styled programs populating Oprah Winfrey's OWN network. These shows marbleize uplift and improvement into their ideology and marketing. They also eschew overt claims to objectivity.

"Although reality TV whets our appetite for the authentic," write Murray and Ouellette, "much of our engagement with such texts paradoxically hinges on our awareness that what we are watching is constructed and contains 'fictional' elements."[16] Part of the buy-in for reality programming hinges on the spectator's willingness to suspend his or her disbelief, accepting that the contrived elements merely heighten the reality instead of standing in for actuality. Hill points out that viewers connect to representations coded as "authentic," whether in personality, in emotion, or in the show's events. She makes the case that an overdetermined use of fiction carries adverse impacts. "The more ordinary people are perceived to perform for the cameras," Hill notes, "the less real the program appears to be to viewers," thereby diminishing its popularity.[17] Shows able to present a sophisticated blend of realness and theatricality not only gain wider viewership but also level a more profound impact on the way spectators comprehend and respond to the program's underlying messages.

One instance of this synergy and its effects occurred in the 2009 season of *Dancing with the Stars*. On this show, notable celebrities pair up with professional ballroom dancers to compete against each another to win prize money for a charity of their choice. The 2009 broadcast featured Kelly Osbourne, daughter of infamous rock musician Ozzy Osbourne. In addition to the show's weekly dance-off, the program includes footage of the teams rehearsing, which is where many of the show's unscripted moments occur and where spectators glimpse the labor and effort involved in constructing the dance routines performed for audiences.

Within the course of these practice sessions Osbourne experienced a number of challenges relating to body image and self-esteem, documented by the reality TV cameras. As Osbourne and her partner successfully advanced through the competition, spectators tracked an alternate narrative emerging from the show: Osbourne's trajectory from a "miserable, lonely, depressed" girl to a confident, healthier person. Osbourne's "real" personal story became intricately bound to the competition. Its emotional and psychological components resonated with many female viewers also experiencing difficulty with their weight or self-images. In many interviews Osbourne credited the program and the support of her partner with fundamentally changing her life. Osbourne's actual issues merged seamlessly with the show's focus on dance performance, glamour, and spectacle, which boosted ratings, helped propel the pair to the finale, and established Osbourne as a fan favorite and an icon of self-empowerment.

Increasingly, reality television has used affective discourses as signifiers of the realism absent from the program's final product. Depictions of people in emotionally vulnerable situations form provocative images that help spectators identify with the individuals and engage with the show's foundational tenets. NBC's *The Biggest Loser* puts overweight contestants through grueling exercise and dietary regimes, while also extracting the often highly emotional personal and psychological reasons behind their weight gain in confessionals and confrontations with the program's trainers. A facet of the audition process in the hit franchise *American Idol* involves showcasing many of the contestants' backgrounds. Hardship, tragedy, and extraordinary challenges figure pointedly in the contestant narratives: a 16-year-old man who had spent time growing up in a homeless shelter, a twenty-three-year-old single mother of a special needs child, a twenty-six-year-old Chicago native named Chris Medina whose fiancé, two months prior to the wedding in 2009, suffered traumatic brain, skull, and facial injuries from a car accident. Chris used his audition as a tribute to his fiancé, Juliana. Before giving Medina the coveted "thumbs up" to the next round, the trio of celebrity judges insisted on meeting Juliana. Juliana was brought out in her wheelchair before the emotional judges and, presumably, equally as wrought home audiences. Rocker/judge Steven Tyler kneeled next to the young woman, kissed her on the cheek and said, "I just heard your fiancé sing, and he sings so good, you know, 'cause he sings to you all the time."[18] The power of sentimentalism, no matter how obviously deployed, cannot be underestimated in the interests of reality TV developers, constantly in search of ways to make the content of their shows more credible. For *Extreme Makeover: Home Edition*, the meticulously managed constructions of sentimentalism do more than enhance the show; they *are* the show, in both connotations of the word.

By virtue of its reliance on benevolence as a crucial narrative and representational through-line, *Extreme Makeover: Home Edition* evidences a complexity lacking from other reality shows. It traffics in what Hill identifies as "border territories," hybrid conglomerations that marry together often antithetical ideological elements.[19] The show purports a return to traditional

American values in its singling out of a deserving family upon whom to administer uplift (echoing the Horatio Alger "rags to riches" metaphor for the American dream) and in its insistence on the role of the community in performing benevolence. Over the course of these narratives, it celebrates and enforces commodity and the role of the material as the driving force behind charity and personal transformation. The program takes an unproblematic stance on the capitalism necessary to produce the show and to make the family's "dreams come true." It disarms this issue by subsuming capitalism into an overarching narrative that espouses the Christian tenets of good works and American ideals. Despite or because of these tensions, *Extreme Makeover: Home Edition* remains an immensely popular show that distinguishes itself from other reality TV offerings in its altruistic agenda. The new performance and representational modes driven by reality TV help to account for the show's wide-ranging appeal and elucidate its role in changing the way Americans participate in charity.

"MEET THE CARTER FAMILY": DEMONSTRATIONS OF THE DESERVING

On the *Extreme Makeover: Home Edition* web site, producers describe their ideal candidates as families "usually living under extraordinary circumstances such as unusual disadvantage, disease, or disability." A family is "chosen from hundreds of thousands of applicants to receive the surprise of a lifetime when Pennington and his dream making design crew appear on their door step."[20] Producers send the family on an all-expenses-paid trip to a place such as New York City, Disney World, or San Francisco for the duration of the renovation. Executive producer Denise Cramsey describes breaking down the applicant pool into "desperat[e] and deserving" but also points out that the show's producers give equal weight to the family's level of community involvement: "producers want to say 'this family has done so much for you.'"[21] Applicants must download and fill out a written application and include a video with their submission. The visual component of the application process is vital; it allows the family to tell their story in its most rudimentary yet appealing terms, and it also provides insight for the television audience, who participate from home in judging the family's worth alongside the design team. As Hill points out, "When audiences watch reality TV, they are also engaged in critical viewing of the attitudes and behaviors of ordinary people in the programmes."[22] With the high stakes of dream houses and fantasy vacations involved, it becomes imperative not only for the family to prove their worthiness but also for the spectator to approve of their worthiness in kind.

The presentation of the distressed family brokers a unique set of meanings that the spectator is entreated to manage. In keeping with historical trends on the display of need, producers visually and rhetorically code the family in terms of lack, tragedy, and pathos. Initially, this framework permits a conventional understanding of the reality show subjects as Other: a television viewer may sympathize with their plight but may not likely identify with them or their situation. However, the stability of this dynamic begins to fray as Pennington discloses the family members' good works and community involvement so that distinctions of "needy" or "helpless" become volatile. For instance, the show's second season featured Larry and Judy Vardon, Deaf individuals with one hearing-capable child and another who is blind and autistic. Judy volunteers at the community center working with blind and Deaf children, and Larry, an automotive welder, fixes cars for free in his spare time. In another episode, Pennington and his crew help Clara Ward, a woman with a degenerative muscle disease who uses a wheelchair and runs a family daycare center out of her cramped, cluttered, dilapidated quarters. Ward gives children and families in the depressed community a safe place to go; despite her disability and her lack of assistance and resources, she collects donated food, clothing, and household items for needy families.[23]

The heroic efforts on the part of these individuals to serve their communities elevates them so that they become endowed with a kind of superiority and uniqueness reserved for celebrities and humanitarian icons. These are not the actions of the "pathetic," "tragic" figure dependent upon collective benevolence to survive; these people are representatives of exceptional American ideals such as social responsibility and charity despite their dire circumstances. *Extreme Makeover: Home Edition* makes this point salient and in doing so disallows spectators from dismissing these people as charity objects and frustrates the impetus to disidentify out of fear or anxiety. However, the ideological gains made by this dynamic, the invitation to empathize rather than sympathize, are quickly mitigated by the show's conceptual bent: in order for the show to fulfill its altruistic principles, the family's selfless actions must never surpass those of Pennington and his legion of community and corporate "do-gooders."

Performance conventions such as the framing of shots, the formulaic way that the show introduces its distinguished families, and the reiteration of proscribed rhetoric enforcing both the subject's plight and the cast's responsibility to provide assistance constitute *Extreme Makeover: Home Edition's* fundamental organizing elements. These devices support the program's narrative framework, while also bolstering the emotional, sociological, and ideological principles that drive and configure the series as a program invested in using charity to further social good. On a more rudimentary level, its use of performance culture amplifies its dramatic properties. The documentary-influenced aesthetic undergirding reality television allows producers a great deal of control over where to direct spectators' visual attention while concurrently granting the illusion of naturalness. Media scholars Madeleine Shofeld and Kendra Gale discuss the show's attention to filming and editing for reality TV. They argue that producers are conscious about policing "any differences of interpretation about what that reality should be."[24] Producers make technological and performance choices in order to invite spectators' immersion in the televisual display. The guise of immediacy and simulated liveness displaces viewers from their living rooms to the scene of distress, inviting a kind of mediatized witnessing to another's extraordinary situation that is then softened and contained through editing, shooting techniques, lighting, and music.

This begins immediately in the intro to the episode that features B-roll shots of geographic exteriors of the primary location. Mountains and wide shots of rolling plains feature in episodes shot in the Midwest; footage of "Main Street" and local churches figure in scenes of small American towns in Ohio or North Carolina. The visual narrative continues with Pennington's introduction to the family via their submission reel, always presented with Pennington's folksy intonation of one of his signature lines, "Meet the Carter family."

This mediatized witnessing extends to and is heightened by the live introduction to the family. Viewers, along with Pennington and his crew, meet the designated family at the site of their current residence. In what has become one of the show's trademarks, Pennington exits his large tour bus and summons the family using a bullhorn. Near hysteria and ecstatic joy over their good fortune, the family races outside to meet the design team, often hugging, crying, and uttering religious praise. Though the moment is meant to evoke utter surprise and shock, a crew member conceded to Halpern that it is "unrealistic" to think the family has remained ignorant about their participation in the show. The producers, he added, most likely threatened the family with disqualification should they disclose any information about their involvement with the show to friends or family.[25]

Following this emotional outpouring, Pennington asks the family for a tour of their house. The tour is less for the design team, who, based on the family's audition materials, have already formulated preliminary renovation ideas that may undergo further modifications, and more for television viewers. Spectators experience a "live" firsthand account of the family's tragic existence as cameras follow Pennington to capture every aspect of the family's living situation.

In the episode featuring the Carter family from Billings, Montana, living in a renovated chicken coop, the camera pans across the small living space, littered with furniture and household goods. In one room, the floor shows visible signs of rot. A designer presses on the soft floor with his boot and pointedly remarks, "This can't be good for people with a condition where people stumble and lose their balance."[26] Pennington expresses surprise and horror over the family's home, pointing out the exposed concrete, wire, and remnants of poultry habitation. The camera closes in on this graphic evidence, forcing spectators to train their gaze on the family's abject conditions. Through these visual and graphic articulations, the danger facing the family becomes amplified. The concept of home is effaced in exchange for a more frightening environment that threatens the family's personal, physical, and economic stability. Consequently, *Extreme Makeover: Home Edition* positions itself, and by extension its volunteers, corporate sponsors, and viewer fans, as not just building renovators but saviors.

Every episode features this stylized walking tour of the family's dwelling, making their need and its urgency palpable to the home spectator. Part of the issue facing the Marshall family in Dallas involved the lack of accessibility in the house. Carleton Marshall, a police officer paralyzed from a shooting and a wheelchair user, lacks the ability to comfortably maneuver through his home's rooms and hallways. A long shot depicts two of Pennington's designers standing close together at the end of a long, narrow hallway. Due to the framing of the shot, the pair appears unusually hampered within the confines of the small space. The visual set-up gestures toward the kind of difficulties Carleton experiences, providing spectators with perspective and an opportunity to imaginatively cast themselves in the same living space as the disabled man and his family. They discuss how Carleton is unable to enter his children's rooms to "tuck them in." In a voiceover, Pennington remarks that the house came with existing structural problems, adding, "Now with Carleton's disability, it's become a trap."[27]

This word choice is particularly evocative for the way it resonates with the images of the space and with cultural misconceptions about the limitations imposed on disabled people in wheelchairs. Indeed, many of the statements the show makes about disability are carefully nuanced to strike the right balance between anxiety about physical difference and recognition of the potential contained in alternate forms of embodiment. *Extreme Makeover* does a remarkable job of renovating homes, like the Carter home, specifically to accommodate disability. Technological innovations, structural marvels, and state-of-the-art equipment all become organic facets of the new domestic space so that the disabled individual may perform any and all activities without what ableist culture would characterize as "limitations." However, this spatial transformation and its concurrent emotional impact on the individual restore the illusion of normative practices to effectively alleviate the spectator from engaging with the experience of disability on a more profound level.

The instance of the Marshall clan offers additional insight on how these representational nuances unfold. Cameron, the Marshalls' young son, has leukemia. The house contains serious mold problems that present a novel set of challenges for an individual with a compromised immune system. During a confessional-style interview to the camera, Pennington remarks, "The scariest thing for the Marshalls is this house could actually take Cameron's life."[28] Halpern illuminates the engineered quality of these types of observations, disclosing that the chosen families undergo interview preparation: "As Ricketts told me, it was essential for the family to describe how all the staircases, narrow hallways, and cramped bedrooms made them prisoners in their own homes."[29] Such statements not only heighten the drama of *Extreme Makeover: Home Edition;* they help dispel critical questions about the show's ethics and its emphasis on materialism and commodity by enforcing a classic ideological imperative underlying all charity endeavors: the very lives of these disadvantaged individuals *depend* on benevolent intervention.

Emotional exhibitionism and intimacy constitute another important component of the predemolition walking tour. Typically, Pennington pauses in his wanderings to prompt the family in sharing personal information, making themselves vulnerable for Pennington and viewers. Julie Carter, the mother living with a rare disease that shrinks her skull, tearfully tells Pennington, "If we didn't have the stress of living in the house over us, we could concentrate on people who are suffering."[30] James Tarpenning, a disabled man and wheelchair user attempting to take care of his wife, children, and adopted brother, who is also a wheelchair user with cerebral palsy, also lives in an inaccessible house. He tells Pennington and the other *Extreme Makeover: Home Edition* personalities that he desperately needs their help, "not for me, but I need your help to help me take care of my family."[31]

Just like the telethon's telemonial, these brief interludes give individuals an opportunity to speak in their own words about their respective situations. Pennington's questions and comments, however, often belie a level of manipulation, as he makes inquiries guaranteed to elicit an intense emotional response from the interview subject. When speaking with Julie Carter, whose oldest daughter, Jade, possesses the same type of condition as Julie, Pennington asks, "As a mom, when you found out Jade had the same disease and you had given it to her, how did that make you feel?" The camera cuts to a closeup shot of Julie. Beginning to cry, she manages to tersely reply: "Guilty."[32]

Over the course of this brief part of the show, the family generates the feel of a close connection with Pennington and, more important, viewers. Due to the cinematic properties of reality TV, spectators experience the emotional and material gravity of the family's hard-luck story in a way that is highly personal, provoking the spectator's investment in witnessing the subsequent uplift of these unfortunate people. The executive vice president of research for Lifetime Television, a network that features similar personal makeover shows, stated that these types of reality programs, including *Extreme Makeover: Home Edition*, are so successful because they "touch a nerve." "It's the viewers watching themselves on the screen in a way," Tim Brooks states. "They can relate to a house that's cluttered, a son with a disability."[33]

In the process of creating sympathetic engagement with the beleaguered family, the show inevitably tracks into the kind of emotional exploitation of both participants and viewers that critics accused the MDA of using in the telethon event. The difference is that *Extreme Makeover: Home Edition* promises and delivers a cure for its recipients. Telethons can only speculate at this type of end game, which is part of what gives that kind of charity event its ideological and affective potency. Conversely, the new vanguard of charity television gives viewers and volunteers a complete experience that charts an evolution from heartbreak to healing to eventual triumphant transformation, meticulously monitored and presented through the camera's surveillance.

DEUS EX CONSTRUCTION MACHINA: THE POLITICS AND PERFORMANCE OF TRANSFORMATION

In her article on *Extreme Makeover* and its implications for remaking narratives of American domesticity, media critic Kristin Jacobson traces the show's indebtedness to a Christian ethos that posits personal and social conversion. "*Extreme Makeover* is a miracle," writes Jacobson, "that creates a new world for a family in seven days."[34] Halpern agrees that the premise behind the show, along with the crew and cast's approach to benevolence, acquires a quasi-religious sentiment that allows people to embark on a journey where they may "reconnect with their faith."[35] In an interview with the UK-based home improvement channel Love Home, Pennington calls revelations of families' new homes "moments of grace."[36] This pervasive attitude translates into a show suitable for family-friendly prime-time programming, which accords with the wholesome image of ABC's parent company, the Walt Disney Corporation. It also joins religious ideals with secular volunteerism to diffuse the importance of materialism, proffered throughout the broadcast. Moreover, this pseudo-religious discourse establishes a transparent dichotomy between the "good" moral forces of Pennington and his team and the "evil" entities of disease, disability, and seemingly inexplicable misfortune or bad luck that makes the program and its featured individuals comprehensible and infinitely appealing. By injecting a spiritual component into the show's polarizing dynamics, its creators justify the need for extraordinary, aggrandized transformation as part of its larger, existential purpose.

Though Pennington and others constantly reiterate that the evolution from demolition to dream house takes place over the course of one week, it unfolds for spectators in highly compressed, faux liveness. Despite the guise of the real infused into reality television, the artificiality of performance is critical and pervasive. Producers make endless choices regarding shots, camera angles, and editing. They even coach cast members and design teams on what to say and how to deliver their dialogue. Producer Anthony Dominici communicates with Pennington via a wireless headset connected to technology inside a utility truck outfitted with computers and more than a dozen monitoring screens that allow the production team to track the designers' activities. In one episode, Dominici gives Pennington clear directions: "I want you to tell me that this is a very green energy source, and I want you to stick the hose into the ground." He told Halpern, "[The cast] are willing to do a scene 20 times if need be. Until I get it right, they're not in the show."[37]

As previously noted, viewers watching reality TV accept a certain level of contrivance in its programming. One could argue that the production of content matters less than its ultimate effects. Biressi and Nunn point out, "Audiences often gauge the authenticity or truthfulness of reality TV on a scale of emotional realism and personal revelation."[38] Given this formula, *Extreme Makeover: Home Edition* is as real as it gets. The affective spectacle often overshadows the literal conversion of the family's house, beginning with the family's ecstatic demonstration upon greeting Pennington and the rest of the team.

Another moment that has become a hallmark of the show, in terms of both its graphic display and its emotional fever, involves what producers characterize as "Braveheart Day." Referring to the 1995 film starring Mel Gibson about the life of Scottish revolutionary William Wallace, producers stage a sequence reminiscent of the film where Wallace leads his army on a sweeping charge against English soldiers. *Extreme Makeover* revisits this emotionally charged event in a sequence where they rally the design team, cast, crew, and thousands of ordinary volunteers to essentially lay siege to the family's home. A wide shot shows the massive swarm of people, dressed in matching show t-shirts, hard hats, gloves, and protective eyewear, cheering, chanting, and working themselves into a frenzy. Pennington usually cues a demolition truck to begin ripping apart the house and then unleashes the mob upon its remnants.

In later seasons, "Braveheart Day" has become even more theatricalized in its presentation of destruction. Carleton Marshall's episode featured his fellow SWAT teammates in the "Braveheart Day" sequence, executing a graphic raid on his home reminiscent of a scene lifted right from a Bruce Willis action movie. Policemen crashed through windows, broke down doors, and destroyed the home's interior, leaving little work for the demolition trucks. In another show, Pennington initiated his destruction by way of an elaborate mousetrap type of invention. Large pieces of plywood created a domino effect, knocking into oversized levers to eventually discharge a handle on a truck containing a wrecking ball. Pennington used a small hand-held camera to stream the event "live" to the Montgomery family, watching on a laptop from their vacation in Disney World.[39]

John MacAloon points out that part of what makes spectacles appealing are their visual "grandeur" and their "symbolic codes." From a performance perspective, spectacles gain effectiveness by "institutionalizing" the roles of the participants and spectators, making them "normative, organically linked, and necessary to the performance."[40] The extraordinary demolition of the family's house not only offers a startling and exciting display for volunteers and television viewers alike; it also unites all parties as a conglomerate, benevolent entity. That is to say, this spectacular scene operates metonymically for charitable practices; it speaks to the symbolic destruction of the inequities this family and all those in need face. It is a sequence that ironically depersonalizes the individual benefactor in order to re-present them as a signifier of moral and spiritual ideals. Spectators may shift their attempt to reconcile the contradictory meanings put forth by the chosen family to, conversely, identify with the thousands of ordinary citizens, the fleet of "saviors," working together for the greater good of this family.

As a moment like "Braveheart Day" discloses, *Extreme Makeover: Home Edition* elevates the pleasure and permissibility of deploying performance to enact its benevolent aims. Palmer makes the case that despite producers' claims to the show's altruism and its spontaneous provocation of inspiration and goodwill outside of the broadcast, it cannot escape its reliance on productive hypocrisy to deliver its goals. He notes that several cast members and designers working on the show's third season possessed acting experience in television and theater. "They know how to emote on screen," Palmer writes. He goes on to state, "Those on screen know how to enhance their performances of concern. Television works here because the effects on all the participants are plain to see—crying, hugging, laughing, etc."[41] To this I would add that the tension between buildup and release manufactured throughout the show is not only apparent but anticipated. Just as many spectators tuned into the MDA telethon to witness Lewis's overwrought physical and emotional demonstrations, millions of viewers watch *Extreme Makeover: Home Edition* for its predictable, sentimental highs and lows and its ultimate payoff in the form of the family's ecstatic gratitude.

The show's climax, its uninhibited denouement, consists of the design team's reveal of the family's new house. This is the broadcast's emotional summit and the act that completes the family's conversion and offers satisfying resolution for spectators, volunteers, and Pennington's team. Each episode delivers its reveal in the same iconic manner: producers park Pennington's giant tour bus in front of the house, obscuring it from witnesses and cameras. When the atmosphere reaches a palpable level of tension, Pennington invites all those gathered (and presumably the viewer at home) to shout: "Move that bus!" As the crowd erupts, the family collapses into tearful screams and shouts, holding one another, hugging Pennington and the other show personnel. Cutaway shots capture other volunteers and cast members crying along with the family. Temporarily released from this initial shock, Pennington invites the family members inside to "check out their new home," where the process of emotional exhibitionism repeats in various degrees as the individuals explore their state-of-the-art, vastly modified new house.

To return to Palmer's assessment, the television apparatus, with its panoptic technology and capacity to provide immediacy and proximity in any situation, is partly responsible for the extreme impact of *Extreme Makeover: Home Edition*. Television, as organizations such as the MDA discovered, provides a broad reach to the populace, exacerbated in the last decade by the pairing of television and web technology. The Internet makes episodes of *Extreme Makeover* available to spectators on a continuous basis. People may relieve their favorite moments by viewing clips and photo galleries; reading testimonials and user comments; and acquiring information about the show's stars, as well as about the products, goods, and services featured in any given episode. The web helps to permanently sustain the "do-good" narrative and ethos of the show.

The proliferation of reality shows and their mixture of contrived elements engender a greater degree of self-awareness for those participating in many of these programs. Competition-based genres, dating or relationship genres (often incorporating principles of competition), and lifestyle genres are among the more notorious reality TV offerings, where participants effect exaggerated, outlandish, or dangerous behavior for the sake of the cameras. Couched in terms of its social good, *Extreme Makeover: Home Edition* may escape association with these more gauche or tasteless artifacts of reality TV culture. However, it nevertheless feeds the same appetite for recognition and for the power inherent in making need visible and charitable intervention demonstrable.

With such extensive and elaborate renovations, the show counts on volunteers. Many individuals come from the family's community, and these people often earn camera time, explaining why they feel compelled to lend a hand to a family who gives so much to the community.[42] Other volunteers travel across the country explicitly to participate in a given project. According to Halpern, many of these people travel on their own time, using vacation time off from work, and at their own expense. In several cases, volunteers for *Extreme Makeover: Home Edition* have also worked on similar endeavors, such as with Habitat for Humanity, an organization that builds homes for needy families. Halpern reports that volunteers told him that "working on those projects failed to deliver the emotional jolt they got from [*Extreme Makeover: Home Edition*]." He also states, "Volunteers loved the pressure that came from building something that would be seen by millions of viewers. When the show was broadcast, they could see the skillfully packaged reaction of the family."[43] Consequently, the concept of the reveal works on several levels: it makes for compelling television predicated on its spectacular nature alone; it showcases the feats of craftsmanship delivered primarily by the design team and its cohort of licensed, professional builders; and it completes the individual's conversion from anonymous citizen to a valued player in the drama of charity television.

"Fairy tale," "magical," and "the work of God" are phrases that often pass through the lips of humbled recipients of *Extreme Makeover*'s conspicuous compassion. However, what viewers fail to witness when the cameras depart and Pennington's sleek missionary on wheels departs for its next pit stop is an unseemly side to that fairy tale. In 2008 the *Washington Post* reported on a story about the Harper family from Georgia. The show had descended upon the Harpers' home, which, among other issues, was toxic because of extensive septic problems. More than eighteen hundred volunteers worked on the house, and as an added caveat, the Harpers received money to help pay property taxes and establish college funds for their children. Despite these efforts, the Harpers ended up taking on a risky loan, putting up their house as collateral. Their *Extreme Makeover: Home Edition* dream house is currently under foreclosure.[44] To date, at least six *Extreme Makeover* families are either facing foreclosure or in the process of selling their houses due to the enormous financial strain that accompanies the mortgage, property taxes, and utilities.

The fact that several of these worthy families find themselves facing hardships while surrounded by state-of-the-art technology and fine home goods elucidates part of the problem with this type of conspicuous, performance-based approach to charity. It necessarily obscures the realities of social and economic disparities and ineffective political policies operating in the public sphere. As journalist Rob Walker states in his article "Entertainment Poverty," *Extreme Makeover: Home Edition* fails to fully treat issues of class and race that factor into the socioeconomic situations of these families. Instead, the show "neatly reconciles" these factors through "the forces of tasteful consumption."[45] *Extreme Makeover: Home Edition* and other similarly- themed charity programs traffic in "fairy-dust economics" that insists there is "no problem that the miracle of sponsored entertainment cannot solve."[46]

Reality TV enters into the modern charity movement bearing a politically contentious message: it purports to be more appealing and passes itself off as more effective than other forms of cultural, financial, or humanitarian practices. In the case of *Extreme Makeover: Home Edition*, the show also attempts to demonstrate that it can act as a credible substitute for badly needed social and economic policies such as welfare or housing assistance. Murray and Ouellette confirm this assessment: "For better or worse, reality TV enacts a highly visible new form of market-based social welfare, as commercial life-style experts, product sponsors, and TV networks pick up where the state, in its role of public service provider, has left off."[47] *Extreme Makeover* fuels this shift in its ever-expanding feats of building ingenuity and lavish secondary prizes that grow more sophisticated and elaborate with each show. There seem to be few obstacles that cannot be overcome through the use of motorized closets, adult-sized tree houses, and lifetime supplies of diapers and baby formula.

Media theorists John McMurria and Leigh Edwards extend this criticism of the show's proclivity toward whitewashing or Disney-fying the more complicated facets of producing a program predicated on outrageous acts of benevolence. Both critics situate the show within neoliberalism. McMurria describes this political attitude as one "which advocates corporate benevolence, individual volunteerism, and personal responsibility as principle means for solving serious social issues."[48] According to McMurria, the show rewards its families for being "model neoliberal citizens whose problems are no fault of their own."[49] Edwards offers the same assessment, noting how this view impacts the family in particular. The awarding of "domestic palaces" and consumer goods to people not only glosses over the problems of the state but sends the message that goods may "effortlessly heal any family troubles."[50] Rather than discuss more entrenched problems affecting these people, such as the lack of affordable health care or access to adequate social programs, *Extreme Makeover: Home Edition* elevates the families' resourcefulness and ingenuity as distinctly American merits, further proof of their uniqueness and leverage for the show's emotional and psychological exploitation of its subjects and spectators.

It is these types of charges leveled at the show that elucidate the ongoing tension it produces. At its heart (a deliberate word choice here) are not the twenty-first-century innovations of design, technology, or construction, not the luxury vacations or fantastic goods. At the core of this charity endeavor are people, the same type of people who look back at citizens from an NFIP billboard or who speak into the camera at a telethon event. In this case, consumerism distracts from this fact, threatening to efface the productive qualities of difference, what Siebers's theory of "complex embodiment" offers to enhance our interpersonal and sociocultural experiences.

While McMurria's and other critics' distrust of *Extreme Makeover*'s seemingly inexhaustible capacity for wish-fulfillment and its increasingly influential role in an already floundering welfare state bears significance, these assessments misunderstand the show's position vis-à-vis the public's changing attitudes toward benevolence. *Extreme Makeover: Home Edition* smartly trades on various aspects of American mythology such as the American dream of personal homeownership, the legacy of the self-made individual, and the belief in the power of community. Performance culture serves as the conduit through which to package these ideas in order to produce an emotionally powerful drama that reifies the most simplistic and engaging of all cultural narratives: triumph over tragedy. In the wake of prolonged international conflict, economic instability, and unease with the effectiveness and role of bureaucracies, the instant gratification delivered through *Extreme Makeover* is more palatable than the slow, laborious change that comes from implementing political and legislative policies.

McMurria suggests reinstating the "realism" in reality TV to move away from the more spectacular and glamorized aspects of Good Samaritan television and to create programs predicated on "demonstrative instruction." He writes:

> A vibrant public television service could cover hundreds of extreme community makeovers, replete with melodrama and suspense, all made possible not only by the voluntary contributions of individual viewers like you but through the billions of tax dollars, social service programs, housing subsidy initiatives, job training programs, urban planning coalitions, and state health care boards.[51]

The challenge of this imagined approach lies in its execution. What might this television service look like? If, as McMurria suggests, it could resist the allure of glamorization, exhibitionism, and sentimental display, would it contain the same type of popular appeal? After all, the twenty-first century's atmosphere of media saturation and technological surveillance creates the imperative to literally and metaphorically stage benevolent activities. Implicit in this formula is a desire to make that staging as exciting, interesting, compelling, and concurrently awe-inspiring as possible. This has been a consistent through-line of benevolent activities from Gallaudet's educational performances to Lewis's outlandish spectacle of need. The mainstream popularity and financial success of a show like *Extreme Makeover* belies a cultural willingness to invest in and accept the more insidious, exploitative, or flawed aspects of television and web technology in order to reap its commodified rewards.

Conclusion

A pink bloom spreads across the ten-foot-wide wall of the home store *Bed, Bath & Beyond* like a psychedelic fungus. The unnatural fauna come in the form of nearly every gadget invented: spatulas, mixing spoons, pizza cutters, garlic presses, can openers, vegetable peelers, rubber oven mitts, measuring cups, and measuring spoons. If it belongs in a kitchen cupboard or drawer, then the good people at the Susan G. Komen for the Cure Foundation have found a way to color it pink. Since its inception in 1982, the charity organization has raised over $1.5 billion to fund research toward the eradication of breast cancer and to provide resources for those battling the disease. Apart from the American Cancer Society, it is the most formidable and powerful nonprofit health organization operating within the United States. Nancy G. Brinker, Susan Komen's sister, founded the organization in memory of her sibling after Komen lost her battle with breast cancer during a decade where treatment and knowledge of the disease were both severely lacking. In press materials about the foundation's history, a detail appears repeatedly like a mantra passed down from one charity health organization to another throughout history: the foundation, Nancy Brinker stated, is a "promise to a dying sister," a vow to fight and put an end to this dreaded pathogen.[1]

Within the historical spectrum of organized benevolence, the Komen Foundation's narrative is a familiar one. The way Brinker characterizes her mission—she is the dedicated foot solider inwhat has become a crusade—aligns itself with the rhetoric and ideology established by the NFIP. Disease is once again at the center of a war, wreaking havoc on another of the nation's most precious resources: women. However, this is where the similarities end.

After all, America has moved on from the patriotic fervor that made it palatable to link military pride to everything from education and car buying to charity. The country has demonstrated a new set of sensibilities toward the way people want to engage with and experience their benevolent causes. This is particularly salient in the mainstream culture's embrace of reality television as a salve for social ills and in the permissibility of making consumerism and benevolent fellow-feeling inextricably joined. The Komen Foundation represents a seminal barometer of the contemporary charity moment, knitting together complex alliances between the marketplace and the social cause. As a forerunner of organized benevolence in the new century, the Komen Foundation's practices encapsulate the driving forces that have converged to make up the contemporary charity landscape: mass media, spectacle, and consumerism.

What the NFIP did for one week in January each year, the Komen Foundation achieves for an entire month. October is National Breast Cancer Awareness Month, and for thirty-one days Komen aggressively concentrates its efforts on saturating the cultural consciousness with promotions and events. *New York Times* business reporter Natasha Singer identifies this trend as the "pinking," or in other factions known as "pink washing" of America: "In marketing circles, 'to pink' means to link a brand or a product to one of the most successful charity campaigns of all times."[2] The joining of product with cause is a formidable way to induce investment in the charity process because it produces a complex internal dynamic that obscures our ability to engage in critical thinking about this relationship between consumer good and benevolence. Sara Ahmed's notion of "happy objects," those products that hit our feel-good pleasure centers, accounts for part of what makes this strategy successful.

> We are moved by things. An object can be affective by virtue of its own location and the timing of its appearance. To experience an object as being affective or sensational is to be directed not only toward the object, but to whatever is around that object, which includes what is behind the object.[3]

For example, a line of pink Komen for the Cure yoga clothes displayed in a city boutique may make a young woman feel good about exercising, advocating for the health of fellow women, and demonstrating her own fashion sense by buying trendy clothes. In this scenario, breast health may be only one of a number of factors "behind" the object that incentivizes the compassionate consumer and might not be one that the individual considers for longer than the time it takes to purchase and wear the item of clothing.

The Komen Foundation is not the first charity to capitalize on consumerism for the sake of the greater good; it is merely one of the most highly organized foundations that has been able to fully realize the power of inextricably linking consumer desire with the production of charitable sentiment. The first company officially credited with employing cause-related marketing (CRM) was American Express in 1983. As part of a campaign to help restore the Statue of Liberty, the credit card company pledged to donate a small portion of every new or existing credit card account toward the Statue of Liberty restoration fund. The initiative proved incredibly successful; American Express's business grew, and the public began to readjust its mindset around the relationship between consumerism and social good. Products became the conduits to providing uplift and reflected upon the identity of the individual as a good consumer and citizen.

In a 1995 study on CRM conducted in Great Britain, researchers found that people also believed that a product associated with a worthy cause reflected positively on the company. According to the same study, 86 percent of people surveyed declared that given a set of products of equal price and quality, the designation that one benefited a certain cause swayed their consumer decision.[4] This mindset was evident as early as the 1970s in the MDA telethon. A public relations representative from the McDonald's Corporation articulated this phenomenon to writer Harry Shearer during the 1976 telethon. He remarked that in a competitive market "people will be influenced by—and I hate to use this word—the image of the company. When the question comes down to Big Mac or Whopper, Jerry's kids can sway the undecideds."[5]

Thus for corporations the CRM concept is a political and economic no-brainer. It undoubtedly boosts bottom-line profits, but more than even this effect, CRM gives the corporation an at times much-needed public relations makeover. The companies that partner with an organization such as the MDA, or the reality show that builds extraordinary dream homes for people in dire need, become the "corporations that care." The companies' participation in charity helps to efface negative attitudes toward big business, especially in the contemporary moment, to temper conceptions of corporations as greedy, callous, unfeeling entities that exploit the middle class for enormous profit. This is, perhaps, a dynamic that Komen not only relies on but exploits for its own ends. With women still controlling more than 80 percent of consumer and domestic spending, who are they more likely to give their money to: a business without investment in social issues or a business that demonstrates its commitment to not just any type of social welfare, but the social welfare of women specifically?

This is not to say that CRM and the rise of more sophisticated campaigns that aggressively promote conspicuous consumption as conspicuous compassion are without their detractors. Critics have voiced concern over the financial transparency behind many of these campaigns (i.e., what percentage of proceeds actually goes to a given cause, how that percentage is rendered, and who is accountable for such transactions), as well as sometimes misleading information about the companies and subsidiaries partnering with a given retail entity.

Mara Einstein's book *Compassion Inc.* divulges the fraught relationships between contemporary marketing machines and the sector of organized benevolence. One of the case studies Einstein examines is the popular (RED) initiative launched in 2006 as part of the Global Fund. The general aim was to raise funds to help populations in Africa and attracted the involvement of high-powered celebrities such as Bono, Oprah Winfrey, and Penelope Cruz. The drive involved intensive branding of the (RED) logo on a slew of products from GAP shirts to Motorola phones to Armani sunglasses and Starbucks coffee. Einstein describes this massive effort as an outcome of the "hypercharity: an organization that is structured and promoted to appeal to large corporations looking to tie in with a charity partner for maximum marketing exposure."[6] The difference between the hypercharity and a more conventional CRM push, notes Einstein, is that these hybrid entities in and of themselves become branded commodities. Brand, profit, bottom line, and image drive these relationships, not cause. Proof of this comes in the dilution of the (RED) message as stated on its web site: "RED: Fighting for an AIDS Free Generation."[7] The nature of this claim is pointed enough to generate interest (everyone wants to eliminate AIDS, right?) and general enough to avoid clouding the consumer's desire for a product with such distractions as facts, statistics, and other complex data.

To return to the example of Komen, pinking products, fashion, jewelry, and tech gadgets has given way to forging symbolic relationships with national franchises such as the National Football League (in 2011 the Dallas Cowboys played for pink, with players wearing pink gear, goal posts wrapped in pink batting, and the infamous Dallas Cowboys cheerleaders shaking pink pom-poms) and political-social entities such as the White House (as a symbol of America's house). Laura Bush was the nation's first First Lady to designate a night to light the White House in shades of pink. The ubiquitous pinking promotes a fun and easy way for individuals to demonstrate their solidarity with the breast cancer crusade, which is the crux of its genius and controversy: visually striking, easy to assign to any good or service, and indelibly connected to the feminine, pinking puts an overly positive emphasis on a grim disease.

"We were going to have to do things to attract people that didn't scare them," states Brinker.[8] As if nodding to the lessons handed down to the public by Lewis and his predecessors in the style of provocation through fear, shock, and unmitigated maudlin ethos, Brinker neatly articulates the twenty-first-century understanding of what resonates with the American public when it comes to soliciting benevolence. Even the most heartwrenching, emotionally anxious moments of *Extreme Makeover: Home Edition* come with the anticipated denouement of collective jubilation and satisfaction that adversity has been bested (albeit temporarily). Komen has been able to revise attitudes about catastrophic illness to draw attention to proactive, life-saving interventions such as encouraging mammograms and promoting public health education. The Komen rubric mitigates the pathology of disease with a new emphasis on individual empowerment and, significantly, the pleasure that accompanies being able to perform mundane tasks such as shopping, dining out, and enjoying leisure activities under the auspices of "fighting" breast cancer.

The assortment of eclectic events and novelty experiences now associated with the Komen Foundation is partly responsible for this transition. Twisted Scissors, a hair salon in North Carolina, ran a "Cut for the Cure" fundraiser in which hairdressers charged ten dollars for both haircuts and pink extensions. Community members in Pinellas Park, Florida, participated in a dog walk that generated over one thousand dollars for the Komen Foundation and featured sponsorships from a local pet supply store. In a historical first, the Illinois State Rifle Association (ISRA) announced its inaugural "Shoot for the Cure" event in 2011 at the ISRA range located near Bonaville, Illinois. "This is a great opportunity for folks to enjoy a day participating in shooting sports, while, at the same time working to eradicate this horrible disease," stated Richard Pearson, ISRA's executive director.[9] One suspects that Roosevelt might have expressed envy over the gimmicky appeal of this last initiative, especially in relation to the many metaphors that link the obliteration of disease with munitions.

These activities and the countless others hosted by local communities across the country transform the happenings of quotidian life into happenings where individuals may stage their participation in benevolence. For instance, the dog walk is not just an occasion to raise money for Komen; it is a chance for people to publicly exhibit their involvement in the cause. The show of solidarity, both in the literal sense and in its relationship to performance culture, is critical to this public health initiative, bolstering its representational and ideological influence. Nowhere is this more evident than in the Komen Foundation's core fundraiser: the 3-Day for the Cure, a sixty-mile walk that takes place simultaneously in cities across the country such as Boston, Philadelphia, Chicago, and San Francisco.

The 3-Day is a massive affair that brings together thousands of participants, both breast cancer survivors and general supporters. Organizers in individual cities plan prewalk rallies designed to further inspire and energize participants. In the 2010 fiscal year alone, 147 races took place, attended by 1.7 million people, who collectively raised $120 million.[10] Staff members erect stages in parks where well-known local or even national personalities appear to give speeches and fire up the crowds with discussion of the foundation's goals and accomplishments. Entertainers help keep the rally's momentum. The fundraiser resembles a fusion of outdoor festival meets social cause meets bachelorette party.

The waves of pink awash in stores and online seem to reach tsunami proportions at these essential occasions. Teams of 3-Day walkers appear in outlandish gear: fuzzy pink hats and feather boas, novelty glasses in the shape and guise of small breasts, pink tutus and tiaras, shaggy pink wigs, and even personal homages to friends or loved ones. Modern aesthetic and sensibilities aside, the Komen 3-Day rallies gesture back to the same type of mass spectacle and public ecstaticism executed by the March of Dimes events. The women's outfits signify an array of meanings that include but are not limited to pride, survival, defiance, support, and the intimate information shared between friends and family members. Participants' sincerity never comes under question. It is this expansive exhibition of "pinking up" that gives the Komen Foundation its influential command in the charity industry. However, it is this same demonstration that has drawn criticism for the way it employs feminized spectacle as a way to flatten out the political, social, and economic intricacies of both the illness and its different treatment methods.

The popular acclaim and the financial success of activities like the Komen 3-Day that bear symbolic as well as economic significance have contributed to an explosion in the number and kinds of walk/run fitness spectacles sponsored by organized charities. The walk/run concept is not a twenty-first-century innovation. The first walkathon was held in 1969 in Bismarck, North Dakota, where several hundred members of a Christian sect walked to raise money for famine relief.[11] However, the import of these events as they exist in their current state of expansiveness, ubiquity, and sophistication deserves discussion for the messages they convey about health, diversity, and the presentation of benevolence.

Despite the Bismarck walkathon's modest size and localization, its format appealed to other entities, especially those focused on health issues. Organizers recognized that the walkathon, like the telethon, generated a sizable amount of money in a short time frame. As such, people could demonstrate their investment in an issue without feeling anxious about an out-of-pocket financial commitment. Even with these parameters, it was not until the mid-1980s that such fitness events began to accrue formidable social and economic weight. The Walk for Hunger, held in Boston in 1985, was the first fundraiser of its kind to raise more than $1 million, due in large part to the participation of corporations that signed up large numbers of employee teams.[12]

Since that unprecedented walkathon, charity organizations have continued to refine and embellish these walk/run endeavors, turning them into industries within the charity industry. According to journalist Anne Kadet for *SmartMoney Magazine*, in the last decade charities have taken on additional employees and created departments exclusively to handle their athletic fundraisers. "These days," writes Kadet, "the walkathon business boasts its own event producers, consultants, trade shows and technology vendors."[13] As the scope of these affairs has increased, so has the extreme nature of their agendas, provoking discussion about their underlying meanings regarding embodiment in relation to health-related causes.

Five-kilometer, three-kilometer, ten-kilometer, and twelve-kilometer races are becoming nearly passé within a fitness-event landscape that includes all-night relays (the American Cancer Society's Relay for Life), three-day

Fig. 10. Rally ceremonies at Susan G. Komen™ 3-Day. Image courtesy of The Susan G. Komen for the Cure.

walks such as the Komen walk, ten-day bike rides, and one-hundred-mile endurance runs. Interspersed are other more unique athletic happenings that play upon high-stakes physical exhibition and novelty: rappelling down skyscrapers, walking over hot coals, and even swimming in freezing waters in the middle of winter.[14] All of these place the figure of the idealized body on display in spectacular fashion. It is the kind of body that exists at the center of every *Rocky* film: engineered for stamina, efficiency, ultimate productivity, and, most important, resistant to deficiency. Psychology researcher Chris Olivola identifies the appeal of witnessing these bodies put through extreme circumstances in service to a greater good as part of a "martydom effect." Olivola contends that individuals will contribute more when they perceive the situation might cause pain or discomfort for their friend or family member, making the event itself "more special and meaningful."[15]

Part of this effect echoes Adam Smith's earliest notions about the relational experience between distressed and nondistressed individuals. However, in this age of display, the proliferation of the hard, athleticized body serving as surrogate for those, such as disabled people, who supposedly lack athleticism throws into relief national ideologies that privilege contained bodies. Their enviable physicalities visually and symbolically connote a desired result: a community of highly functioning bodies, made possible through science and made palatable by collective benevolence.

Yet even these demonstrations given over to the display of a different class of extraordinary bodies are not immune to disruptions that trouble the ideas behind these spectacles of fitness. In June 2011, a young man with Duchenne Muscular Dystrophy named Conrad Reynoldson became the first disabled person to participate in a fundraising event known as the Rock-n-Roll Half Marathon in Seattle. Reynoldson participated as part of a larger initiative called Run for Our Sons, sponsored by Parent Project Muscular Dystrophy, a health nonprofit that promotes resources and research for individuals with Duchenne Muscular Dystrophy. Reynoldson completed the half marathon in his power wheelchair.[16]

His involvement, specifically his physical participation in the occasion, altered the marathon's narrative and conceptual framework. The other people running alongside him were no longer his surrogates, and by extension his saviors, but rather his peers. His body helped neutralize the temptation to lend credibility to a self/Other polarity, to instead acknowledge the spectrum of embodiment that all people must travel upon. Furthermore, Reynoldson, as well as the many other people with disabilities who actively participate in charity events, reifies the kind of productive ideology of embodiment Tobin Siebers envisions. He writes: "Embodiment seen complexly understands disability as an epistemology that rejects the temptation to value the body as anything other than what it was and that embraces what the body has become and will become relative to the demands on it, whether environmental, representational, or corporeal."[17] Understanding the body within this conceptual framework of complex embodiment, with its emphasis on the body's organic and malleable nature, Reynoldson also helps to reconfigure the tenets of benevolence. Simply stated, it becomes increasingly difficult to feel sorry for Reynoldson or view him as distressed, suffering, tragic, or hopeless, the view that typically undergirds charitable fellow-feeling. Instead, spectators must broker a new understanding of this discourse, predicated on another yet to be articulated form of sympathetic identification.

Given the preoccupation with voyeurism, exhibitionism, self-presentation, and inhibition found rampant on the Internet, the web is perhaps a superlative environment for cultivating benevolence in this era of conspicuousness for all things. It offers a nascent arena to play with visual technology as a means to galvanize massive global populations around benevolence, while also raising questions about the ethical and political impacts of this supposedly hyperconnective terrain.

Platforms such as Facebook and Twitter provide a way for people to generate instant support and feedback for their given cause. A site such as Care2, devoted to helping people self-promote charity initiatives, combines the interactivity of social networking with recognizable charity tools (petitions, pledge drives, fundraising endeavors) to help people self-support causes and connect with other like-minded individuals. Care2 draws on individuals' interest in visibly demonstrating their allegiance to a given charity or issue, provides an accessible way to expand outreach, and also encourages people to track and bear witness to the actions of others. It is this brand of voyeurism, combined with a collective drive to amass recognition supported by the Internet, that has the potential to stimulate benevolence to extraordinary levels.

These components also pose new, complicated challenges to the production of charitable sentiment. The issue of sincerity and authenticity comes into play in a free-ranging media arena where people can easily and convincingly slip in and out of multiple identities. Also, the saturation of information, images, and sites competing for acknowledgment and attention makes it progressively difficult for people to prioritize one cause over another, which puts even the most deserving issues at risk at losing support. Where reality TV gives Americans a false sense of accomplishment in relation to the long-term, real-world effects of their "do-goodism," cyberspace steps in to solidify this false sense completely. The alienating forces of the Internet make it steadily more difficult to grapple with the material, political, and social facets of any cause in a responsible, meaningful way.

The controversial Kony 2012 campaign is one instance that offers insight into the tensions produced by an attempt to channel benevolence through new media and to aggressively engage with the web ethos of connectivity. Visual culture has proved a useful arena for human rights activists and organizations to call attention to the particularities of injustices experienced by disenfranchised and victimized populations all over the world. Photographs along with documentary films trade on their legacies of objectivity and truth-telling in an effort to both humanize these persecuted individuals and communicate important factual elements to inform, educate, and ultimately provoke action. This is not to say that these films and photographs are void of emotional heft. Rather, they offer a framework for viewing that attempts to compel through embracing the explicit, while attempting to minimize the aesthetic devices that guide photographic and film gazing. The Kony 2012 initiative disrupted this methodology in the way it made use of the slickest, most visually and emotionally engaging aspects of new media for its ultimately troubled human rights campaign.

Briefly, Kony 2012 is the work of Invisible Children Inc., a San Diego–based nonprofit founded in 2006 by Jason Russell and two other filmmakers who became interested in exposing the crimes of Ugandan warlord Joseph Kony and his band of rebels, the Lord's Resistance Army (LRA). Kony and the LRA are notorious for inflicting terror upon the region and staffing their resistance army with kidnapped and coerced children. As part of the organization's ongoing efforts to help end Kony's vicious reign, Russell released a thirty-minute video in 2012 about Kony and the LRA and, more pointedly, about the plight of the invisible children made to enact Kony's abominations.

With its quick cuts and interspersed footage of Facebook and television, the video resembles a visual text closer to a sophisticated advertisement than to a conventional documentary. Once again, children found themselves at the graphic and emotional epicenter of a charity plea. Russell uses his own young son, Gavin, a blond-haired, blue-eyed picture of idealized health and well-being, as the narrative counterpoint for the tragedy befalling the hundreds of children in Kony's army. Specifically, Russell highlights his friendship with Jacob, a young teen who escaped Kony's regime and whom Russell promised to help in his crusade to stop Kony.

On film, Gavin jumps, runs, dances, and chatters away about his love of playing and making movies with his father. Jacob, on the other hand, speaks tearfully about witnessing the death of his little brother, about conceding that he wished for his own death many times. The two boys are almost literally light and dark personified, with Russell as the benevolent intermediary. In one notably poignant segment, Russell turns the camera to interview Gavin, asking the boy:

RUSSELL: What do I do for a job?

GAVIN: You stop bad guys from being mean.
RUSSELL: Who are the bad guys?
GAVIN: Star Wars people.
Russell puts a photo of Kony in front of Gavin.
GAVIN: He's a bad guy?

Russell explains to his young son that Kony takes children from their parents and forces them to do bad things. "Sad," Gavin responds. To emphasize his point, Russell, over footage of a menacing, shadowy hand making its way toward a sleeping African boy, states, "Kony abducts kids just like Gavin." This last segment echoes the NFIP's *The Crippler* visually and rhetorically as Russell not so subtly suggests, "This could be *your* child."[18]

Russell used simplified messaging (i.e., join with me to stop "the bad man") combined with an appealing digital package to spark an enormous response, which is another unique facet of the Kony 2012 case study. Within days of appearing on YouTube, Russell's video had garnered an initial thirty million hits, with a similar influx of traffic brought to the Invisible Children/Kony 2012 Facebook page and Twitter feed. People seemed eager to shake their collective fists and mobilize to stop Kony's tyranny even if their instructions on how to do so were vague (not to mention the ambiguous nature of the moniker "Kony 2012," which sounds like an election slogan) but included donating to Invisible Children and showing support for Kony 2012 in their own personal way. Regardless, Russell's bid, which also attracted the attention of major news outlets and a host of celebrity supporters, proved the power of a new relationship forged by postmodern media and the contemporary charity endeavor. Berlant characterizes the effects of this era of hyperconnectivity: "Members of mass society witness suffering not just in concretely local spaces, but in the elsewhere brought home and made intimate by sensationalist media, where documentary releases about the pain of strangers is increasingly at the center of both fictional and nonfictional events."[19] While Russell might have been effective in grabbing the attention of the masses and in theoretically bringing the Other, as Berlant suggests, into proximity with the self through extraordinary technology, he nevertheless underestimated the likelihood that the public's willingness to engage critically with an issue would outweigh its appetite for conspicuous compassion.

In the midst of calls for action to shut down Kony, there was an equally loud faction of calls to shut down Russell. Human rights advocates, members of the media, and foreign affairs critics dismissed Russell's film as naive and accused the filmmaker/activist of grossly oversimplifying, among many aspects, the complexities of Ugandan politics, the fraught relationship between Uganda and the American government, and the depiction of the African people as unable to stop Kony. To this last charge, critics unhappily noted Russell's contribution to enforcing the stereotype that pits Westerners as "saviors," a trope also incredibly familiar in regard to organized benevolence.

Members of the media also questioned the Invisible Children organization itself. Many raised concerns about the appropriation of its funds and resources. Though there are claims to the organization's good works, such as sustaining educational programs and building an early-warning radio signal center, a report featured on *ABC World News* cited findings that showed that Invisible Children spent more than $8.6 million in 2011, with 32 percent of funds going to pay for salaries, travel, and film production expenses.[20] Moreover, Russell's pep rally format, while clearly energizing, lacks a cohesive strategy to turn benevolent intention into benevolent *action*. His insistence that putting Kony under the global virtual panopticon will be enough to "smoke him out" in order to bring him to justice amounts to little more than a video game mentality. The "Cover the Night" campaign on April 20, 2012, which encouraged people to banner and sticker their neighborhoods with Kony 2012 materials, came and went with more of a yawn than the collective roar Russell had first managed to generate.

Rights and Views, the forum for the Columbia University human Rrghts community, published a response to Kony 2012 where the authors conceded that despite its flaws the film performs a valuable service in raising awareness. "It also raises the question," the group notes, "'who benefits from the awareness?'"[21] Like the (RED) or Komen endeavors, Kony 2012 muddies the ethical waters of how to create visibility for a given cause and of to what end it is permissible to rest on the "everybody wins" mentality. In other words, this most recent use of new media to steer a charitable cause points to an evolving trend where spectacle, style, trendiness, and a preoccupation with the ideology of excess and volume that contributed to the corrosion of America's financial stability threaten to eclipse the subjective, idiosyncratic, political, social, and personal histories of charity's beneficiaries.

Despite these new challenges, the many and varied paths to benevolence in this contemporary moment make for a fluid landscape that houses vast potential. What some perceive as the missteps of Einstein's "hypercharity" model become opportunities to correct course, to explore new markets and methods, and to restructure seminal cultural and political ideas about "need" by enfranchising the populations, such as the disabled community, made to embody those monikers in more powerful and provocative ways. The image of Reynoldson moving through the half marathon in his electronic chair seems more relevant and powerful than the tentative images of children in leg braces or using walkers. The notion of controlling content, shaping messages, and impacting others in the time it takes to upload a photo or YouTube video is invigorating for the possibilities these activities hold, even at the expense of the anxieties or problems they might produce. These and other innovations already at work seem to suggest the turn into an era where we might build models of charitable sentiment based on democratizing components that prize the human, even as it merges with technologies, to ensure a rich and varied culture of conspicuous compassion.

NOTES

INTRODUCTION

1. Barefoot Contessa, http://www.barefootcontessa.com/about/aspx. Accessed 4/15/11.

2. Marikar, "Barefoot Contessa Reaches Out."

3. Pereda, "March 2011 Update Part 1 & 2," Angels for Enzo, http://www.angels forenzo.com/march2011update2.htm. Accessed 4/15/11.

4. Angelo, "Time for Some Damage Control."

5. Comments are taken from responses on Pop Eater, http://www.popeater .com/2011/03/31/ina-garten-make-a-wish/, and *Business Insider*, http://www.business insider.com/food-network-ina-garten-barefoot-contessa-make-wish-2011-3. Accessed 4/15/11.

6. Marikar, "Barefoot Contessa Reaches Out."

7. Martin, *Virtuous Giving*, 14.

8. "Giving Statistics," Charity Navigator, "Giving Statistics," http://www.charity navigator.org/index.cfm?bay=content.view&cpid=42. Accessed 9/15/11.

9. For a more comprehensive discussion of CRM and its rise in American social and business practices, see Adkins, *Cause Related Marketing*; and W. Smith and Higgins, "Cause-Related Marketing."

10. Mitchell and Snyder, *Cultural Locations of Disability*, 3.

11. Berlant, *Compassion*, 5.

12. Davidson, *Concerto for the Left Hand*, 4.

13. Garland-Thomson, *Staring*, location 34–39.

14. L. J. Davis, *Bending Over Backwards*, 26–29.

15. Siebers, *Disability Theory*, 3.

16. Ibid., 16.

17. Ibid., 22–23.

18. Ibid., 25.

19. Stanley, *From Bondage to Contract*, 103.

20. "New York's Holiday Beggar and His 'Graft,'" *New York Times*, Dec. 25, 1904.

21. See Schechner, *Between Theatre and Anthropology*. Theater historian Marvin

Carlson provides a concise overview of the various disciplines intersecting with and contributing to the development of performance studies in his work *Performance*.

22. This is an admittedly necessarily reductive gloss on the concept of performativity. For a more comprehensive discussion of the idea and its iteration in contemporary scholarship, see Judith Butler, *Gender Trouble*; Judith Butler, *Excitable Speech*; Parker and Sedgwick, *Performativity and Performance*; and Luxley, *Performativity*.

23. Madison and Hamera, *Sage Handbook of Performance Studies*, xii.

24. T. C. Davis, "Theatricality: An Introduction," 33.

CHAPTER 1

1. Nineteenth-century attitudes about Deaf individuals equated their disability with muteness as well, conflating the two in contemporary parlance as "deaf/dumb." Historians of Deaf culture such as Harlan Lane, Douglas Baynton, Bernard Muttez, and John Van Cleve, among others, devote attention in their scholarship to the historical and political significance of this conjunction. I follow the nineteenth-century trend of demarcating Deaf people as "deaf/dumb" in order to maintain a sense of cultural fidelity to this time period.

2. Gallaudet, "Sermon Delivered at the Opening," 35.

3. McCarthy, *American Creed*, 49–50.

4. For a detailed discussion of these early reform efforts such as the establishment of the American Bible Tract Society, see McCarthy, *American Creed*, chap. 3, "The Legacy of Disestablishment." For more on the Second Great Awakening, see Griffin, *Their Brothers' Keepers*.

5. McCarthy, *American Creed*, 52.

6. Bakal, *Charity USA*, 23.

7. Qtd. in Bremner, *American Philanthropy*, 12.

8. McCarthy, *American Creed*, 16. This attitude characterized and continues to characterize charity as an instrument that ideally provides some level of relief but also institutes preventative measures so that problems such as poverty, illness, alcoholism, gambling, or other immoral practices are brokered at the source.

9. Many feminist and historical scholars have published widely on the involvement of women in nineteenth-century charity movements. For more on the work of female charity reformers in antebellum America, see Ginzberg, *Women in Antebellum Reform*; Ginzberg, *Women and the Work of Benevolence*; Stansell, *City of Women*; N. A. Hewitt, *Women's Activism and Social Change*; Scott, *Natural Allies*; and McCarthy, *Lady Bountiful Revisited*.

While I do not engage specifically with this phenomenon, I acknowledge and take into consideration the feminization of charity's affective components, as well as the gendered implications of the charity plea.

10. Qtd. in McCarthy, *American Creed*, 19.

11. Ibid., 33.

12. Wagner, *What's Love Got to Do With It?* 54.

13. "Seeker of Happiness," 2.

14. Klages, *Woeful Affliction*, 17.

15. Todd, *Sensibility*, 8.

16. Ibid., 25.

17. R. H. Brown, *Sentimental Novel in America*, 176.

18. Ibid., 176.

19. Halttunen, *Confidence Men and Painted Women*, 57.

20. Ginzberg, *Women in Antebellum Reform*, 19.

21. Both Stansell and Ginzberg give ample consideration to the way women achieved a level of respectability through their charitable efforts. See Ginzberg's *Women and the Work of Benevolence*, Ginzberg's *Women in Antebellum Reform*, and Stansell's *City of Women*.

22. Samuels, *Culture of Sentiment*, 6.

23. Halttunen, *Confidence Men and Painted Women*, 40.

24. A. Smith, *Theory of Moral Sentiments*, 3–4.

25. Ibid., 3.

26. Ibid., 7.

27. Reid, *Essays on Active Powers of the Human Mind*, 160.

28. Ibid., 158.

29. "Modern Drama" (1829), 297.

30. M. C. Henderson, *City and the Theatre*, 48–49.

31. Marshall, *Figure of Theatre*, 176.

32. Spaulding, "American Drama," 331.

33. For discussion of this strain of cultural and scientific logic, see Deutsch and Nussbaum, *Defects*; Huet, *Monstrous Imagination*.

34. A vast amount of literature exists detailing the history and social/political implications of the American sideshow. For particularly well-researched and theoretically complex discussions of this entertainment venue, see Adams, *Sideshow USA*; Altick, *Shows of London*; Bogdan, *Freak Show*; Chemers, *Staging Stigma*; Garland-Thomson, *Extraordinary Bodies*.

35. Klages, *Woeful Afflictions*, 13.

36. Ibid., 14. Klages goes into further detail on the medical studies conducted on the blind in *Woeful Afflictions*.

37. "The Blind" (1830), 186.

38. Holmes, *Fictions of Affliction*, 30.

39. Bell, *Sentimentalism, Ethics and Culture of Feeling*, 38.

40. Henderson, *City and the Theatre*, 49.

41. *New York Mirror*, Aug. 2, 1823.

42. *New York Mirror*, July 28, 1827.

43. Grimstead, *Melodrama Unveiled*, 12.

44. For a detailed analysis of these types of melodramas, see McConachie, *Melodramatic Formations*.

45. Brooks, *Melodramatic Imagination*, 20.

46. The scholarship conducted on melodrama by twentieth-century theater and cultural historians reflects a trend toward reclaiming melodrama from its pejorative status and examining the social and political effects of this theatrical phenomenon. See McConachie's *Melodramatic Formations*, Brooks's *Melodramatic Imagination*, and Bank's discussion of melodrama and "theatre culture" in the latter half of the nineteenth century in *Theatre Culture in America*. For collections of essays that explore new cultural, artistic, and social perspectives on melodrama in European and American contexts, see Hadley, *Melodramatic Tactics*; Hays and Nikolopoulo, *Melodrama*; and Mason, *Melodrama and the Myth of America*. For a discussion of the influence of melodrama between theater and film, see Bratton, Cook, and Gledhill, *Melodrama*.

47. Mason, *Melodrama and the Myth of America*, 12.

48. Grimstead, *Melodrama Unveiled*, 179.

49. Ibid., 194.

50. For a detailed analysis of the gendered implications of breeches roles, see Mullenix, *Wearing the Breeches*; and Merrill, *When Romeo Was a Woman*.

51. *New York Mirror*, Nov. 14, 1829.

52. Holcroft, *Deaf and Dumb*, 1.1.

53. Ibid., 5.1.

54. Ibid., 1.2.

55. Ibid., 2.1.

56. Klages, *Woeful Afflictions*, 17.

57. Holmes, *Fictions of Affliction*, 30.

58. De l'Epée is a familiar figure to Deaf historians, and his work on what he termed "the living dictionary" is well documented in several sources. See Fischer, "Abbe De L'Eppe and the Living Dictionary"; Lane, *Mask of Benevolence*; Baynton, *Forbidden Signs*.

59. Holcroft, *Deaf and Dumb*, 2.1.

60. Ibid., 3.2.

61. Ibid., 3.2.

62. Diamond, *Broken Sword*, Act I.

63. Ibid., Act. I.

64. Brooks, *Melodramatic Formations*, 59.

65. Shepherd, "Blood, Thunder and Theory," 149.

66. Gallaudet, "Sermon Delivered at the Opening," 35.

67. Lasch, *World of Nations*, 7.

68. Rothman, *Discovery of the Asylum*, 189.

69. Ibid., 13.

70. Griffin, "Religious Benevolence as Social Control," 89.

71. P. Valentine, "Nineteenth-Century Experiment in Education," 362.

72. Ibid., 371. Other states included Ohio, Michigan, Tennessee, Texas, Kentucky, and Virginia.

73. "Asylum for the Deaf and Dumb" (1815), 395.

74. Gallaudet, "Sermon Delivered at the Opening," 361.

75. Stiker, *History of Disability*, 77.

76. Klages, *Woeful Afflictions*, 114 (emphasis mine).

77. "Deaf and Dumb" (1825), 31.

78. "Institution of the Deaf and Dumb at Paris," 19.

79. "Deaf and Dumb" (1821), 252.

80. Ibid., 252.

81. Ibid., 252.

82. Ibid., 252–53.

83. "Deaf Dumb and Blind," 236.

84. Ibid., 236.

85. Ibid., 237.

86. Ibid., 237.

87. Ibid., 237.

CHAPTER 2

1. "Fetes Here to Aid Fight on Paralysis," *New York Times*, Jan. 28, 1940; "Spirit of Carnival Marks Fetes Here," *New York Times*, Jan. 31, 1940.

2. Oshinsky, *Polio: An American Story*, 51.

3. For further discussion of cultural attitudes correlating social ills with Otherness at the turn of the century, see Bremner, *From the Depths*; L. Fried, *Makers of the City*.

4. Sauter, *Theatrical Event*, 65.

5. Dr. Bertram Waters, qtd. in "Bar All Children from the Movies in Paralysis War," *New York Times*, July 4, 1916.

6. "Day Shows 12 Dead by Infant Paralysis," *New York Times*, July 2, 1916.

7. Ibid.; "Paralysis Cripple a Problem for the City," *New York Times*, July 31, 1916; "Oyster Bay Revolts over Poliomyelitis," *New York Times*, Aug. 29, 1916.

8. "Infantile Paralysis Is Found Contagious," *New York Times*, Sept. 28, 1911.

9. Qtd. in T. Gould, *Summer Plague*, 4.

10. "Victims," *New York Times*, July 8, 1916.

11. N. Rogers, *Dirt and Disease*, 21.

12. Sontag, *Illness as Metaphor*, 58.

13. Health officials such as Dr. Emerson and others exacerbated this type of racist paranoia by strongly urging city and town officials to cancel ethnic celebrations and festivals, warning that large crowds in limited confines might hasten the spread of the disease. For discussion of this issue, see N. Rogers, *Dirt and Disease*, 32–37.

14. "39 Die of Paralysis," *New York Times*, July 23, 1916.

15. Donald Armstrong, "Misinformation on Infantile Paralysis," *New York Times*, July 19, 1916.

16. Sontag, *Illness as Metaphor*, 58.

17. "Bar All Children from the Movies"; "31 Die of Paralysis," *New York Times*, July 15, 1916; "10,000 Cases in US," *New York Times*, Aug. 18, 1916.

18. "Who Will Care for the Little Cripples When They Leave the Hospitals?" *New York Times*, July 16, 1916 (emphasis per original).

19. J. S. Smith, *Patenting the Sun*, 43.

20. Qtd. in Houck and Kiewe, *FDR's Body Politics*, 16 (emphasis per original).

21. Ibid., 17. For further discussion of attitudes about and care for the disabled in the early twentieth century, see Gallagher, *FDR's Splendid Deception*.

22. Goldberg, *Making of Franklin D. Roosevelt*, 47.

23. J. Gould, *Good Fight*, 77. Frances Perkins, longtime secretary to Roosevelt, describes FDR's polio experience as one marked by "spiritual transformation." She notes that his trials with the disease "purged the slightly arrogant attitude he had displayed on occasion before he was stricken." See Perkins, *Roosevelt I Knew*, 29.

24. Gallagher, *FDR's Splendid Deception*, 24.

25. Roosevelt's numerous physical and rhetorical strategies have been well documented. See Gallagher, *FDR's Splendid Deception*; Goldsmith, *Conspiracy of Silence*; Houck and Kiewe, *FDR's Body Politics*; J. E. Smith, *FDR*.

26. Oshinsky (*Polio*) details many of the letters President Roosevelt received from polio patients who asked him for advice and expressed their admiration for his ability to overcome the disease. Many of these letters are archived at the Franklin D. Roosevelt Presidential Library and Museum, 4079 Albany Post Road, Hyde Park NY. www.fdr library.marist.edu.

27. T. Gould, *Summer Plague*, 41.

28. Gallagher, *FDR's Splendid Deception*, 35.

29. T. Gould, *Summer Plague*, 41.

30. Many vacationing individuals complained about the inclusion of polio patients at the resort, illuminating pejorative attitudes toward the disabled in general and the polio patient in particular. Roosevelt addressed some of these problems by building a separate dining room where polio patients and their families could dine without scrutiny or prejudice and constructing a smaller treatment pool segregated from the primary pool guests used for recreation. As Warm Springs became more popular as a clinic than as a vacation resort, the number of able-bodied visitors not associated with a polio patient diminished until the property was redeveloped exclusively for polio treatment.

31. Gallagher, *FDR's Splendid Deception*, 41.

32. Ibid., 47. The Georgia Warm Springs Foundation fell under the jurisdiction of the New York State Board of Charities, rather than a similar entity in Georgia, due to Roosevelt's status as a practicing New York lawyer with his partner, Basil O'Connor. O'Connor would play a critical role in the NFIP, maintaining foundation operations from offices in New York City.

33. Oshinsky, *Polio*, 47.

34. J. E. Smith, *FDR*, 69.

35. Cohn, *Four Billion Dimes*, 41.

36. Oshinsky, *Polio*, 49.

37. Glassberg, *American Historical Pageantry*, 43–44.

38. Ibid., 44.

39. Bates, *Pageants and Pageantry*, 4–5.

40. Ibid., 39.

41. "An American Pageant at an American Bayreuth," *New York Times*, Aug. 7, 1910.

42. "Ten Thousand People to Portray Missionary Life," *New York Times*, Jan. 22, 1911.

43. Glassberg, *American Historical Pageantry*, 4.

44. For details on other reform-minded pageants, see Prevots, *American Pageantry*.

45. "40 Parties in City Celebrate the Day," *New York Times*, Jan. 31, 1934.

46. Ibid., 3.

47. Ibid., 3.

48. Ibid., 1.

49. "President's Radio Talk," *New York Times*, Jan. 31, 1934.

50. "Gay Pageant Here Honors President," *New York Times*, Jan. 31, 1935.

51. Glassberg, *American Historical Pageantry*, 284.

52. Mulvey, "Visual Pleasure and Narrative Cinema," 837.

53. The National Foundation for Infantile Paralysis, Inc., "General Statement of Plans and Appointment of Committees," 1937, Fundraising Campaign Materials, March of Dimes Archive, White Plains, NY.

54. Ibid., 2. O'Connor and Roosevelt felt strongly about disallowing doctors and medical researchers a controlling interest in policy making. See Gallagher, *FDR's Splendid Deception*, 147–49, for more information on the foundation's administrative structure.

55. J. E. Smith, *FDR*, 81.

56. Gallagher, *FDR's Splendid Deception*, 149.

57. Some conservative sects criticized this institutional structure as communist. See ibid., 149.

58. Basil O'Connor, radio speech, Dec. 4, 1941 (emphasis per original), Correspondence and Radio Speeches, Fundraising Campaign Materials, March of Dimes Archive.

59. Ibid.

60. J. E. Smith, *FDR*, 80 (my emphasis).

61. Turner, *From Ritual to Theatre*, 10–11.

62. Ibid., 11.

63. Oshinsky, *Polio*, 54.

64. Cohn, *Four Billion Dimes*, 53.

65. For example, the *New York Times* reported more than ten thousand celebrations across the country to cap off the 1940 polio fundraising drive. See "Dimes Begin March to the President," *New York Times*, Jan. 19, 1940.

66. *A Mile O'Dimes Fundraising Guide Booklet*, Jan. 1942, Fundraising Campaign Materials, March of Dimes Archive. It is important to note the novelty of this ploy by pointing out that all proceeds from the booth benefited the local chapter, not the states listed on the bottles.

67. Ibid.

68. Ibid.

69. "Drive Opens Today in Paralysis Fight," *New York Times*, Jan. 12, 1942.

70. "Times Sq. Renamed in Paralysis Drive," *New York Times*, Jan. 22, 1942.

71. "City Urged to Lead in March of Dimes," *New York Times*, Jan. 16, 1945; "Dimes Drive Running 20% to 30% Ahead of '44!" press release, Jan. 29, 1945, Fundraising Campaign Materials, March of Dimes Archive.

72. MacAloon, "Olympic Games and the Theory of Spectacle," 250.

73. Ibid., 265.

74. Turner, *From Ritual to Theatre*, 27.

75. Christopher Lasch, "History Typescript National Administration," unpublished manuscript, Nov. 29, 1956, 13–15, Media Techniques, Fundraising Campaign Materials, March of Dimes Archive.

76. Curtis and Mallach, *Photography and Reform*, 17.

77. Unidentified author, "Biography of Donald Anderson," Jan. 1950, Poster Children, Fundraising Campaign Materials, March of Dimes Archives.

78. "Of Friendship," *National Foundation News* 4, no. 4 (1945): 15.

79. Cutlip, *Fund Raising in the United States*, 384.

80. Dorothy Ducas to Mrs. Eleanor Roosevelt, Jan. 9, 1945, White House Luncheon, Fundraising Campaign Materials, March of Dimes Archive.

81. Lasch, "History Typescript National Administration," 9.

82. W. Berger, "Public Service Advertising in America."

83. Bagozzi and Moore, "Public Service Advertisements," 56.

84. "Extra Effort! Extra Dimes," *Motion Picture Campaign Book*, 1944, Press and Radio Collection, Fundraising Campaign Materials, March of Dimes Archive.

85. *In Daily Battle*, 1945, National Foundation for Infantile Paralysis, Radio and Film Department, Fundraising Campaign Materials, March of Dimes Archive.

86. Ibid.

87. Allen, "Role of the Star in Film History," 549.

88. March of Dimes, Newsreel with Judy Garland and Mickey Rooney, http://www.youtube.com/watch?v=fOkJAIPkxRA&feature=channel. Uploaded by March of Dimes 9/12/07. Accessed 2/22/10.

89. March of Dimes, "Somebody's Darling," PSA script, 1946, Media and Publicity, Fundraising Campaign Materials, March of Dimes Archive.

90. March of Dimes, Newsreel with Lucille Ball and Desi Arnaz, 1954, http://www.youtube.com/watch?v=fOkJAIPkxRA&feature=channel. Uploaded by March of Dimes 2006. Accessed 2/22/10.

CHAPTER 3

1. *Jerry Lewis MDA Labor Day Telethon*, 1976, VHS (personal footage obtained from a private collector). By early 2000, the name of the telethon was truncated to Jerry Lewis MDA Telethon. Following Lewis's parting with the organization in 2011, the 2012 and current iteration of the telethon is titled *MDA Show of Strength*.

2. Ellis, "Star as a Cinematic Phenomenon," 301.

3. Butler, *Star Texts*, 11.

4. Haller, "Misfit and Muscular Dystrophy," 142.

5. Tom Shales, "Send in the Clown: Jerry Lewis's Labor Day of Love," *Washington Post*, Aug. 30, 1997.

6. Garland-Thomson, *Staring*, loc. 157–62.

7. Ibid., loc. 185–90.

8. In her analysis of the United Way's fundraising strategies, Ellen Barton highlights rhetoric used on promotional materials such as "It's just plain good business to support the United Way" and "Here's how your company and employees gain by becoming a chapter company of the United Way." These slogans draw an implicit relationship between reader and charity organization, assuming a proactive stance toward donating (Barton, "Textual Practices of Erasure," 189, 191).

9. Bennetts, "Jerry vs. the Kids," 90.

10. Longmore, "Conspicuous Contribution and American Cultural Dilemmas," 136.

11. Ibid., 135.

12. This term comes from theorist David Thomson. See Thomson, *OverExposures*, 133.

13. The Martin/Lewis partnership is exhaustively probed in several seminal sources: Gheman, *That Kid*; Levy, *King of Comedy*; Krutnik, *Inventing Jerry Lewis*; and Tosches, *Magnificent Dino*.

14. Levy, *King of Comedy*, 65.

15. Qtd. in ibid., 65.

16. Krutnik, "Sex and Slapstick," 114.

17. Museum of Broadcast Communications, http://www.museum.tv/collections section.php?page=16. Accessed 8/15/09.

18. Levy, *King of Comedy*, 140.

19. Lewis and Gluck, *Jerry Lewis in Person*, 222.

20. Levy, *King of Comedy*, 140.

21. Krutnik, *Inventing Jerry Lewis*, 181.

22. Spigel, *Welcome to the Dreamhouse*, 290.

23. Levy, *King of Comedy*, 106–7.

24. *Dean Martin and Jerry Lewis Radio and TV Party for Muscular Dystrophy*, 1953, videocassette (VHS). All descriptions of this telethon are taken from my own VHS copy of the broadcast, obtained from a private collector.

25. Esslin, "Theatre of the Absurd," 323.

26. Ibid., 323.

27. Ibid., 323.

28. Levy, *King of Comedy*, 273.

29. Krutnik, *Inventing Jerry Lewis*, 182.

30. Levy, *King of Comedy*, 273.

31. In 1963 Lewis's solo television show, *The Jerry Lewis Show*, a weekly two-hour variety/talk show, was a disastrous flop and was canceled after little more than four

weeks. Similarly, critics declared Lewis's 1964 film *The Patsy* a screen failure, questioning Lewis's ability to achieve the same kind of success sans Martin.

32. Levy, *King of Comedy*, 387. See also Krutnik, *Inventing Jerry Lewis*, for commentary on this issue. Lewis also describes this period in his autobiography: "Everybody crying out for happy entertainment, while everything in sight was being tainted by the grime of 'realism' and magnified on celluloid. A decaying process . . . and that's what they were doing to our industry. It was eroding under a heavy flood of X-rated films. So I backed off. I wouldn't play the game" (Lewis and Gluck, *Jerry Lewis in Person*, 272).

33. Krutnik, *Inventing Jerry Lewis*, 182.

34. Lewis and Gluck, *Jerry Lewis in Person*, 270.

35. Levy, *King of Comedy*, 388.

36. Spigel, *Welcome to the Dreamhouse*, 40–41.

37. *Jerry Lewis MDA Labor Day Telethon*, 1976.

38. Jerry Lewis, interview, *CBS Morning*, May 20, 2001.

39. Hevey, *Creatures That Time Forgot*, 35.

40. Though the term "poster child" is still in popular use, promotional items from individual state-based chapter offices suggest a migration to the term "Goodwill Ambassador," in an attempt to rebrand the poster-child phenomenon in less pejorative and infantilized terms.

41. Barton, "Textual Practices of Erasure," 184.

42. *Jerry Lewis MDA Telethon*, 1976, videocassette (VHS). Private collection.

43. Cindy Johns, qtd. in Block, *Beyond Affliction*.

44. Lillian Gonzales, former poster child for a Christian charity organization, qtd. in Block, *Beyond Affliction*; Laura Hershey, "From Poster Child to Protester," Crip Commentary, http://www.cripcommentary.com. Accessed 4/22/04.

45. Sowell, "Memories."

46. *The Jerry Lewis MDA Labor Day Telethon*, 1989, videocassette (VHS).

47. *Jerry Lewis MDA Labor Day Telethon*, 1987, videocassette (VHS).

48. Hershey, "From Poster Child to Protester."

49. Smitt, "'Please Call Now,'" 702; Hershey, "From Poster Child to Protester."

50. Spigel, *Welcome to the Dreamhouse*, 46.

51. *Jerry Lewis MDA Labor Day Telethon*, 1989.

52. Hershey, "From Poster Child to Protester."

53. *Jerry Lewis MDA Labor Day Telethon*, 1987.

54. *Jerry Lewis MDA Telethon*, 2000, videocassette (VHS) (personal collection).

55. Farson, "Funny Men Dean Martin and Jerry Lewis," 22.

56. Qtd. in Farson, "Funny Men Dean Martin and Jerry Lewis," 22.

57. Kass, "Jerry Lewis Analyzed," 122.

58. Durgnat, *Crazy Mirror*, 234.

59. Murray Pomerance, "Introduction," in Pomerance, *Enfant Terrible!* 4.

60. Jenkins, *Pistachio*, 68.

61. Most film historians consolidate this type of humor under the rubric "slapstick," conflating this locution with a concept of popular "low" comedy evinced in vaudeville,

burlesque, carnival, and film. This formulation perpetuates a misappropriation of the term's original meaning, which the *Oxford English Dictionary* defines as a device made from two flat pieces of joined wood used in pantomime to produce the loud noise that accompanies a violent strike. For this reason I prefer to use the term "physical comedy" instead of slapstick; the latter describes a performance *effect* rather than a comic operation and curtails the tendency toward overdetermination. My thanks to Tracy Davis, who brought the misunderstanding and misuse of this concept to my attention. See *Oxford English Dictionary*, 2nd ed., s.v. "slapstick."

62. Dale, *Comedy Is a Man in Trouble*, 16.

63. Jenkins, *Pistachio*, 217.

64. Dale, *Comedy Is a Man in Trouble*, 14–15.

65. Durgnat, *Crazy Mirror*, 234.

66. Bukatman, "Paralysis in Motion," 188; Kass, "Jerry Lewis Analyzed," 122.

67. Shaviro, *Cinematic Body*, 114.

68. Early in his tenure as telethon host, Lewis developed a penchant for deviating from the telethon's proscribed format, such as scripted copy for introductions of guests or for particular segments. On more than one occasion Lewis voiced resistance to material written for him by MDA officials, preferring instead to ad lib or perform his own material. Levy describes an event in 1960 that involved a cabaret show featuring Lewis and various celebrities asked to promote the MDA at the close of their show. Art Zigouras recalled, "We wrote material for Jerry [who] came in and just threw it out. Egotistically: 'No, no [Lewis stated] tell me what you want me to say and I'll do my own stuff'" (qtd. in Levy, *King of Comedy*, 274). Despite Lewis's notorious reputation as a megalomaniac, the benefits for the MDA (i.e., exposure, credibility, and financial gains) outweigh any conceivable losses.

69. *Jerry Lewis MDA Labor Day Telethon*, 1990, videocassette (VHS).

70. *Jerry Lewis MDA Telethon*, 2000, videocassette (VHS).

71. Examples of this behavior are taken from telethon broadcasts in 1990, 1992, and 2000.

72. Shaviro, *Cinematic Body*, 118–19.

73. These instances are taken from a compilation of telethon "moments" assembled for the 1990 twenty-fifth anniversary broadcast.

74. *Jerry Lewis MDA Labor Day Telethon*, 1986, videocassette (VHS).

75. *Jerry Lewis MDA Labor Day Telethon*, 1991, videocassette (VHS).

76. *Jerry Lewis MDA Labor Day Telethon*, 1985, videocassette (VHS).

77. Jenkins, *Pistachio*, 217.

78. Garland-Thomson, *Staring*, loc. 166–71.

79. Burke, *Attitudes toward History*, 171 (emphasis per original).

80. Lipton, "Jerry's Encore."

81. *Jerry Lewis MDA Labor Day Telethon*, 2000, videocassette.

82. Garland-Thomson, *Staring*, loc. 387–91.

83. Evan J. Kemp, "Aiding the Disabled: No Pity Please," *New York Times*, Sept. 3, 1981.

84. In a piece printed in the *New York Times* entitled "Do-Good Pitythons," writer Robert Bernstein echoed Kemp's initial claims, focusing on the fact that until the telethon addressed its own culpability in allowing archaic attitudes toward the disabled to remain, it would continue to face opposition. See Robert Allen Bernstein, "Do-Good Pitythons," *New York Times*, Sept. 6, 1983.

85. In previous telethons, Lewis or other guest hosts had made general and broad statements that telethon donations funded summer camps, provided wheelchairs for individuals, and supported research.

86. Edmund S. Tijerina, "Protesters Call Jerry Lewis Telethon Exploitive," *Chicago Tribune*, Sept. 2, 1991.

87. Robert A. Jones, "Jerry's Kids: It's a Pity but It Works," *Los Angeles Times*, Sept. 4, 1991.

88. Bennetts, "Jerry vs. The Kids," 93.

89. Jerry Lewis, interview, *Primetime Live*, ABC, Sept. 3, 1992, videocassette (VHS).

90. Cripchick, "Protest the Jerry Lewis MDA Telethon." Cripchick's weblog, http://misscripchick.wordpress.com/2007/08/28/protest-the-jerry-lewis-mda-telethon-by-blogging-about-the-charity-model-of-disability-and-why-the-telethon-oppresses-people-on-labor-day/. Accessed 9/25/07.

91. Laura Hershey, "Last Word on the MDA Telethon (at least for this year, 2010)," Laura Hershey: Writer, Poet, Activist, Consultant, http://www.laurahershey.com/?p=401. Accessed 9/16/10.

92. L. J. Davis, *Bending Over Backwards*, 13.

93. Ritter, "Jerry Lewis Retiring from MDA Telethon."

94. Ibid.

95. Steven Zeitchik and Deborah Vankin, "Jerry Lewis Ousted as MDA Telethon Host," *Los Angeles Times*, articles.latimes.com/2011/aug/05/entertainment/la-et-jerry-lewis-20110805. Accessed 9/1/11.

96. M. E. Williams, "What's Labor Day without Jerry Lewis?"

97. "MDA Spokesperson and Honorees," http://www.mda.org/commprog/good will.html. Accessed 9/1/11.

CHAPTER 4

1. *Extreme Makeover: Home Edition* (*EM: HE*), dir. David Dryden, season 5, episode 5 (Buena Vista Home Entertainment, 2007).

2. For information on these and other families chosen by *EM: HE*, visit recaps at abc.go.com/shows/extreme-makeover-home-edition/episode-guide. As of December 2011 ABC announced plans to cancel the show at the end of its ninth season with four "special" episodes set to air beginning November 29, 2012. As such, information about the show is limited to abc.go/com/shows/extreme-makeover-home-edition/index. Original access of recap info 6/22/10. Updated access of recap and current info 11/12/12.

3. Murray and Ouellette, "Introduction," in *Reality TV*, 2.

4. *EM: HE* web site: http://abc.go.com/primetime/xtremehome/index?pn=about. Accessed 6/22/10.

5. Halpern, "Emotional Buildup."

6. Palmer, "*Extreme Makeover: Home Edition*: An American Fairy Tale," 168.

7. *EM: HE* web site: http://abc.go.com/prime. Accessed 6/22/10.

8. The early surge around reality television prompted FOX to create the Reality Channel. A report posted in Oct. 2009 on the web site realitytvworld.com noted that FOX planned to discontinue the reality cable channel in Mar. 2010. According to the piece, FOX execs claim there is not enough of a consolidated market for this programming to warrant an entire channel. See http://www.realitytvworld.com/news/fox-cable-shutting-down-fox-reality-channel-cable-network-9742.php. Accessed 4/2/10.

9. These numbers are based on Nielsen ratings, found at http://www.zap2it.com/tv/ratings/. Many television ratings according to Neilsen data can be found in major newspapers or entertainment/media publications. Accessed 10/18/09.

10. Hill, *Reality TV*, 6.

11. Murray and Ouellette, *Reality TV*, 3.

12. Biressi and Nunn, *Reality TV*, 3.

13. Murray and Ouellette, *Reality TV*, 5.

14. Biressi and Nunn, *Reality TV*, 36.

15. Ibid., 4.

16. Murray and Oullette, *Reality TV*, 7.

17. Hill, *Reality TV*, 57.

18. Roy Trakin, "American Idol Breaks Out the Hankies," Xfinity TV Blog. Posted 1/27/11. Accessed 11/13/12. http://xfinity.comcast.net/blogs/tv/2011/01/27/american-idol-breaks-out-the-hankies/.

19. Hill, *Reality TV*, 2.

20. *EM: HE* web site: http://abc.go.com/primetime/xtremehome/index?pn=about. In 2006 the show came under intense scrutiny when a production memo was leaked to the Smoking Gun web site detailing a "wish list" of ideal candidates suffering from unusual and extraordinary conditions, such as Lou Gherig's disease (ALS); progeria, which causes a child to rapidly age; and anhidrosis, which makes a child immune to pain. See http://www.thesmokinggun.com/documents/crime/abcs-extreme-exploitation. Posted 3/27/06. Accessed 10/18/09.

21. Hal Boedeker, "So How Does ABC'S Extreme Makeover: Home Edition Pick the Families It Helps?" *Orlando Sentinel*, Sept. 29, 2007.

22. Hill, *Reality TV*, 9.

23. *EM: HE*, season 2, episode 7; season 6, episode 23; season 7, episode 14.

24. Shofeld and Gale, "Under the (Glue) Gun," 267.

25. Halpern, "Emotional Buildup."

26. *EM: HE*, season 5, episode 5.

27. *EM: HE*, season 7, episode 3.

28. *EM: HE*, season 7, episode 11.

29. Halpern, "Emotional Buildup."

30. *EM: HE*, season 5, episode 5.

31. *EM: HE*, season 7, episode 7.

32. *EM: HE*, season 5, episode 5.

33. Felicia Lee, "Home Edition Shows the Softer Side of Reality TV," *New York Times*, Nov. 4, 2004.

34. Jacobson, "Renovating the American Woman's Home," 109.

35. Halpern, "Emotional Buildup."

36. Lovehome.co.uk. http://uktv.co.uk/home/item/aid/602573/displayVideo/hi. Posted 3/25/10. Accessed 6/18/10.

37. Halpern, "Emotional Buildup."

38. Biressi and Nunn, *Reality TV*, 4.

39. *EM: HE*, season 7, episode 6.

40. MacAloon, "Olympic Games and the Theory of Spectacle," 243.

41. Palmer, "*Extreme Makeover: Home Edition*," 175.

42. It is worth noting that these volunteers do not offer information about ways they might have helped out the family in the past, if at all. Instead, they appear to rally around the show and its legion of high-profile Good Samaritans.

43. Halpern, "Emotional Buildup."

44. Hank Stuever, "The Extreme Reality Makeover Show," *Washington Post*, July 29, 2008, http://www.washingtonpost.com/wp-dyn/content/article/2008/07/28/AR2008072802587.html.

45. Rob Walker, "Entertainment Poverty," *New York Times*, Dec. 4, 2005.

46. Stuever, "Extreme Reality Makeover Show"; Walker, "Entertainment Poverty."

47. Murray and Ouellettte, *Reality TV*, 9.

48. McMurria, "Desperate Citizens and Good Samaritans," 305.

49. Ibid., 320.

50. Edwards, "Reality TV and the American Family," 134.

51. Ibid., 327.

CONCLUSION

1. See http://ww5.komen.org. Accessed 2/12/09.

2. Natasha Singer, "Welcome Fans to the Pinking of America," *New York Times*, Oct. 16, 2011, http://www.nytimes.com/2011/10/16/business/in-the-breast-cancer-fight-the-pinking-of-america.html?_r=2&hp.

3. Ahmed, "Happy Objects," 33.

4. W. Smith and Higgins, "Cause-Related Marketing," 305.

5. Shearer, "Mid-Section: Telethon," 40.

6. Einstein, *Compassion Inc.*, 72.

7. (RED), http://www.joinred/aboutred. Accessed 8/20/11.

8. Shearer, "Mid-Section," 40.

9. Leslie Chester, "Cut for a Cure," *Cary Citizen*, Oct. 13, 2011, carycitizen.com/2011/10/13/cut-for-a-cure/; Juliana Torres, "Dog Walk Benefits Cancer Fund," *Pinellas Park Beacon*, Oct. 13, 2011, www.tbnweekly.com/pubs/pinellas_park_beacon/content_articles/101311_par-03.txt.; "ISRA Announces First Annual Susan G. Komen Shoot for the Cure," *PR Newswire*, Sept. 26, 2011, www.prnewsire.com/news-releases/isra-announces-first-annual-susan-g-komen-shoot-for-the-cure-130607453.html.

10. Singer, "Welcome Fans to the Pinking of America."

11. Kadet, "Are Charity Walks and Races Worth the Effort?"

12. Ibid.

13. Ibid.

14. Ibid.

15. Quoted in ibid.

16. "Community: Run for Our Sons," *End Duchenne ENews*, June 11, 2011, www.parentproject.org/site/PageNavigator/end_duchenne_enews_june11.

17. Siebers, *Disability Theory*, 27.

18. "Kony 2012," Jason Russell, invisiblechildren.com/videos/Kony-2012/.

19. Berlant, *Compassion*, 4.

20. Francis and Patinkin, "Kony 2012 Charity Invisible Children Addresses Its Critics."

21. "Mapping the Kony 2012 Controversy."

BIBLIOGRAPHY

ARCHIVES

Fundraising Campaign Materials. March of Dimes Archives. White Plains, NY
Media Files. Muscular Dystrophy Association. Bedford, NH.
Photography. Franklin D. Roosevelt Library. Hyde Park, NY. Franklin D. Roosevelt
 Presidential Library and Museum. www.fdrlibrary.marist.edu.

MEDIA

Dean Martin and Jerry Lewis Radio and TV Party for Muscular Dystrophy. 1953. Video-
 cassette (VHS), 90 minutes. Private collection.
Extreme Makeover: Home Edition. Dir. David Dryden. Buena Vista Home Entertain-
 ment, 2003–10. DVD. Burbank, CA.
FDR: Years of Crisis. A&E Home Video, release date 9/27/05.
Jerry Lewis: The Last American Clown. A&E Biography Series. Soapbox Productions,
 1996. Videocassette (VHS). 100 minutes. Distributed by A&E Home Video. Nar-
 rated by Alan King.
Jerry Lewis MDA Telethon. 2000. Videocassette (VHS). Private collection.
Jerry Lewis MDA Labor Day Telethon. 1976. Videocassette (VHS).
Jerry Lewis MDA Labor Day Telethon. 1985–90. Videocassette (VHS).
Lewis, Jerry. Interview. *Primetime Live,* ABC. September 3, 1992. Videocassette (VHS).
Lewis, Jerry. Interview. *CBS Sunday Morning.* 2001. Videocassette (VHS).

PERIODICALS EXTENSIVELY CONSULTED

National Foundation News
New York Mirror
New York Times
Survey

NINETEENTH-CENTURY NEWSPAPER AND JOURNAL ARTICLES

American Monthly Magazine and Critical Review. April 28, 1817, 135."Annual Report of the Trustees of the New-England Institution." *New England Magazine* (April 1835): 321–29.

"Asylum for the Deaf and Dumb." *Weekly Recorder,* June 14, 1815, 395–96.

"Asylum for the Deaf and Dumb: A Letter." *Weekly Recorder,* September 30, 1820, 45.

"The Blind." *American Monthly Magazine* 2, no. 3 (June 1830): 186–92.

Carey, J. "The Railroad Boy's Appeal." Hay Broadsides. Brown University, 1880.

"Cincinnati Asylum for the Education of the Deaf and Dumb." *Philanthropist; A Weekly Journal Containing Essays on Moral and Religious Subjects,* December 11, 1821, 96.

"Deaf and Dumb." *Cincinnati Literary Gazette,* January 22, 1825, 31.

"Deaf and Dumb." *Philanthropist; A Weekly Journal Containing Essays on Moral and Religious Subjects,* February 17, 1821, 251–54.

"Deaf and Dumb Asylum." *Atlanson's Saturday Evening Post,* October 22, 1831, 2.

"The Deaf Dumb and Blind." *New England Telegraph and Eclectic Review,* May 1836, 236–39.

"The Drama." *American Anthenaeum,* April 21, 1825, 15–17.

"The Drama." *Port Folio* (October 1810): 336–40.

"The Drama: Letter from a Gentleman." *Port Folio* (December 1812): 635–43.

"The Drama vs. the Saints." *Correspondent,* April 7, 1827, 173–75.

"Dumb Creatures." *Weekly Visitor or Ladies Miscellany,* October 25, 1806, 414.

"Education of the Blind." *New England Magazine* (March 1833): 177–81.

"From an Essay on the Institution of the Blind." *New York Literary Journal and Belles-Lettres Repository* (November 1820): 70–72.

Gallaudet, Thomas H. "Sermon Delivered at the Opening of the Connecticut Asylum for the Education and Instruction of Deaf and Dumb Persons." *American Monthly Magazine and Critical Review* (November 1817): 34–40.

"The Imposter." *New York Weekly Museum,* July 1, 1815, 136.

"Institution of the Deaf and Dumb at Paris." *National Recorder,* July 8, 1820, 17–19.

"Interesting Correspondence." *Weekly Recorder,* August 7, 1816, 14.

"The Lame Labor to Live." Hay Broadsides. Brown University, 1895.

"Literature for the Blind." *Cincinnati Mirror, and Western Gazette of Literature, Science, and the Arts,* September 12, 1835, 365–66.

"The Modern Drama." *Philadelphia Monthly Magazine,* March 1829, 297–309.

"The Modern Drama." *Port Folio* (August 1813): 213–15.

"The Morality of the Stage—No. II." *Correspondent,* March 17, 1827, 119–20.

"New England Institution for the Blind." *New England Magazine* (February 1833): 154.

"Pennsylvania Institution for the Deaf and Dumb." *Port Folio* (November 1824): 414.

"School for the Instruction of the Blind." *Cincinnati Mirror, and Western Gazette of Literature, Science, and the Arts,* January 25, 1834, 115–16.

"A Seeker of Happiness." *Weekly Museum,* September 29, 1792, 2.

Spaulding, J. K. "The American Drama." *American Quarterly Review* 1, no. 2 (June 1827): 331–57.

Starr, Allen. "Memorial of Professor Jean-Marie Charcot." *Medical News,* October 4, 1893, 436.

"Theatre." *Port Folio* (March 1809): 254–55.

PUBLISHED SOURCES

Adams, Rachel. *Sideshow USA: Freaks and the American Cultural Imagination.* Chicago: University of Chicago Press, 2001.

Adkins, Sue. *Cause Related Marketing: Who Cares Wins.* Oxford: Butterworth-Heinemann, 1999.

Ahmed, Sara. "Happy Objects." In *The Affective Theory Reader,* ed. Melissa Gregg and Gregory J. Seigworth, 29–51. Durham: Duke University Press, 2010.

Alland, Alexander, Sr. *Jacob A. Riis: Photographer and Citizen.* New York: Aperture, 1974.

Allen, Robert C. "The Role of the Star in Film History." In Braudy and Cohen, *Film Theory and Criticism,* 547–62.

Alter, Jean. *A Sociosemiotic Theory of Theatre.* Philadelphia: University of Pennsylvania Press, 1990.

Altick, Richard. *The Shows of London.* Cambridge: Belknap Press, 1978.

Anderson, Nels. *The Hobo: The Sociology of the Homeless Man.* Chicago: University of Chicago Press, 1923.

Andrew, Dudley. "The Neglected Tradition of Phenomenology in Film Theory." In *Movies and Methods,* vol. 2., ed. Bill Nichols. Berkeley: University of California Press, 1985.

Angelo, Megan. "Time for Some Damage Control, Food Network: Ina Garten Just Snubbed a Make-A-Wish Kid." *Business Insider.* http://www.businessinsider.com/food-network-ina-garten-barefoot-contessa-make-wish-2011-3#ixzz1HuDbo TBx. Accessed 4/15/11.

Asbel, Bernard. *The F.D.R. Memoirs.* New York: Doubleday and Company, 1973.

Aston, Elaine, and George Savona. *Theatre as Sign System: A Semiotics of Text and Performance.* New York: Routledge, 1992.

Auerbach, Jonathan. "Chasing Film Narrative: Repetition, Recursion, and the Body in Early Cinema." *Critical Inquiry* 26 (Summer 2000): 798–820.

Auslander, Philip. *Liveness: Performance in a Mediatized Culture.* London: Routledge, 1999.

Bagozzi, Richard, and David Moore. "Public Service Advertisements: Emotions and Empathy Guide Prosocial Behavior." *Journal of Marketing* 58, no. 1 (1994): 56–70.

Bakal, Carl. *Charity USA*. New York: Times Books, 1979.

Bank, Rosemarie K. *Theatre Culture in America, 1825–1860*. Cambridge: Cambridge University Press, 1997.

Bank, Rosemarie K. "Women in Melodrama." In *Women in American Theatre*, ed. Helen Krich Chinoy and Linda Walsh Jenkins. New York: Theatre Communications Group, 1981.

Barnett, D., and S. Hammond. "Representing Disability in Charity Promotions." *Journal of Community and Applied Psychology* 9 (July–August 1999): 309–14.

Barol, Bill. "I Stayed Up with Jerry Lewis." *Newsweek*, September 21, 1987, 66–68.

Barstch, Shardi. *Actors in the Audience: Theatricality and Double Speak from Nero to Hadrian*. Cambridge: Harvard University Press, 1994.

Barton, Ellen L. "Textual Practices of Erasure: Representations of Disability and the Founding of the United Way." In Wilson and Lewiecki-Wilson, *Embodied Rhetoric*.

Bates, Esther Willard. *Pageants and Pageantry*. Boston: Gin and Co., 1912.

Baynton, Douglas C. *Forbidden Signs: American Culture and the Campaign against Sign Language*. Chicago: University of Chicago Press, 1996.

Baynton, Douglas C. "A Silent Exile on This Earth:" The Metaphorical Construction of Deafness in the Nineteenth Century." *American Quarterly* 44 (June 1992): 216–43.

Bederman, Gail. *Manliness and Civilization: A Cultural History of Gender and Race in the United States*. Chicago: University of Chicago Press, 1996.

"Begging on Boston's Streets." *Survey*, October 2, 1909, 3.

Bell, Michael. *Sentimentalism, Ethics, and the Culture of Feeling*. New York: Palgrave, 2000.

Bennetts, Leslie. "Jerry vs. the Kids." *Vanity Fair*, September 1993, 26–37.

Bentley, Eric. *The Life of the Drama*. New York: Atheneum, 1964.

Berger, John. *Ways of Seeing*. New York: Penguin Books, 1972.

Berger, Warren. "Public Service Advertising in America." *Kaiser Family Foundation Forum*, February 2002. http://www.kaisernetwork.org/health_cast/hcast_index.cfm?display=detail&hc=464.

Berlant, Lauren, ed. *Compassion: The Cultural Politics of an Emotion*. London: Routledge, 2004.

Bilken, Douglas, and Lee Bailey, eds. *Rudely Stamp'd: Imaginal Disability and Prejudice*. Washington, DC: University Press of America, 1981.

Biressi, Anita, and Heather Nunn. *Reality TV: Realism and Revelation*. London: Wallflower Press, 2005.

Bishop, Jim. *F.D.R.'s Last Year, April 1944–April 1945*. New York: William Morrow Co., 1974.

Block, Lori. *Beyond Affliction: The Disability History Project.* Narr. Lori Block. National Public Radio, May 1998. Audiocassette.

Bogdan, Robert. *Freak Show.* Chicago: University of Chicago Press, 1988.

Bolton, Richard, ed. *The Contest of Meaning: Cultural Histories of Photography.* Cambridge: MIT Press, 1999.

Booth, Michael. *English Melodrama.* London: Herbert Jenkins, 1965.

Boyer, Paul. *Urban Masses and Moral Order in America, 1820–1920.* Cambridge: Harvard University Press, 1978.

Brandt, Lillian. *How Much Shall I Give?* New York: Frontier Press, 1921.

Bratton, Jacky, Jim Cook, and Christine Gledhill, eds. *Melodrama: Stage, Picture, Screen.* London: BFI Press, 1994.

Braudy, Leo, and Marshall Cohen, eds. *Film Theory and Criticism.* Oxford: Oxford University Press, 1999.

Brecht, Bertolt. *Brecht on Theatre: The Development of an Aesthetic.* Trans. John Willett. New York: Hill and Wang, 1964.

Bremner, Robert Hamlett. *American Philanthropy.* Chicago: University of Chicago Press, 1960.

Bremner, Robert Hamlett. *From the Depths: The Discovery of Poverty in the United States.* New York: New York University Press, 1956.

Brooks, Peter. *Melodramatic Imagination.* New Haven: Yale University Press, 1976.

"Brotherly Love and Professional Beggars." *Survey,* April 17, 1909, 105–6.

Brottman, Mikita. "The Imbecile Chic of Jerry Lewis." In Pomerance, *Enfant Terrible!*

Brown, Allston T. *History of the American Stage.* New York: Benjamin Bloom, 1870.

Brown, Ross Herbert. *The Sentimental Novel in America.* Durham: Duke University Press, 1940.

Bukatman, Scott. "Paralysis in Motion: Jerry Lewis's Life as a Man." In *Comedy/Cinema/Theory,* ed. Andrew S. Hurton. Berkeley: University of California Press, 1991.

Bukatman, Scott. "Terminal Idiocy: The Comedian is the Message." In Pomerance, *Enfant Terrible!*

Burke, Kenneth. *Attitudes toward History.* California: Hermes Publication, 1959.

Burns, Elizabeth. *Theatricality: A Study in Convention in the Theatre and Social Life.* London: Longman, 1972.

Butler, Jeremy, ed. *Star Texts: Image and Performance in Film and Television.* Detroit: Wayne State University Press, 1991.

Butler, Judith. *Bodies That Matter.* New York: Routledge, 1993.

Butler, Judith. *Excitable Speech: A Politics of the Performative.* London: Routledge, 1997.

Butler, Judith. *Gender Trouble: Feminism and the Subversion of Identity.* London: Routledge, 1990.

Campbell, Jane, and Mike Oliver, eds. *Disabled Politics.* London: Routledge, 1996.

Canguilhelm, Georges. *The Normal and the Pathological.* Trans. Carolyn R. Fawcett. New York: Zone Books, 1989.

Carlson, Marvin. *Performance: A Critical Introduction.* London: Routledge, 1996.

Carlson, Marvin. "The Resistance to Theatricality." *Substance* 31 (2002): 238–50.

Carlson, Marvin. "Theatre Audiences and the Reading of Performance." In *Interpreting the Theatrical Past: Essays in the Historiography of Performance,* ed. Thomas Postlewait and Bruce McConachie. Iowa City: University of Iowa Press, 1989.

Carlson, Marvin. *Theatre Semiotics: Signs of Life.* Bloomington: Indiana University Press, 1990.

Chambers, Clarke A. *Paul U. Kellogg, and the Survey: Voices for Social Welfare and Social Justice.* Minneapolis: University of Minnesota Press, 1971.

Charney, Leo, and Vanessa R. Schwartz, eds. *Cinema and the Invention of Modern Life.* Berkeley: University of California Press, 1995.

Chemers, Michael. *Staging Stigma: A Critical Examination of the American Freak Show.* New York: Palgrave MacMillion, 2008.

Cohn, Victor. *Four Billion Dimes.* Minneapolis: Minneapolis Star and Tribune, 1984.

Connell, R. W. *Masculinities.* Berkeley: University of California Press, 1995.

Corrigan, John. *Business of the Heart: Religion and Emotion in the Nineteenth Century.* Berkeley: University of California Press, 2002.

Crutchfield, Susan, and Marcy Epstein, eds. *Points of Contact: Disability, Art, and Culture.* Ann Arbor: University of Michigan Press, 2000.

Currie, Barton W. "The Nickel Madness." *Harper's Weekly,* August 24, 1907, 246–47.

Curtis, Verna Posever, and Stanley Mallach. *Photography and Reform: Lewis Hines and the National Child Labor Commission.* Milwaukee: Milwaukee Art Museum, 1984.

Cutlip, Scott. *Fund Raising in the United States.* New Brunswick: Rutgers University Press, 1965.

Dale, Alan. *Comedy Is a Man in Trouble.* Minneapolis: University of Minnesota Press, 2000.

Danesi, Marcel. *Understanding Media Semiotics.* London: Oxford University Press, 2002.

Davidson, Michael. *Concerto for the Left Hand: Disability and the Defamiliar Body.* Ann Arbor: University of Michigan Press, 2008.

Davis, Brion David, ed. *Antebellum Reform.* New York: Harper and Row, 1967.

Davis, Lennard J. *Bending Over Backwards: Disability, Dismodernism, and Other Difficult Positions.* New York: New York University Press, 2002.

Davis, Lennard J. *The Disability Studies Reader.* London: Routledge, 1997.

Davis, Tracy C. "Theatricality: An Introduction." In Davis and Postlewait, *Theatricality.*

Davis, Tracy C., and Tom Postlewait, eds. *Actresses as Working Women: Their Social Identity in Victorian Culture.* London: Routledge, 1991.

Davis, Tracy C., and Tom Postlewait, eds. *Theatricality.* Cambridge: Cambridge University Press, 2004.

Davis, Tracy C. "Theatricality and Civil Society." In Davis and Postlewait, *Theatricality.*

Debord, Guy. *Society of the Spectacle*. Detroit: Black and Red, 1970.

Del Valle, Christina. "Some of Jerry's Kids Are Mad at the Old Man." *Business Week*, September 14, 1992, 39.

Deutsch, Helen, and Felicity Nussbaum, eds. *Defects: Engendering the Modern Body*. Ann Arbor: University of Michigan Press, 2000.

Devine, Edward Thomas. *The Practice of Charity*. New York: Lentilton, 1907.

Devine, Edward Thomas. *When Social Work Was Young*. New York: Macmillan, 1939.

Diamond, William. *The Broken Sword*. New York: David Longworth, 1817.

Diderot, Denis. *The Paradox of Acting*. New York: Hill and Wang, 1967.

Dimock, George. "Children of the Mills: Re-reading Lewis Hines' Child-Labor Photographs." *Oxford Art Journal* 16, no. 2 (1993): 37–54.

Dimock, George. *Priceless Children: American Photography 1890–1925: Child Labor and the Pictorialist Ideal*. Greensboro: Weatherspoon Art Museum, University of North Carolina, 2002.

Doherty, Jonathan L. *Lewis Wickes Hines' Interpretive Photography: The Six Early Projects*. Chicago: University of Chicago Press, 1978.

Douglas, Mary. *Purity and Danger: An Analysis of Concepts of Pollution and Taboo*. New York: Praeger, 1966.

Dudden, Faye E. *Women in the American Theatre*. New Haven: Yale University Press, 1994.

Dunlap, William. *A History of the American Theatre*. New York: J. J. Harper, 1832.

Durgnat, Raymond. *The Crazy Mirror: Hollywood Comedy and the American Image*. London: Faber and Faber, 1969.

Eastman, Crystal. *Work-Accidents and the Law*. Ed. Paul Underwood Kellogg. New York: Russell Sage Foundation, 1910.

Edwards, Leigh. "Reality TV and the American Family." In *The Tube Has Spoken: Reality TV and History*, ed. Julie Anne Taddeo and Ken Dvorak. Kentucky: University Press of Kentucky, 2010.

Einstein, Mara. *Compassion Inc.* Berkeley: University of California Press, 2012.

Elam, Keir. *Semiotics of Theatre and Drama*. London: Methuen, 1980.

Elliot, Timothy R., and E. Keith Byrd. "Media and Disability." *Rehabilitation Literature* 43, nos. 11–12 (November–December 1982): 348–55.

Ellis, John. "Star as a Cinematic Phenomenon." In *Star Texts*, ed. Jeremy Butler. Detroit: Wayne State University Press, 1991.

Elsaesser, Thomas, ed. *Early Cinema Space, Frame, Narrative*. London: BFI, 1990.

Esslin, Martin. "The Theatre of the Absurd." In *Essays in the Modern Drama*, ed. Morris Freedman. Boston: D. C. Heath and Co, 1964.

Everson, William K. *American Silent Film*. New York: Oxford University Press, 1978.

Fahy, Thomas, and Kimball King, eds. *Peering behind the Curtain: Disability, Illness, and the Extraordinary Body in Contemporary Theatre*. New York: Routledge, 2002.

Fairchild, Amy. "The Polio Narratives: Dialogues with FDR." *Bulletin of the History of Medicine* 75, no. 3 (2001): 488–534.

Farson, Daniel. "Funny Men Dean Martin and Jerry Lewis." *Sight and Sound* 22, no. 1 (July–September 1952): 32–33.

Fell, John L. *Film before Griffith.* Berkeley: University of California Press, 1993.

Feral, Josette. "Forward." *Substance* 31 (2002): 1–15.

Feral, Josette. "Performance and Theatricality: The Subject Demystified." Trans. Terese Lyons. *Modern Drama* 25 (1982): 170–81.

Feral, Josette. "Theatricality: The Specificity of Theatrical Language." *Substance* 31 (2002): 94–109.

Ferris, Leslie. *Acting Women: Images of Women in Theatre.* New York: New York University Press, 1989.

Fiebach, Joachim. "Theatricality: From Oral Traditions to Televised 'Realities.'" *Substance* 31 (2002): 17–41.

Fisch, Edith L., Doris Jonas Freed, and Esther R. Schactner. *Charities and Charitable Foundations.* New York: Lond Publishing, 1974.

Fischer, Renate. "Abbe De L'Eppe and the Living Dictionary." In *Deaf History Unveiled,* ed. John Van Cleve. Washington, DC: Gallaudet University Press, 2002.

Fisher, P. J. *Polio Story.* London: Heinemann Company, 1967.

Fiske, John, and John Hartley. *Reading Television.* New York: Methuen, 1978.

Fleischer, Davis Zames, and Frieda Zanes. *The Disability Rights Movement: From Charity to Confrontation.* Philadelphia: Temple University Press, 2001.

"For or Against Jerry?" *Accent on Living* 36 (Fall 1991): 50–54.

Foster, Hal. *Vision and Visuality.* Seattle: Bay Press, 1988.

Foucault, Michel. *Birth of a Clinic.* Trans. A. M Sheridan Smith. New York: Vintage Books, 1973.

Foucault, Michel. *Discipline and Punish.* Trans. Alan Sheridan. New York: Vintage Books, 1977.

Fox, Daniel M., and James Terry. "Photography and the Self Image of American Physicians, 1880–1920." *Bulletin of the History of Medicine* 52 (Fall 1978): 435–57.

Francis, Enjoli, and Felicia Patinkin. "Kony 2012 Charity Invisible Children Addresses Its Critics." *ABCNews.com.* abcnews.go.com/International/Kony-2012-charity-invisible-children-addresses-critics/story?id=15877622#.UkFqZIVKI6O. Posted 3/8/12.

Freedman, Morris, ed. *Essays in Modern Drama.* Boston: D. C. Heath and Co, 1964.

Fried, Lewis F. *The Makers of the City.* Amherst: University of Massachusetts Press, 1990.

Fried, Michael. *Absorption and Theatricality: Painting and Beholder in the Age of Diderot.* Berkeley: University of California Press, 1980.

Friedberg, Ann. "A Denial of Difference: Theories of Cinematic Identification." In *Psychoanalysis and Cinema,* ed. E. Ann Kaplan. New York: Routledge, 1990.

Friedel, Frank. *FDR. Vol. 2, The Ordeal.* Boston: Little Brown, 1954.

Friedman, Lawrence J., and Mark D. McGarvie, eds. *Charity, Philanthropy, and Civility in American History.* Cambridge: Cambridge University Press, 2003.

Fulton, A. R. *Motion Pictures: The Development of an Art from Silent Films to the Age of Television*. Norman: University of Oklahoma Press, 1960.

Fuoss, Kirk. "Lynching Performances, Theatres of Violence." *Text and Performance Quarterly* 19, no. 1 (January 1999): 1–37.

Furnham, A. "The Just World, Charitable Giving and Attitudes toward Disability." *Personality and Individual Differences* 19 (October 1995): 577–85.

Gallagher, Hugh Gregory. "FDR: An Unusual Look at a Hero." *Disabled USA* (Spring 1982): 23–26.

Gallagher, Hugh Gregory. *FDR's Splendid Deception*. Arlington, VA: Vandamere Press, 1999.

Gan, Anne-Britt. "The Fall of Theatricality in the Age of Modernity." *Substance* 31 (2002): 251–64.

Garcia, Oskar. "MDA Telethon Host Lythgoe: Jerry Lewis 'Always Welcome.'" *Today Television MSNBC*. Today.msnbc.msn.com/id/44397546/ns/today-entertainment/t/mda-telethon-host-lythgoe-jerry-lewis-always-welcome/#.ToyebHGzfo. Accessed 8/10/11.

Garland-Thomson, Rosemarie. *Extraordinary Bodies: Figuring Physical Disability in American Culture and Literature*. New York: Columbia University Press, 1997.

Garland-Thomson, Rosemarie. *Staring: How We Look*. Kindle ed. Oxford: Oxford University Press, 2009.

Garner, Stanton B. *Bodied Spaces: Phenomenology and Performance in Contemporary Drama*. Ithaca: Cornell University Press, 1994.

Gerould, Daniel C. *American Melodrama*. New York: Performing Arts Publishers, 1983.

Gheman, Richard. *That Kid*. New York: Avon, 1964.

Ginzberg, Lori D. *Women and the Work of Benevolence: Morality, Politics, and Class in Nineteenth-Century United States*. New Haven: Yale University Press, 1990.

Ginzberg, Lori D. *Women in Antebellum Reform*. Illinois: Harlan Davidson, 2000.

Glassberg, David. *American Historical Pageantry*. Chapel Hill: University of North Carolina Press, 1990.

Godley, Dan. *Disability Studies: An Interdisciplinary Introduction*. London: Sage Publications, 2011.

Goffman, Erving. *Frame Analysis: Essays on the Organization of Experience*. Cambridge: Harvard University Press, 1974.

Goffman, Erving. *The Presentation of Self in Everyday Life*. New York: Doubleday, 1959.

Goffman, Erving. *Stigma: Notes on the Management of Spoiled Identity*. New Jersey: Prentice-Hall, 1963.

Goldberg, Richard Thayer. *Making of FDR: Triumph over Disability*. Cambridge, MA: Abt Books, 1981.

Goldsmith, Harry. *A Conspiracy of Silence: The Health and Death of Franklin D. Roosevelt*. Lincoln, NE: iUniverse Inc., 2008.

Goodwin, Jeff, and James M. Jasper, eds. *Passionate Politics: Emotions and Social Movements*. Chicago: University of Chicago Press, 2001.

Gordon, Rae Beth. *Why the French Love Jerry Lewis: From Cabaret to Early Cinema.* Stanford: Stanford University Press, 2001.

Gould, Jean. *A Good Fight: The Story of F.D.R.'s Conquest of Polio.* New York: Dodd, Mead and Company, 1960.

Gould, Lewis L. *America in the Progressive Era, 1890–1914.* England: Pearson Education Limited, 2001.

Gould, Lewis L., ed. *The Progressive Era.* New York: Syracuse University Press, 1974.

Gould, Tony. *A Summer Plague: Polio and Its Survivors.* New Haven: Yale University Press, 1995.

Gregg, Melissa, and Gregory J. Siegworth, eds. *The Affective Theory Reader.* Durham: Duke University Press, 2012.

Griffin, Clifford S. "Religious Benevolence as Social Control, 1815–1860." In *Antebellum Reform,* ed. Brion Davis. New York: Harper and Row, 1967.

Griffin, Clifford S. *Their Brothers' Keepers: Moral Stewardship in the United States, 1800–1865.* New York: H. Wolff, 1960.

Grimstead, David. *Melodrama Unveiled.* Chicago: University of Chicago Press, 1968.

Grosz, Elizabeth. *Volatile Bodies: Toward a Corporeal Feminism.* Indianapolis: Indiana University Press, 1994.

Gunning, Tom. "The Whole Town's Gawking: Early Cinema and the Visual Experience of Modernity." *Yale Journal of Criticism* 7, no. 2 (1994): 189–201.

Gutman, Judith Mora. *Lewis Hines and American Social Conscience.* New York: Walker, 1967.

Gutwirth, Marcel. *Laughing Matter: An Essay on the Comic.* New York: Cornell University Press, 1993.

Hadley, Elaine. *Melodramatic Tactics: Theatricalized Dissent in the English Marketplace 1800–1885.* Stanford: Stanford University Press, 1995.

Hahn, Harlan. "Advertising the Acceptably Enjoyable Image: Disability and Capitalism." *Policy Studies Journal* 15 (March 1987): 551–71.

Hales, Peter B. *Silver Cities: The Photography of American Urbanization.* Philadelphia: Temple University Press, 1984.

Haller, Beth. "The Misfit and Muscular Dystrophy." *Journal of Popular Film and Television* 21 (Winter 1994): 142–49.

Halpern, Jake. "Emotional Buildup." *New York Times Magazine,* Oct. 5, 2008. www.nytimes.com/2008/10/05/realestate/keymagazine/105Extreme-t.html?pagewanted=all&_r=0.

Halttunen, Karen. *Confidence Men and Painted Women: A Study of Middle-class Culture in America, 1830–1870.* New Haven: Yale University Press, 1982.

Hammett, Jennifer. "Essentializing Movies: Perceiving Cognitive Film Theory." *Wide Angle* 14 (January 1992): 86–94.

Hammond, Michael, Jane Howarth, and Russell Keat. *Understanding Phenomenology.* Oxford: Basil Blackwell, 1991.

Handler, Glenn. *Public Sentiments: Structures of Feeling in Nineteenth-Century American Literature.* Chapel Hill: University of North Carolina Press, 2001.

Hansen, Miriam. *Babel and Babylon: Spectatorship in American Silent Film.* Cambridge: Harvard University Press, 1991.

Haskell, Thomas L. "Capitalism and the Origins of the Humanitarian Sensibility, Part One." *American History Review* 90, no. 2 (April 1985): 339–61.

Haskell, Thomas L. "Capitalism and the Origins of Humanitarian Sensibility, Part Two." *American History Review* 90, no. 3 (June 1985): 547–66.

Hassett, William D. *Off the Record with F.D.R. 1942–1945.* New Brunswick: Rutgers University Press, 1958.

Hays, Michael, and Anastasia Nikolopoulo, eds. *Melodrama: The Cultural Emergence of A Genre.* New York: St. Martin's Press, 1996.

Heilman, Robert. *Tragedy and Melodrama: Versions of Experience.* Seattle: University of Washington Press, 1968.

Heller, Dana Alice, ed. *Makeover Television: Realities Remodeled.* London: I. B. Tauris and Co., 2007.

Henderson, George, and Willie V. Bryan. *Psychosocial Aspects of Disability.* Springfield, IL: Charles C. Thomas, 1984.

Henderson, Mary C. *The City and the Theatre: New York Playhouses from the Bowling Green to Times Square.* New York: James T. White and Co., 1973.

Hershey, Laura. "False Advertising: Let's Stop Pity Campaigns for People with Disabilities." *Ms.*, April–May 5, 1995, 96–97.

Hevey, David. *The Creatures That Time Forgot.* Routledge: London, 1992.

Hewitt, Barnard. *Theatre USA: 1668–1957.* New York: McGraw-Hill Co., 1959.

Hewitt, Nancy A. *Women's Activism and Social Change: Rochester New York, 1822–1872.* Ithaca: Cornell University Press, 1984.

Hill, Annette. *Reality TV: Audiences and Popular Factual Television.* London: Routledge, 2005.

Hine, Lewis. "How the Camera May Help in Social Uplift." In *Classic Essays in Photography*, ed. Alan Trachtenburg. New Haven: Leek's Island Books, 1980.

Holcroft, Thomas. *Deaf and Dumb; or, The Orphan Protected.* In *London Stage: A Collection of the most reputed Tragedies, Comedies, Operas, Melo-dramas, Farces and Interludes.* London: G. Balne, 1825.

Holmes, Martha Stoddard. *Fictions of Affliction: Physical Disability in Victorian Culture.* Ann Arbor: University of Michigan Press, 2004.

Holmes, Martha Stoddard. "Working (with) the Rhetoric of Affliction: Autobiographical Narratives of Victorians with Physical Disabilities." In Wilson and Lewiecki-Wilson, *Embodied Rhetoric.*

Houck, Davis W., and Amos Kiewe. *FDR's Body Politics: The Rhetoric of Disability.* College Station: Texas A&M University Press, 2003.

Huet, Marie-Helene. *Monstrous Imagination.* Cambridge: Harvard University Press, 1993.

Husserl, Edmund. *Cartesian Meditations: An Intro to Phenomenology*. Trans. Durian Carrns. The Hague: Martinus Nijhoff, 1960.

Ingstad, Benedicte, and Susan Reynolds Whyte, eds. *Disability and Culture*. Berkeley: University of California Press, 1995.

Ireland, Joseph N. *Records of the New York Stage: 1750–1860*. New York: Benjamin Bloom, 1866.

"ISRA Announces First Annual Susan G. Komen Shoot for the Cure." *PR Newswire*, September 26, 2011. www.prnewswire.com/news-releases/isra-announces-first-annual-susan-g-komen-shoot-for-the-cure-130607453.html.

Jacobs, Lewis. *The Rise of American Film: A Critical History*. New York: Harcourt Brace, 1947.

Jacobson, Kristin. "Renovating the American Woman's Home: American Domesticity in *Extreme Makeover: Home Edition*." *Legacy* 25, no. 1 (2008): 105–20.

James, Reese D. "Old Drury of Philadelphia." PhD dissertation. University of Pennsylvania, 1932.

Jay, Martin. *Downcast Eyes: The Denigration of Vision in Twentieth-Century French Thought*. Berkeley: University of California Press, 1993.

Jay, Martin. "Scopic Regimes of Modernity." In *Vision and Visuality*, ed. Hal Foster. Seattle: Bay Press, 1988.

Jenkins, Henry. *What Made Pistachio Nuts?: Early Sound Comedy and the Vaudeville Aesthetic*. New York: Columbia University Press, 1992.

Johnson, Mary. "Jerry's Kids." *Nation*, September 7, 1992, 232–34.

Johnson, Mary. "A Test of Wills: Jerry Lewis, Jerry's Orphans, and the Telethon." In *The Ragged Edge*, ed. Barnett Shaw. Kentucky: Advocado Press, Louisville, KY, 1994.

"Joseph Kony 2012 Video: Stop Kony Campaign Draws Criticism." *Huffington Post*. www.huffingtonpost.com/2012/03/08/joseph-kony-video-stop-kony_n_1332427.html.

Kadet, Anne. "Are Charity Walks and Races Worth the Effort?" *SmartMoney*, June 21, 2011, www.smartmoney.com/spend/travel/are-charity-walks-and-races-worth-the-effort-1306536923690/?zone=intromesage#tabs.

Kaplan, E. Ann. "Theories of Melodrama: A Feminist Perspective." *Women in Performance: A Journal of Feminist Theory* 1 (Spring–Summer 1983): 40–49.

Kass, Robert. "Jerry Lewis Analyzed." *Films in Review* 4, no. 3 (1953): 119–23.

Keil, Charlie. *Early American Cinema in Transition: Story, Style and Filmmaking 1907–13*. Madison: University of Wisconsin Press, 2001.

Kenney, James. *The Blind Boy: A Melo-drama in Three Acts*. London: Lacey Thomas Hailes, 1801.

Kibler, Alison. *Rank Ladies: Gender and Cultural Hierarchy in American Culture*. Chapel Hill: University of North Carolina Press, 1999.

Klages, Mary. *Woeful Afflictions: Disability, Sentimentality in Victorian America*. Philadelphia: University of Pennsylvania Press, 1999.

Klaver, Elizabeth. "Spectatorial Theory in the Age of the Media Culture." *New Theatre Quarterly* 44 (November 1995): 309–21.

Kleinhans, Chuck. *Continuous Entertainment: Short Works.* S.1: Chuck Kleinhans, 1992.

Kony 2012. Dir. Jason Russell. 2012. Online at the site invisiblechildren.com/videos/Kony-2012/.

Kracuer, Siegfried. *Theory of Film: The Redemption of Physical Reality.* Oxford: Oxford University Press, 1960.

Krauss, Rosalind. "Tracing Nadar." *October* 5 (Summer 1978): 24–47.

Kriegel, Leonard. "The Wolf in the Pit in the Zoo." *Social Policy* (Fall 1982): 16–23.

Kristeva, Julia. *Powers of Horror: An Essay on Abjection.* Trans. Leon S. Roudiez. New York: Columbia University Press, 1982.

Krutnik, Frank. *Inventing Jerry Lewis.* Washington, DC: Smithsonian Institution, 2000.

Krutnik, Frank. "Jerry Lewis: The Deformation of a Comic." *Film Quarterly* 48 (Fall 1994): 12–26.

Krutnik, Frank. "Sex and Slapstick: The Martin and Lewis Phenomenon." In Pomerance, *Enfant Terrible!,* 109–22.

Kuppers, Petra. *Bodies on Edge: Disability and Contemporary Performance.* London: Routledge, 2003.

Landy, Marcie, ed. *Imitations of Life: A Reader in Film and TV Melodrama.* Detroit: Wayne State University Press, 1991.

Lane, Harlan. *The Mask of Benevolence: Disabling the Deaf Community.* New York: Alfred A. Knopf, 1992.

Lasch, Christopher. *The World of Nations: Reflections on American History, Politics, and Culture.* New York: Alfred A. Knopf, 1973.

Lash, Joseph. *Eleanor and Franklin.* New York: Norton, 1971.

Levy, Shawn. *The King of Comedy: The Life and Art of Jerry Lewis.* New York: St. Martin's Press, 1996.

Lewis, Jerry. "If I Had Muscular Dystrophy." *Parade Magazine,* September 2, 1990.

Lewis, Jerry. *Total Film-maker.* New York: Random House, 1971.

Lewis, Jerry, and Herb Gluck. *Jerry Lewis in Person.* New York: Pinnacle Books, 1985.

Linton, Simi. *Claiming Disability: Knowledge and Identity.* New York: New York University Press, 1998.

Lipton, Michael A. "Jerry's Encore." *People Online.* http://www.people.com/people/archive/article/0,,20138719,00.html. Posted 12/9/02.

Longmore, Paul K. "Conspicuous Contribution and American Cultural Dilemmas." In *The Body and Physical Difference,* ed. David T. Mitchell and Sharon L. Snyder. Ann Arbor: University of Michigan Press, 1997.

Longmore, Paul K. "The Cultural Framing of Disability: Telethons as a Case Study." *PMLA* 120, no. 2 (March 2005): 502–8.

Longmore, Paul K. "Screening Stereotypes: Images of Disabled People in Television and Motion Pictures." In *Images of the Disabled, Disabling Images*, ed. Alan Gartner and Tom Joe. New York: Praeger Production, 1987.

Longmore, Paul K. "Uncovering the Hidden History of People with Disabilities." *Reviews in American History* 15 (September 1987): 355–64.

Longmore, Paul K., and Lauri Umansky, eds. *The New Disability History: American Perspectives*. New York: New York University Press, 2001.

Looker, Earle. "Is Franklin D. Roosevelt Physically Fit to Be President?" *Liberty Magazine*, July 25, 1931, 6–10.

Lubin, Sigmund. *The Fake Blind Man*. Prod. and dir. Sigmund Lubin. 1905. 1 minute. Videocassette (VHS).

Lubove, Roy. *The Progressive and the Slum: Tenement House Reform in New York City, 1890–1917*. Pittsburgh: University of Pittsburgh Press, 1962.

Luxley, James, ed. *Performativity*. London: Routledge, 2007.

MacAloon, John. "Olympic Games and the Theory of Spectacle in Modern Societies." In *Rite, Drama, Festival, Spectacle*, ed. John MacAloon. Philadelphia: ISHI, 1984.

MacCabe, Colin, ed. *High Theory/Low Culture: Analyzing Pop Television and Film*. Manchester: Manchester University Press, 1986.

"Mapping the Kony 2012 Controversy." *Rights and Views: Opinion and Research from the Columbia University Human Rights Community*, March 12, 2012. Blogs.cuit.columbia.edu/rightsviews/2012/03/12/mapping-the-kony-2012-controversy-what-does-it-mean-for-huma-rights-advocacy/.

Madison, D. Soyini, and Judith Hamera. *The Sage Handbook of Performance Studies*. London: Sage Publications, 2006.

Marikar, Sheila. "Barefoot Contessa Reaches Out to Make-A-Wish Kid She Snubbed." *ABC News*. http://abcnewsgo.com/Entertainment/barefoot-contess-turns-make kid/story?id=1323857#.UKF2m4VKI6U. Posted 03/28/11.

Markley, Robert. "Sentimentality as Performance: Shaftesbury, Sterne, and the Theatrics of Virtue." In *The New Eighteenth Century: Theory, Politics, English Literature*, ed. Felicity Nussbaum and Laura Brown. New York: Methuen, 1987.

Marshall, David. *The Figure of Theatre: Shaftesbury, Defoe, Adam Smith and George Eliot*. New York: Columbia University Press, 1986.

Marshall, David. *The Surprising Effects of Sympathy*. Chicago: University of Chicago Press, 1988.

Martin, Mike W. *Virtuous Giving: Philanthropy, Voluntary Service and Caring*. Bloomington: Indiana University Press, 1994.

Mason, Jeffrey D. *Melodrama and the Myth of America*. Bloomington: Indiana University Press, 1993.

Mason, Jeffrey D. "Street Fairs: Social Space, Social Performance." *Theatre Journal* 48 (1996): 301–19.

McCarthy, Kathleen D. *American Creed: Philanthropy and the Rise of Civil Society, 1700–1865.* Chicago: University of Chicago Press, 2003.

McCarthy, Kathleen D., ed. *Lady Bountiful Revisited: Women, Philanthropy and Power.* New Brunswick: Rutgers University Press, 1990.

McConachie, Bruce. *Melodramatic Formations: American Theatre and Society 1820–1870.* Iowa City: University of Iowa Press, 1992.

McIntire, Ross T. *White House Physician.* New York: G. P. Putnam and Sons, 1946.

McLuhan, Marshall. *Understanding Media: The Extensions of Man.* New York: American Library, 1964.

McMurria, John. "Desperate Citizens and Good Samaritans: Neoliberalism and Makeover Reality TV." *Television and New Media* 9, no. 4 (July 2008).

"MD Telethon Is Not a Pity Party." *Accent of Living* 36 (Winter 1991): 54.

Medhurst, Martin J., et al., eds. *Cold War Rhetoric: Strategy, Metaphor, and Ideology.* New York: Greenwood Press, 1990.

Meredith, George. *An Essay on Comedy.* Ed. Wylie Sypher. New York: Doubleday Anchor Books, 1956.

Merleau-Ponty, Maurice. *Phenomenology of Perception.* Trans. Colin Smith. London: Routledge and Kegan Paul, 1962.

Merrill, Lisa. *When Romeo Was a Woman.* Ann Arbor: University of Michigan Press, 2000.

Miall, David S., ed. *Metaphor: Problems and Perspectives.* Sussex: The Harvester Press, 1983.

Miller, Joseph. "The Mask of Charity." *Arena,* September 1902, 263.

Miller, Mark Crispin. *Boxed In: The Culture of TV.* Evanston: Northwestern University Press, 1988.

Miller, Mark Crispin. "Sickness on TV." *New Republic,* October 7, 1981, 27–29.

Mintz, Stephen. *Moralists and Modernizers: America's Pre–Civil War Reformers.* Baltimore: Johns Hopkins University Press, 1995.

Mitchell, David T., and Sharon Snyder. *The Body and Physical Difference: Discourses of Disability.* Ann Arbor: University of Michigan Press, 1997.

Mitchell, David T., and Sharon Snyder. *Cultural Locations of Disability.* Chicago: University of Chicago Press, 2006.

Mitchell, David T., and Sharon Snyder., eds. *Narrative Prosthesis: Disability and the Dependencies of Discourse.* Ann Arbor: University of Michigan Press, 2000.

Moody, Jane. "Illusions of Authorship." In *Women and Playwrighting in Nineteenth-Century Britain,* ed. Tracy C. Davis and Ellen Donkin. Cambridge: Cambridge University Press, 1999.

Morgan, Ted. *FDR: A Biography.* New York: Simon and Schuster, 1985.

Morse, William R. "Desire and the Limits of Melodrama." In *Themes in Melodrama,* ed. James Redmond. Cambridge: Cambridge University Press, 1992.

Mullenix, Elizabeth Reitz. *Wearing the Breeches: Gender on the Antebellum Stage.* New York: St. Martin's Press, 2000.

Mulvey, Laura. "Visual Pleasure and Narrative Cinema." In Braudy and Cohen, *Film Theory and Criticism.*

Murray, Susan, and Laurie Ouellette, eds. *Reality TV: Remaking Television Culture.* New York: New York University Press, 2002.

Musser, Charles. *The Emergence of Cinema: The American Screen to 1907.* Berkeley: University of California Press, 1990.

Norden, Martin. *The Cinema of Isolation: A History of Physical Disability in the Movies.* New Brunswick: Rutgers University Press, 1994. Accessed 4/15/11.

Norten, James. "The High-Tech Smearing of Ina Garten." *Chow Hound.* www.chow .com/food-news/77531/the-high-tech-smearing-of-ina-garten.

Odell, George. *Annals of the New York Stage.* Vols. 2–4. New York: Columbia University Press, 1931.

"Of Friendship." *National Foundation News* 4, no. 4 (1945): 15.

Oliver, Kelly. *Witnessing: Beyond Recognition.* Minneapolis: University of Minnesota Press, 2001.

Oliver, Michael. *The Politics of Disablement.* New York: St. Martin's Press, 1990.

Oshinsky, David. *Polio: An American Story.* Oxford: Oxford University Press, 2005.

Palmer, Gareth. "*Extreme Makeover: Home Edition:* An American Fairy Tale." In *Makeover Television: Realities Remodeled,* ed. Dana Alice Heller. London: I. B. Tauris and Co., 2007.

Parker, Andrew, and Eve Kosofsky Sedgwick, eds. *Performativity and Performance.* London: Routledge, 1995.

Pavis, Patrice. *Language of the Stage: Essay on the Semiotics of Theatre.* New York: Performing Arts Journal Publications, 1982.

Pavis, Patrice. *Theatre at the Crossroads of Culture.* London: Routledge, 1992.

Perkins, Francis. *The Roosevelt I Knew.* New York: Viking, 1946.

Phillips, Marilyn J. "Damaged Goods: Oral Narratives of the Experience of Disability in American Culture." *Social Science and Medicine* 30 (1990): 849–59.

Pixérécourt, Guilbert. *The Forest of Bondy; or, The Dog of Montagris.* Trans Daniel Gerould. In *American Melodrama,* ed. Daniel Gerould. New York: Performing Arts Journal, 1983.

Pointon, Ann. *Framed: Interrogating Disability in the Media.* London: BFI, 1997.

Pomerance, Murray, ed. *Enfant Terrible! Jerry Lewis in American Film.* New York: New York University Press, 2002.

Prevots, Naima. *American Pageantry: A Movement for Art and Democracy.* Ann Arbor: UMI Research Press, 1990.

Pultz, John. *Photography and the Body.* London: Union House, 1995.

Quinn, Arthur Hobson. *A History of the American Drama from the Beginning to the Civil War.* New York: F. S. Crofts and Co, 1946.

Read, Alan. *Theatre and Everyday Life: An Ethics of Performance*. New York: Routledge, 1993.

Redmond, James, ed. *Melodrama*. Cambridge: Cambridge University Press, 1992.

Reese, James D. *Old Drury of Philadelphia*. Oxford: Oxford University Press, 1932.

Reid, Thomas. *Essays on the Active Powers of the Human Mind*. London: Kessinger Publishing, 2005.

Riis, Jacob. *How the Other Half Lives*. Intro. Donald N. Bigelow. New York: Hill and Wang, 1957.

Ritter, Ken. "Jerry Lewis Retiring from MDA Telethon." *Huffington Post*. www.huffing tonpost.com/2011/05/16/jerry-lewis-retiring-from-mda-telethon_n_862844 .html. Accessed 5/30/11.

Rodgers, Daniel T. *The Work Ethic in Industrial America, 1850–1920*. Chicago: University of Chicago Press, 1974.

Rogers, Linda J., and Beth Blue Swadener, eds. *Semiotics and Dis/Ability: Interrogating Categories of Difference*. Albany: State University of New York Press, 2001.

Rogers, Naomi. *Dirt and Disease: Polio before FDR*. New Brunswick: Rutgers University Press, 1992.

Rosen, George. "Disease, Disability and Death." In *The Victorian City: Images and Realities*, vol. 2, ed. H. J. Dyus and Michael Wolff. London: Routledge, 1973.

Rosenblum, Walter, Naomi Rosenblum, and Alan Trachtenberg. *America and Lewis Hines*. New York: Aperture, 1977.

Ross, Winston. "Kony 2012 Creators Seek to Shift Focus Back to Africa with New Video." *Daily Beast*. www.dailybeast.com/articles/2012/04/02/Kony-2012-creators.html. Accessed 5/1/12.

Rothman, David J. *The Discovery of the Asylum: Social Order and Disorder in the New Republic*. Boston: Little Brown and Co., 1990.

Russell, Marta. *Beyond Ramps: Disability at the End of the Social Contract*. Monroe, ME: Common Courage Press, 1998.

Samuels, Shirley, ed. *The Culture of Sentiment: Race, Gender, and Sentimentality in Nineteenth-Century America*. New York: Oxford University Press, 1992.

Sauter, Willmar. *The Theatrical Event: Dynamics of Performance and Perception*. Iowa City: University of Iowa Press, 2000.

Schechner, Richard. *Between Theatre and Anthropology*. Philadelphia: University of Philadelphia Press, 1985.

Schindler, Merrill. "Jerry's Revenge." *Los Angeles Magazine*, August 5, 1980, 25–29.

Schwartz, Harold. *Samuel Gridley Howe: Social Reformer, 1801–1876*. Cambridge: Harvard University Press, 1956.

Scott, Anne Firor. *Natural Allies: Women's Associations in American Society*. Urbana: University of Illinois Press, 1991.

Seavey, Nina Gilden, Jane Smith, and Paul Wagner. *A Paralyzing Fear: The Triumph over Polio in America*. New York: TV Books, 1998.

Sekula, Allan. "On the Invention of Photographic Meaning." *Art Forum* (January 1975): 36–46.

Sennett, Richard. *The Fall of the Public Man*. New York: W. W. Norton, 1992.

Shakespeare, Tom. "Art and Lies? Representations of Disability on Film." In *Disability Discourse*, ed. Marian Corker and Sally French. Philadelphia: Open University Press, 1999.

Shapiro, Joseph P. *No Pity: People with Disabilities Forging a New Civil Rights Movement*. New York: Times Books, 1993.

Shaviro, Steven. *The Cinematic Body*. Minneapolis: University of Minnesota Press, 1993.

Shearer, Harry. "Mid-Section: Telethon." *Film Comment* 15 (May–June 1976): 33–48.

Shepherd, Simon. "Blood, Thunder and Theory: The Arrival of English Melodrama." *Theatre Research International* 24, no. 2 (Summer 1999): 145–51.

Shofeld, Madeleine, and Kendra Gale. "Under the (Glue) Gun: Containing and Constructing Reality in Home Makeover TV." *Popular Communications* 5, no. 4 (2007): 263–82.

Siebers, Tobin. *Disability Theory*. Ann Arbor: University of Michigan Press, 2008.

Simmell, Georg. *The Metaphors of Mental Life: The Sociology of Georg Simmell*. Trans. Kurt H. Wolff. Glencoe: Free Press, 1950.

Simmell, Georg. "On Visual Interaction." In *Introduction to the Science of Sociology*, ed. Robert E. Paul and Ernest W. Burgess. Chicago: University of Chicago Press, 1924.

Singer, Ben. *Melodrama and Modernity: Early Sensational Cinema and Its Contexts*. New York: Columbia University Press, 2001.

Slide, Anthony. *Aspects of American Film History Prior to 1920*. New York: Scarecrow Press, 1978.

Smith, Adam. *Theory of Moral Sentiments*. Ed. D. D. Raphael and A. L. Macfie. Oxford: Clarendon Press, 1976.

Smith, Jane S. *Patenting the Sun*. New York: Doubleday, 1990.

Smith, Jean Edward. *FDR*. New York: Random House, 2008.

Smith, Warren, and Matthew Higgins. "Cause-Related Marketing: Ethics and the Ecstatic." *Business and Society* 39, no. 3 (September 2000): 305–25.

Smitt, Christopher. "'Please Call Now before It's Too Late': Spectacle Discourse in the Jerry Lewis Muscular Dystrophy Telethon." *Journal of Popular Culture* 36, no. 4 (Spring 2003): 687–703.

Sobchak, Vivian. *The Address of the Eye: A Phenomenology of Film Experience*. Princeton: Princeton University Press, 1992.

Solenburger, Alice Willard. *One Thousand Homeless Men: A Study of Original Records*. New York: Russell Sage Foundation, 1911.

Sontag, Susan. *Illness as Metaphor*. New York: Farrar, Straus, and Giroux, 1977.

Sourtorious, Rolf, ed. *Paternalism*. Minneapolis: University of Minnesota Press, 1983.

Sowell, Carol. "Memories: The Way They Were: MDA Goodwill Ambassadors."

MDA Publications. http://www.mda.org/publications/quest/q22memories.html. Accessed 10/10/09.

Spigel, Lynn. *Welcome to the Dreamhouse: Popular Media and Postwar Suburbs.* Durham: Duke University Press, 2001.

Stange, Maren. *Symbols of Ideal Life: Social Documentary Photography in America 1890–1950.* Cambridge: Cambridge University Press, 1989.

Stanley, Amy Dru. *From Bondage to Contract: Wage Labor, Marriage, and the Market in the Age of Slave Emancipation.* Cambridge: Cambridge University Press, 1998.

Stansell, Christine. *City of Women: Sex and Class in New York, 1789–1860.* New York: Alfred A. Knopf, 1986.

Starr, Allen M. "Memorial of Professor Jean-Marie Charcot." *Medical News,* October 14, 1893, 433–38.

States, Bert O. *Great Reckonings in Little Rooms.* Berkeley: University of California Press, 1985.

Stein, Sally. "Making Connections with the Camera: Photography and Social Mobility in the Career of Jacob Riis." *AfterImage* 10 (May 1983): 9–16.

Steinorth, Karl. *Lewis Hines: Passionate Journey, Photography from 1905–1937.* Zurich: Edition Stemmle, 1996.

Stevens, Ruth. *Hi-Ya Neighbor.* Atlanta: Foote and Davies, 1947.

Stiker, Henri-Jacques. *A History of Disability.* Trans. William Sayers. Ann Arbor: University of Michigan Press, 1997.

Sugiera, Malguizata. "Theatricality and Cognitive Science: Audience's Perception and Reception." *Substance* 31 (2002): 225–37.

Szasz, Ferenc, and Ralph H. Bogardus. "The Camera and the American Social Conscious: The Documentary Photography of Jacob A. Riis." *New York History* 55, no. 4 (October 1974): 409–36.

Tagg, John. *The Burden of Representation: Essays on Photographies and Histories.* Minneapolis: University of Minnesota Press, 1988.

Taussig, Michael. *Mimesis and Alterity: A Particular History of the Senses.* New York: Routledge, 1993.

Thomas, Carl. "The Body and Society: Some Reflections on the Concepts of Disability and Impairment." In *Reframing the Body,* ed. Nick Watson and Sarah Cunningham Burley. New York: Palgrave, 2001.

Thomson, David. *OverExposures: The Crisis in American Filmmaking.* New York: William Morrow and Co., 1981.

Todd, Janet. *Sensibility: An Introduction.* London: Methuen, 1986.

Tosches, Nick. *The Magnificent Dino: Living High in the Dirty Business of Dreams.* New York: Doubleday, 1992.

Trachtenberg, Alan, ed. *Classic Essays on Photography.* New Haven: Leete's Island Books, 1980.

Trachtenberg, Alan. "Photography: The Emergence of a Keyword." In *Photography in Nineteenth-Century America*, ed. Martha A. Sandweiss. New York: Harry N. Abrams, 1991.

Trachtenberg, Alan. *Reading American Photographs: Images as History*. New York: Hill and Wang, 1989.

Transtadt, Ragnhild. "Could the World Become a Stage? Theatricality and Metaphorical Structures." *Substance* 31 (2002): 216–24.

Trattner, Walter I. *From Poor Law to Welfare State: A History of Social Welfare in America*. 2nd ed. New York: Free Press, 1979.

Traube, Leonard. "Martin and Lewis Write Show Biz History in 16 ½ -Hour Telethon." *Variety*, March 16, 1952, 1.

Turner, Victor. *Dramas, Fields and Metaphors: Symbolic Action in Human Society*. New York: Cornell University Press, 1974.

Turner, Victor. *From Ritual to Theatre: The Human Seriousness of Play*. New York: Performing Arts Journal Publications, 1982.

Turnley, Walker. *Roosevelt and the Warm Springs Story*. New York: Wyn, 1953.

Valentine, Gill. "What It Means to Be a Man: The Body, Masculinities, Disability." In *Mind and Body Spaces: Geographies of Illness, Impairment and Disability*, ed. Ruth Butler and Hester Parr. New York: Routledge, 1999.

Valentine, Phyllis Klein. "A Nineteenth-Century Experiment in the Education of the Handicapped: American Asylum for the Deaf and Dumb." *New England Quarterly* 64, no. 3 (September 1991): 355–75.

Van Cleve, John Vickrey, ed. *Deaf History Unveiled*. Washington, DC: Gallaudet University Press, 2002.

Van Till, Jon, and Associates. *Critical Issues in American Philanthropy*. San Francisco: Jossey-Bass Publishers, 1990.

Wagenknect, Edward. *Movies in the Age of Innocence*. Norman: University of Oklahoma Press, 1962.

Wagner, David. *What's Love Got to Do with It? A Critical Look at American Charity*. New York: W. W. Norton, 2000.

Walters, Carole. "The Complete Jerry Lewis Telethon Party Guide." *Villiage Voice*, September 1, 1987, 47–48.

Walters, Ronald G. *American Reformers: 1815–1860*. Toronto: McGraw-Hill Ryerson, 1978.

Ward, Geoffrey C. *A First-Class Temperament: The Emergence of Franklin Roosevelt*. New York: Harper and Row, 1989.

Warner, Landon H., ed. *Reforming American Life in the Progressive Era*. New York: Jerome S. Ozer Publishing, 1971.

Wendell, Susan. *The Rejected Body*. London: Routledge, 1996.

White, Graham J. *F.D.R. and the Press*. Chicago: University of Chicago Press, 1979.

Wiebe, Robert H. *The Search for Order, 1877–1920*. New York: Hill and Wang, 1967.

Williams, Linda, ed. *Viewing Positions: Ways of Seeing Film*. New Brunswick: Rutgers University Press, 1995.

Williams, Mary Elizabeth. "What's Labor Day without Jerry Lewis?" *Salon.com*. www .salon.com/2011/08/04/labor-day-without-jerry-lewis. Posted 8/4/11. Accessed 8/30/11.

Williams, Raymond. *Marxism and Literature*. Oxford: Oxford University Press, 1977.

Wilson, Daniel J. "A Crippling Fear: Experiencing Polio in the Era of FDR." *Bulletin of History of Medicine* 72, no. 3 (1998): 464–98.

Wilson, James C., and Cynthia Lewiecki-Wilson, eds. *Embodied Rhetoric: Disability in Language and Culture*. Carbondale and Edwardsville: Southern Illinois University Press, 2001.

"Without Jerry Lewis, MDA Telethon Raises More Money?" *International Business Times*. www.ibtimes.com/articles/209269/20110906/jerry-lewis-telethon-2011-mda .htm. Accessed 9/11/11.

Wolter, Jurgen C. *The Dawning of American Drama: American Dramatic Criticism, 1746–1915*. Westport, CT: Greenwood Press, 1993.

Wood, William B. *Personal Recollections of the Stage*. Philadelphia: Henry Carey Baird, 1855.

Woods, Robert Archey. *The Poor in Great Cities*. New York: Scribner and Sons, 1895.

Woolf, S. J. "The Roosevelt of 1929." *North American Review* 227, no. 3 (March 1929): 261–62.

Zola, Kenneth. "Depictions of Disability: Metaphor-Message." *Social Science Journal* 22 (1985): 5–17.

INDEX

Able-bodied, 57, 72, 79, 109–11, 121
Active Powers of the Human Mind, 26
Affect: theories of, 22, 25, 26; in nineteenth-century melodrama, 36, 44; in NFIP campaigns, 75, 80, 90, 137
ALS, 111
American Cancer Society, 152
American Idol, 133, 134, 137
American Orthopedic Association, 58
American Pageant Association, 60
American Red Cross, 50
Anarchistic comedy, 114, 115, 119. *See also* Jerry Lewis comedic style
Anderson, Donald, 76, 77, 79, 130
Antebellum: culture, 22; beliefs, 41
Arnaz, Desi Jr., 85, 86
Asylum, Education for Deaf and Dumb, 18, 20; educational concept of, 19, 41–43

Ball, Lucille, 85, 86
Barefoot Contessa, 1, 3, 9. *See also* Ina Garten
Beggars, 10, 36
Benevolence: acts of, 19, 24, 110, 119, 151, 164; concept of, 3, 4, 10, 13, 15–17, 19–22, 24, 25; contemporary context, 153, 156–58, 160, 161, 164; context of MDA telethon, 89, 91, 93, 103, 105, 108, 112, 124, 127; context of nineteenth-century culture, 31, 33, 35–37, 40–42, 45, 48; in era of reality television, 130, 131, 133, 137–39, 142, 144, 146, 149, 150; intervention, 8, 27, 31, 96, 100, 162; organized, 5, 8, 13, 19, 49, 93, 104, 152, 153, 155, 164; patron and patriarchs, 3, 12, 26, 34, 45, 47, 48, 101, 105, 123; in relation to NFIP and

polio crisis, 51, 63, 65, 69, 74; spectacular, 14, 87, 132
Birthday Ball, 59, 62, 63, 65, 66, 70, 74, 75. *See also* pageants
Blind: individuals, 13, 18, 28–31, 34, 35, 40–43, 46, 47, 139; public exhibition of, 43
Body: about Jerry Lewis, 113–18, 120, 121, 134, 136, 159, 160; Roosevelt and polio, 56, 57, 64, 65, 78, 80, 83, 87, 89, 91, 104, 107, 108; theories of, 8–10, 17, 26
Breast cancer, 152, 156, 157. *See also* Susan G. Komen for the Cure Foundation
Breeches actresses, 39
Brinker, Nancy G., 152, 156
The Broken Sword, 38
Brooklyn Committee on Crippled Children, 55
Byoir, Carl, 59

Campobello Island, 56
Cantor, Eddie, 69, 98
Capitalism, 131, 138
Cause Related Marketing (CRM), 4, 16, 154, 155
Charity: with the advent of the charity telethon, 89, 90, 92, 96, 99–101, 104, 105, 119, 124; advertising, 78, 82, 104; contemporary attitudes about, 150, 152, 153, 154, 158, 161, 163; the crusade against polio, 48–51, 68, 70, 72, 75, 76, 79, 80, 83, 87; definition and theories of, 2, 4–6, 8–10, 12–14, 16, 17; in era of reality television, 128–32, 134, 138–40, 142–44, 147, 148, 149, 150; events, 60, 98, 160; industry, 3, 8, 89, 90, 93, 101, 102,